Asthma

Asthma

Stop Suffering, Start Living

THIRD EDITION

M. Eric Gershwin, M.D.
E. L. Klingelhofer, Ph.D.

PERSEUS PUBLISHING
Cambridge, Massachusetts

Copyright © 2001 by M. Eric Gershwin, M.D., and E. L. Klingelhofer, Ph.D.

Cataloging-in-Publication Data is available from the Library of Congress
ISBN 0–7382-0398–X

Perseus Publishing is a member of the Perseus Books Group.
Find us on the World Wide Web at http://www.perseuspublishing.com
Perseus Publishing books are available at special discounts for bulk purchases in the U.S. by corporations, institutions, and other organizations. For more information, please contact the Special Markets Department at the Perseus Books Group, 11 Cambridge Center, Cambridge, MA 02142, or call (617) 252-5298.

Text design by Trish Wilkinson
Set in 12-point Goudy by Perseus Publishing Services

First printing, September 2001

1 2 3 4 5 6 7 8 9 10—03 02 01

*This is for our wives, Laurel and Jean—mothers
who have dealt with their children's asthma with
matchless patience, resourcefulness, and imperturbability.*

To Our Readers

This book can help you and your family greatly. Its suggestions about health care reflect the best and most up-to-date medical information and opinion available. As with all medical advice, however, cases—and therefore treatments—may vary.

The authors and publisher therefore disclaim any responsibility for consequences resulting from following advice or procedures set forth in this book. It is not intended to be an alternative to or substitute for your own doctor's recommendations. In particular, the treatment of severe, protracted, or stubborn symptoms or use of any drug or medication should be undertaken only after consultation with your own physician.

Contents

Caring for Your Asthma

Acknowledgments

Many hands and minds went into this book. We owe more than we can tell to:

- The medical researchers who are gradually unlocking the mysteries of allergy and making it more treatable
- The medical practitioners, upon whose day-to-day experience and wisdom we have drawn heavily
- The American Lung Association chapters and other groups and societies that enthusiastically responded to our requests for information and advice.

We owe special thanks to Nikki Phipps, who typed the manuscript and whose energy, intelligence and matchless skills really made this book happen. We also thank Dr. Judy Van de Water for help with illustrations and proofreading sections of the manuscript.

Finally, members of the faculty of the Division of Allergy and Clinical Immunology at the University of California Medical School at Davis contributed importantly to the manuscript. We are enormously grateful to Drs. Rahmat Afrasiabi, Christopher Chang, Katherine Gundling, Gary Incaudo, Sarah Kuhl, Stanley Naguwa, Bruce Ryhal, Robert Saunders, and Arif Seyal, whose informed, careful, and helpful suggestions caught errors of fact and rhetoric and helped us to make the book much better. The mistakes that remain are ours alone.

M.E.G.
E.L.K.

Introduction to the
Third Edition

What This Book Aims to Do

Nine years have passed since the second edition of *Asthma: Stop Suffering, Start Living* appeared. Over those nine years enormous changes have taken place in our understanding of the nature of the disease, the way it affects its victims, and the treatments available to respond to it. Accordingly, this new, completely revised version will help readers to understand and to make informed decisions about:

- The disease's underlying causes
- The symptoms of the disease and when, in whom, and why they appear
- The substances, activities, and conditions that can trigger asthma's symptoms
- The best, most effective preventive measures and treatments to follow in caring for the disease
- Some especially ineffectual, risky, or inappropriate therapies to avoid
- The surest, most promising caregivers and care delivery systems to choose

In this updated version we single out the following important and troubling topics for completely new or greatly expanded coverage:

- The implications of disproportionate increases in the incidence and the death rate from asthma—particularly among the elderly.
- The treatment options, limited though they are, available to the poor, the uninsured, and the elderly seeking adequate care for their symptoms.
- What steps victims or their caregivers can take to overcome the single most important bar to the effective, competent management of asthma—the failure to stick with treatment recommendations and prescriptions.

People often ask us why we've chosen to write about asthma and allergies.[1] Eric Gershwin has two answers ready. "As a doctor you can do something about asthma," he replies. "With lots of medical conditions you're simply helpless." Eric had to deal with severe allergies in two of his children and that experience brought him to his specialization as an allergist.

As a child, Ed Klingelhofer was often and sometimes seriously sick with attacks of moderate persistent asthma. Those episodes happened back in the days when understanding of and treatment for the disease hardly existed. His symptoms (as asthma symptoms often do) relented as he grew older but both of his children (and, now, his granddaughters) have relived parts of his past. "No kid and no parent ought to go through what happened to me," he says to explain his interest in doing something about the disease.

This book is our full answer to that simple wish; our experiences underline our firm conviction that asthma can be tamed and controlled.

---

[1]See also our *Taking Charge of Your Child's Allergies* (Totowa, N.J.: Humana Press, 1998) and *Living Allergy Free* (Totowa, N.J.: Humana Press, 1992).

We know how difficult it is to be a patient with a chronic disease. It is always important to remember that people with asthma are living with asthma, not dying of it. This book aims to make that living much easier.

You will not find any miracle cures spelled out in the book; there are no miracle cures for asthma. We do provide current, solid, scientifically based information about the disease and the means available to manage and control it. We stress throughout the book our conviction, borne out by decades of experience with thousands of patients, that asthma, faithfully and aggressively looked after, can be kept under wraps and need not be a bar to leading an active and satisfying life.

How to Use This Book

Asthma: Stop Suffering, Start Living, has three parts. Part 1 defines and describes asthma. That section traces the all-important link between allergy and asthma, sketches the typical course of the form of asthma that starts in childhood, and contrasts this early onset version with symptoms that first turn up in adolescence or adulthood. We spell out how the disease differs from other conditions whose symptoms resemble asthma, thus enabling you or your care provider to determine whether or not you have asthma and, if you do, what steps you can take to identify its cause or causes.

Part 2 focuses on the heart of asthma care—avoiding the disease's causes and the complications associated with it. Asthma's triggers vary enormously according to the routes they follow to enter the body or the conditions inside or outside of the body that provoke the symptoms. Thus, knowing and keeping clear of these agents demands both knowledge and vigilance. The several chapters in this part outline strategies that tell how to avoid the substances or conditions that trigger symptoms—substances or conditions found at home or school, at work or play, inside or out of doors. This part also offers information and suggestions about assessing and dealing with the added risks and complications that may trouble asthmatics contemplating surgery or pregnancy.

Part 3 is all about treating and living with asthma—managing symptoms, finding appropriate medical care and using it effectively, getting, taking, and sticking with medications properly, and coping with acute attacks. We also cover other elements of asthma care in this section, including the place and the use of allergy shots, the interplay of asthma and routine child immunization, and precautions to take during travel. The section concludes by noting that by its very nature asthma encourages its victims to consider and to experiment with alternative and nontraditional modes of treatment. Generally speaking, folk or alternative treatments are not nearly as effective as standard medical options; indeed, some of the home remedies we cite can be hazardous to the asthmatic's health. There is also much misinformation that can impede the quality of care. Asthma has no quick and easy "fixes" and you, the sufferer, should be wary of buying into miracle overnight cures.

In earlier editions of this book, we included appendixes to help asthma sufferers. These addenda included detailed maps and tables identifying allergy and asthma-causing pollens, their locales, and their seasons. Also included were diets that, when followed, would have the asthma sufferer avoid certain asthma-causing foods, food additives, and chemicals. Wherever possible these aids to the reader now appear as sidebars along with the relevant text. We have retained a greatly expanded and web-oriented roster of help sources and suggestions about suppliers of products for asthmatics as appendixes.

This expanded and updated edition has several features designed to help you find the information you need to manage asthma successfully. We have relied extensively on decision or flow charts—algorithms—that take you step by step from recognition of a problem or question to its resolution. We have revised charts that appeared in earlier editions to make them easier to follow and use.

We have tried to chain and coordinate information on a topic or issue by telling you exactly where to look for additional data or recommendations by inserting a cross reference to a certain page in another part of the text.

As noted, we have put together a comprehensive list of web-based help sources or resources for many aspects of the disease and explain how to connect with them. Exploiting that list will help you to touch base with organizations or agencies concerned with all aspects of the care and treatment of asthma.

In using this book you will almost certainly turn directly to the sections that cover the problems or issues that puzzle or trouble you. However, this does not mean that you should pass over other topics. For instance, if you have asthma, you already know about wheezing, shortness of breath, coughing and mucus production, its major symptoms. But do you really know what causes your asthma? If your symptoms turn up during a cold, do you know what is happening in your body and why it reacts in the way it does? Understanding the physiological basis for asthma will help you to develop an early warning system for the onset of the disease and identify what triggers symptoms or makes them worse—and how best to treat them.

This book tells you how to approach your illness proactively; that is its most important feature. In spite all of the information and all of the medications that are available, too many asthmatics or their parents take a passive, reactive approach. By doing this they put asthma in charge of their lives rather than the other way around.

The first step in taking charge of your asthma is to answer each of the following key questions honestly and straightforwardly. If you cannot say "yes" to any question, search for the motivation and information you need to answer it in the affirmative in the pages that follow. Getting to the place where you have your asthma under firm control will take serious effort, diligence, and the stubbornness to see the task through. Once there, though, the payoff is huge: a fuller, happier, and healthier life. Go for it, and good luck!

Finally, if we haven't listed a question or problem with asthma that troubles you, where do you turn for help? Take what troubles you to your physician or nurse practitioner or your pharmacist (especially for questions about medications, their side effects, and what to do in the event of a

FIGURE I.1   Key Questions About Asthma—and Where to Look for Answers

Do you know what's happening in your body during an asthma attack?	NO →	See Chapter 1, pages 12–17
Do you know what triggers your asthma and how to avoid it?	NO →	See Chapter 5, pages 65–74
Do you know the early warning signs of an asthma attack?	NO →	See Chapter 5, pages 68–70
Do you know what steps to take to prevent or ease an asthma attack?	NO →	See Chapter 12, pages 158–160 and Chapter 14
Do you know exactly what medication or medications you are taking?	NO →	See Chapters 2, 12, and 14
Do you know why and when you need to take your asthma medications?	NO →	See Chapter 12, pages 157–161
Do you have trouble taking your medications?	NO →	See Chapter 12 and Chapter 14, pages 189–192
Do you have trouble remembering to take your asthma medications?	NO →	See Chapter 12, pages 164–168
Students, does the school know about your asthma and how you care for it?	NO →	See Chapter 9, pages 137–138
Do you know what to do if you need emergency treatment for your asthma?	NO →	See Chapter 12, page 159, and Chapter 16
Do you keep your medications with you without fail?	NO →	See Chapter 18, page 225
Do you have a regular doctor?	NO →	See Chapter 13, pages 172–175
Does your doctor know about your asthma and treat it seriously?	NO →	See Chapter 13, page 181

(continues)

FIGURE I.1   *(continued)*

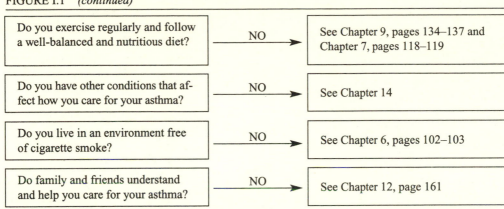

Do you exercise regularly and follow a well-balanced and nutritious diet?	NO →	See Chapter 9, pages 134–137 and Chapter 7, pages 118–119
Do you have other conditions that affect how you care for your asthma?	NO →	See Chapter 14
Do you live in an environment free of cigarette smoke?	NO →	See Chapter 6, pages 102–103
Do family and friends understand and help you care for your asthma?	NO →	See Chapter 12, page 161

reaction). Also, look in the index to this book, pages 251–262 or turn to Appendix B, where we list some extremely useful asthma help resources on the World Wide Web and give addresses, web addresses, and phone numbers of organizations or agencies that offer advice and help to individuals with asthma or other respiratory diseases. Answers are out there; you can find them if you go to the right places and make your needs known.

PART ONE

Understanding Your Asthma

1

What Is Asthma?

One in sixteen Americans—18 million individuals altogether—have asthma.

More than any other chronic illness, asthma:

- Claims more victims
- Causes more days of absence from work or school
- Carries a higher price tag
- Results in more days spent in hospital or emergency rooms

Asthma can show up at any age, although it commonly appears before the fifth birthday. In childhood it is three times more common and more severe in boys, but after puberty its incidence in the sexes evens out. More often found in people who live in urban, industrialized settings or colder climates, it also affects the urban poor—especially African Americans—disproportionately. But no ethnic nor age nor economic group stands immune to the disease.

Asthma represents an immense and growing public health problem. Over the past twenty years the number of cases of self-reported asthma has almost doubled, far outstripping the growth in population. During the same period the rate of asthma-caused deaths has shot up nearly 50 percent, from 11.5 deaths per million in 1980 to an estimated 18 in 1999.

That's the bad news.

The good news?

- In younger sufferers, symptoms of asthma tend to ease and may disappear altogether by late adolescence.
- Recent medical discoveries have brought about a much better understanding of the nature of the disease and its underlying causes.
- Treatment and control of symptoms of asthma has also improved dramatically, aided by the development of potent new medications.

Consequently, asthma sufferers, given proper care and counsel, can confidently expect to control their symptoms effectively and to lead full, active lives.

Symptoms of Asthma

Symptoms of asthma result from interactions among inflammatory cells, mediators, and the structures and tissues that make up the airways—the trachea, bronchial tubes, lungs. Those symptoms are:

- Shortness of breath
- Wheezing
- Coughing
- Increased production of mucus

Shortness of Breath

Asthmatic shortness of breath results when the airways become inflamed and go into spasm, causing the layer of smooth muscle that surrounds the tubes to constrict. This constriction cuts the flow of air to the lungs. Breathing air, like delivering water through pipes, depends on the diameter of the delivery tubes; the larger the tube, the more efficient and easier the delivery.

Airways resemble the complex root structure of a tree with the tubes dividing, becoming smaller and smaller, and proliferating, the farther they descend into the chest (see Figure 1.1).

When the smooth muscle sheaths that surround the airways go into spasm, the flow of air is cut and the telltale breathlessness and high-pitched wheezing of asthma follows.

FIGURE 1.1   The Respiratory Airways

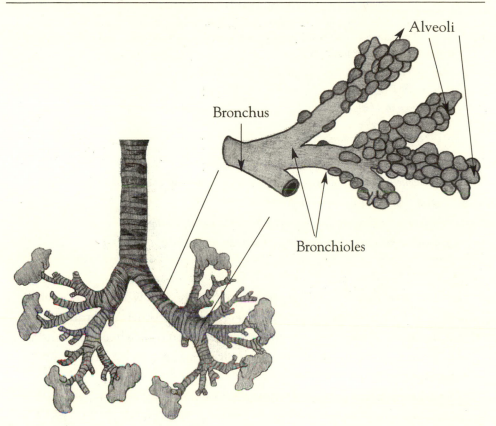

Heredity usually catches the blame for airways hypersensitive to inflammation and prone to going into spasm. In some children that tendency is present with their very first breath; in others it shows up on only a handful of occasions over an entire lifetime. However, an inherited tendency for airways to go into spasm can be made worse or triggered by a raft of substances or conditions, some of which are listed below.

In time, most asthmatics come to identify the major triggers of their symptoms. However, they may know only the major or obvious cause; minor or incidental contributors can go unnoticed.

Kevin has had asthma since early childhood. Although he had a rough time when he was younger, his symptoms gradually eased. While he still had oc-

---

Conditions or Substances That Trigger Airway Spasm

Inhaling airborne irritants including cigarette smoke, pollens, animal dander, dust and dust mites, particulate matter including smoke, pollutants like sulfur dioxide, ozone, smog, and many fumes or vapors found in the home or workplace.

Coming down with upper respiratory infections including common colds, influenza, and other infections of the airways or the sinuses.

Ingesting any of an almost endless list of foods, food additives, dyes, preservatives, "flavor enhancers," or other chemicals.

Exercising, hyperventilating, breathing in cold air.

Experiencing intense emotion, particularly sustained laughing and crying.

Encountering chemicals found in some workplaces—such as latex products found in hospitals.

Inhaling pungent odors such as incense and perfume.

Taking aspirin and other nonsteroidal anti-inflammatory drugs (like Ibuprofen).

During nighttime when breathing problems tend to appear or intensify.

---

casional episodes, he could manage them comfortably by staying out of harm's way by avoiding cigarette smoke, dust, and other airborne triggers and using a metered dose inhaler when he started to wheeze. He didn't worry much about being asthmatic, though, figuring he had things under control.

But, Kevin had a rude awakening. One night he was partying with a few friends and suddenly began to have serious trouble breathing. He used his inhaler but it didn't help; despite the medication his breathing worsened. Soon he was literally fighting for breath. A friend drove him to the emergency room where he was given nebulized Albuterol, steroids and fluids. These kicked in quickly and brought relief.

Kevin went to his physician to report the incident and to try to establish its cause. He had had no symptoms that day and, apart from the partying, had done nothing out of the ordinary. No one at the party was a smoker. The doctor asked Kevin if he had eaten anything that evening. "I had a few glasses of wine and some snacks," Kevin replied.

"What were the snacks?" the doctor asked.

"The usual. Peanuts. Crackers. Cheese. Chips. Salsa."

"Probably something you ate," the doctor said. "Ever had any trouble with any of those things before?"

"Never!"

Even though Kevin said he had had no problems with the foods he'd eaten, the doctor advised him to be careful when he ate those foods in the future. Kevin had a second, milder attack a few weeks after the first one. The circumstances were much the same except that he had eaten only tortilla chips with salsa. Playing a hunch, the doctor requested Kevin to give the brand name of the foods involved. She then checked the list of ingredients on the labels; there were no common allergens listed; still, she asked an old friend and colleague at the medical school to run a series of test looking for possible triggers. The salsa, it turned out, contained an enormous load of the preservative metabisulfite, even though the label on the bottle said "fresh." The doctor correctly concluded that the sulfite-laced salsa combined with sulfite-laden wine had produced Kevin's symptoms.

Kevin's case is typical of individuals who suddenly react asthmatically to something that had never troubled them before. In his case, the sulfite from the salsa and the red wine did the damage.

Wheezing

Asthmatic wheezing, a breathy, whistlelike sound heard during inhalation or exhalation, is a distinctive trademark of the disease. To test yourself for wheezing, breathe in and out as deeply as you can to clear your throat. Next, take a deep breath by inhaling as fully as you can, then exhale forcibly, listening carefully to the sound you are making. If you do not have asthma all you should hear is the movement of air in and out of your mouth; no sound or noise should occur below the level of the throat. If you have someone with asthma go through the same set of maneuvers and put your ear to the back of his or her chest during the exhalation stage, you will hear a high-pitched, reedy sound. But beware—this maneuver can make the airways of sensitive asthmatics go into spasm. In other cases the deep breath will not elicit wheezing but rather will precipitate a series of violent coughs. When people with asthma feel relatively good, the wheezing will happen only during the breathing-out phase, and then only when it is done forcibly and deeply.

It is important to distinguish an asthmatic wheeze from the ordinary sounds associated with breathing. Children with colds or other respiratory infections often develop significant swelling and inflammation of their adenoids as well as congestion of the nasal passages. These children may seem to snore when they sleep or have a snuffly nose, but listening to the chest can readily distinguish the noise arising from nasal obstruction from the asthmatic wheeze.

Mucus Production and Coughing

In addition to the spastic muscle tissue surrounding the airways, the airways contain mucus-producing cells, goblet cells, that contribute to asthma's symptoms, particularly its persistent, deep cough. Everybody, asthmatic or not, has these goblet cells; asthmatics have many more of these mucus-producing cells than nonasthmatics do. People with severe asthma have the most goblet cells of all.

Mucus is important because it transports the enzymes and chemicals that help the lungs fight infection. In asthmatics, however, these cells produce an excess of mucus that clogs airways and obstructs the flow of air, especially in the small airways in the bottom of the lungs. The persistent asthmatic cough is the body's effort to rid itself of the mucus.

Mucus is a major lurking problem in asthma. People with persistent asthma build up large amounts of mucus in the airways; if the mucus is not cleared, it can cause severe breathing difficulties and even death. Mucus and asthma remind us that the best approach to good asthma care is prevention; it is much easier to prevent the symptoms of asthma and therefore the buildup of mucus than it is to treat a case that is out of control.

A persistent cough, especially at night, sometimes represents the sole asthmatic symptom.

Jenny, 35, has had a nighttime cough for over two years. She has never had any health problems although a brother had child onset asthma. Jen tried virtually every cough medicine imaginable. Her doctor ordered a chest X ray, lung tests and a sinus X ray, and finally referred her to a specialist. With all tests negative, the specialist put her on a trial of Azmacort, an inhaled corticosteroid, and within two weeks the cough was gone. Jen had joined the ever increasing group of adult-onset asthmatics. Her only manifestation was the annoying cough.

An annoying cough, in the absence of other obvious causes, can signal the presence of asthma.

The Different Types of Asthma

Symptoms of asthma do not vary, but their severity and the agents causing them do.

The National Heart, Lung, and Blood Institute of the National Institutes of Health has identified four levels of severity when classifying asthmatic symptoms. Those levels are:

- Severe persistent
- Moderate persistent
- Mild persistent
- Mild intermittent

We discuss the features of each of these classifications fully in Chapter 14.

Asthma has so many different causes that they defy neat cataloging. One rough but useful way to do this spells out three different types or categories of causes—extrinsic, intrinsic, and mixed. This classification, once widely used by doctors, helps our understanding of asthma, although we now believe that the causes of asthma in most people evolve over time, the causes going from extrinsic to intrinsic or vice versa. For most people, their asthma is probably "mixed."

1. Extrinsic ("from without") asthma refers to episodes that follow exposure to substances in the environment—dusts, pollens, and the like. It is usually associated with high levels of allergen-specific IgE (immunoglobulin E) and represents a "true" allergic reaction (see Chapter 3, pages 42–45 for more about IgE and its relationship to allergy and asthma). Extrinsic asthma, usually reliably diagnosed by skin or blood tests (called RAST) or

provoked by challenge tests, commonly shows up in childhood, often along with eczema and hay fever. Curiously, people with extrinsic asthma tend to wheeze following exertion or exercise. They will often have hay fever, eczema, or both and are sometimes said to be atopic.

Mary's asthma began at about 8 and lasted until she reached 13. It always showed up in the springtime and was worse on windy days. She and her parents quickly tied her symptoms to days with high pollen counts. Although Mary's asthma proved difficult to manage during the pollen season, it got easier to handle with age and the use of medications that suppressed the pollens' effects. Nonetheless, even as an adult she often wheezed after vigorous exercise and has always had problems around cats.

Mary has mild intermittent asthma.

2. Intrinsic ("inherent") asthma, found in both children and adults, follows or can be made worse by infection, stress, or changes in environment or climate. Allergy tests are not as useful here, but the typically close correspondence between wheezing and the activities or events that trigger the symptoms make it easy to spot the cause.

Arthur's asthma began suddenly, twenty years ago, when he was 3. It hasn't let up since. He has to take several medications just to remain reasonably comfortable and must see his physician several times a year. Although many factors make Arthur's asthma worse, viral infections always trigger the symptoms that make him extremely ill. Arthur once had to go to the hospital when asthma followed a bout of sinusitis, and a common cold will send him to the emergency room. Arthur now has asthma year around and an extensive battery of allergy tests was negative.

Arthur has moderate persistent asthma.

3. Mixed asthma may have both extrinsic and intrinsic elements.

Jim had eczema in infancy but it went away around age 4. However, at age 6 he began to show signs of hay fever and, at age 7, asthma. His asthma, like his hay fever, always came on during the spring and fall; his mother kept the windows closed and made Jim stay indoors on windy days. As he grew older, Jim's seasonal symptoms eased but did not go away. Then, in his early 20s Jim began to wheeze when exposed to cigarette smoke and, on occasion, during a cold. His asthma, seasonal and extrinsic in childhood, now shows up in response to intrinsic triggers like respiratory infections as well as pollens.

Jim's mild intermittent asthma has both extrinsic and intrinsic triggers. Figure 1.2 diagrams the differences between those two categories, although it pays to remember that, regardless of cause, the symptoms of asthma, shortness of breath, wheezing, coughing, and mucus production, do not change.

Why Me?

Why me? is the asthma sufferer's first question. The doctor who makes that diagnosis will have asked if other family members, such as grandparents, parents, or siblings, have a history of asthma or allergies. In fact, more than two-thirds of asthmatics can point to a close family member who has or has had asthma and this statistic encourages the conclusion that heredity plays an important role in asthma. However, the precise nature of that role remains something of a puzzle. Some individuals from families riddled with asthma never show the disease; others from seemingly asthma-free backgrounds inexplicably turn up with it. Arthur, the intrinsic asthmatic described above, has absolutely no family history of asthma. He has six brothers and three sisters, not one of whom has asthma, and his parents, likewise, do not have the disease.

On the other hand, Jim, with mixed asthma, has two brothers and one sister. One brother and the sister have asthma; the sister's started at nearly the same age that Jim's did and she has had severe eczema her entire life. Jim's mother also has asthma while his father has no asthma or allergies. Jim's asthma clearly has a family connection but the exact part that heredity plays in the disease remains a mystery.

Some genes likely make one more prone to develop allergies; other genes may determine how extensive and severe these allergies may be. The ongoing growth in genetic research and especially the Human

FIGURE 1.2   Extrinsic and Intrinsic Asthma

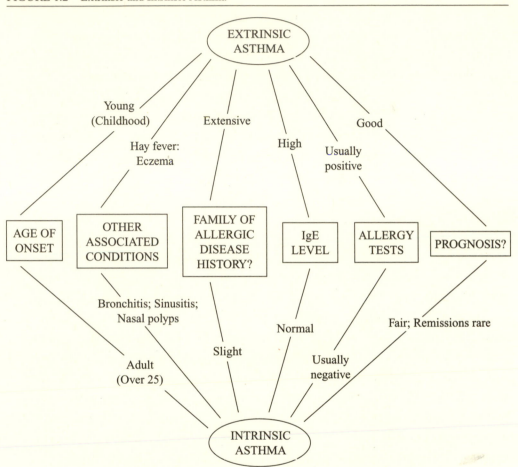

Genome Project will doubtless clarify the role that heredity plays in the development of asthma although atopy, the genetic condition that disposes one to manufacture excessive amounts of immunoglobulin E, the substance associated with allergic reactions to many substances or conditions, plays an important part. And atopy is a complex hereditary condition. We have already mentioned IgE in connection with extrinsic asthma and deal with this important topic fully in Chapter 3, pages 42–45. One theory suggests that exposure to pollution, especially early in life, may explain the increase in incidence of asthma.

Asthma and Panic

Asthma's symptoms, obvious and seemingly life-threatening, regularly throw sufferers and their families into panic. For the asthmatic, panic can intensify the spasms of the smooth muscle of the airways and further impair breathing. The panic can spread to family members who, in their concern and anguish, suggest inappropriate remedies or procedures—remedies or procedures that only serve to make matters worse. Two common ill-considered tactics are to advise the sufferer to breathe slowly and deeply or to have him or her take sedatives or tranquilizers.

Having the asthmatic breathe deeply or "try to cough it up" causes hyperventilation that further constricts the airways and makes the wheezing and shortness of breath worse, forcing mucus into the airways and blocking them even more. Caregivers should remember that the acute shortness of breath that defines asthma attacks usually appears to be more dangerous than it actually is. Advice should directly address the asthmatic's symptoms, not the caregiver's needs or unfounded beliefs. In any event, do not wait to see if symptoms abate; at the first sign of a crisis, go directly to your doctor or to an emergency room. Remember that peak flow meter readings indicate how well or badly you are doing. We cover peak flow meter use in Chapter 5.

Having asthmatics take tranquilizers or sedatives (a once common and extremely dangerous mistake) grew out of the mistaken belief that overexcitement or emotional upset triggers asthma. Not so. People having severe attacks need to keep awake just to breathe harder and more often to get the air they need. Sedating an asthmatic can bring on sleep that ends in suffocation and death.

Asthma Imposters

Several complaints have symptoms that closely resemble those of asthma. These look-alike conditions require different treatments from the ones prescribed for asthma, and mistaking them for asthma can have dangerous results. Accordingly, the symptoms of wheezing and shortness of breath must first undergo a careful and all-bases-covered differential diagnosis.

Conditions that imitate asthma include:

- Emphysema
- Chronic bronchitis
- Gastroesophogeal reflux (GER)
- Cystic fibrosis
- Foreign objects in the lung

Emphysema, a loss in elasticity of the lung tissue, most often results from cigarette smoking or longtime exposure to polluted air. Its external symptoms are shortness of breath that gets worse over time accompanied by a persistent, dry cough. Emphysema almost never affects children; it shows up most often in middle-aged smokers.

John began smoking at age 16 and soon developed a pack-a-day habit. At about age 45 he noticed that whenever he got a cold it settled into his chest and seemed to hang on forever. Still, he kept on smoking. Then at age 50, what started out as an ordinary cold turned ugly; John became acutely short of breath, turned blue, and collapsed. His wife called 911; the EMTs took him to the emergency room. John was breathing very rapidly and the ER doctor, while listening to his chest, heard some wheezing. He had John admitted to the hospital and ordered an X ray. It revealed a tremendous amount of swelling of the air sacs in his lungs. Further studies showed severely damaged air tubes and the presence of large, air-filled cysts that greatly impaired his breathing.

Treatment for this severely disabling and near-epidemic disease may include regular inhalation of oxygen. People with emphysema wheeze, and although their wheezes are treated much like those of asthmatics, the similarity breaks down at that point. Emphysema always shows irreversible damage to the lungs; moderate persistent or severe cases of asthma, improperly treated over a period of time, may also show lung abnormalities. However, in mild or moderate intermittent asthma—or properly and aggressively treated forms of the disease—the lung remains intact and the tissue returns to normal.

Chronic bronchitis also mimics asthma. Like emphysema, it frequently turns up in people who smoke. Workers in industries that expose them to dusts, gases, or vapors often develop bronchitis, as do residents of pollution-plagued cities like Houston or Los Angeles.

Carl has chronic bronchitis. He smoked heavily for about 20 years and worked on and off in Pennsylvania's coal mines. Injured on the job, he gave up the mines and moved to be with his daughter in Los Angeles. There his chronic cough worsened whenever he traveled the freeways. When the doctor listened to Carl's chest he sometimes heard wheezing but, unlike people with asthma, Carl's wheezing, cough, and bronchitis never let up. He can only hope that his condition will not deteriorate further and that, after flare-ups, he will return to his borderline status.

Gastroesophogeal reflux (GER) occurs more often in children than it does in adults. The "reflux" or backing up of the stomach's contents into the esophagus leads to stimulation of the nerves in the esophagus and this nerve reaction presumably precipitates the wheezing that accompanies the condition. Other companion symptoms include burping, belching, and heartburn.

Jerome, age 35, wakes up every night wheezing. His wife notices that he has chronic bad breath. Jerome's doctor recognizes the symptoms of GER and recommends raising the head of the bed 6 to 8 inches and prescribes Prilosec, a drug that reduces stomach acid. Jerome follows these simple instructions; the reflux improves substantially and the wheezing stops.

GER can be treated surgically, but this alternative ought to be avoided except for aggravated and stubborn cases.

Cystic fibrosis, a severe hereditary disease affecting children, sometimes passes for asthma. The disease runs in families and occurs in boys and girls; its cause remains unknown. Children with cystic fibrosis produce an enormous quantity of exceptionally thick mucus in the airways as well as an increase of mucus in all bodily secretions. Even the sweat of cystic fibrosis victims is thicker than that of other people and salt crystals often form on their skin. Children with cystic fibrosis experience severe, recurrent bacterial infections that gradually destroy the lungs. After many years of research, hope may be on the horizen for victims of cystic fibrosis. The gene that produces cystic fibrosis has been identified and the future will likely lead to gene therapy and a possible cure. Children with cystic fibrosis often have asthma as well, so often that when asthma sets in during early childhood—earlier than the usual age of onset—physicians may routinely suspect cystic fibrosis and order a sweat chloride test to rule out its diagnosis.

Penny had her first bout of pneumonia when she was only five months old. Hospitalized and given antibiotics, she recovered without incident. At the age of one year, she went back to the hospital with a second attack of pneumonia. Then, at eighteen months, a cold accompanied by severe wheezing put her in the hospital yet again. At this point her doctor got suspicious— too many serious respiratory illnesses at too early an age in too short a period of time. He ordered a sweat chloride test and it came back positive. Penny had cystic fibrosis. Even though Penny and her parents had to face a difficult future, early diagnosis of the disease meant she could have immediate and more aggressive treatment of infections whenever they occurred.

Foreign objects lodged in the lung can produce asthmalike symptoms. Usually the victims of this kind of accident have somehow inhaled a small object, typically bits of candy or peanuts, although the harvest of objects that doctors pull out of lungs is amazing—M&Ms, nails, hair balls, paper clips, seeds, cigarette butts, fruit pits. Even when X rays fail to pick up the invading object, the affected lung will show inflammation or the doctor's examination will reveal that the wheezing occurs in only one lung. Asthma, playing no favorites, affects both lungs, so that makes one-lung wheezes caused by foreign objects easy to detect.

Six-year-old Robin wolfed some peanuts. Several days after the episode her mother (who did not know of the peanut gobbling) noticed that Robin started coughing a lot, had a wheeze, and her skin seemed a little blue.

Mother and child went to the doctor who listened to Robin's chest, heard the wheeze, thought she might have asthma, but it didn't sound quite right. He ordered an X ray that showed that a lobe in her left lung had collapsed. This suggested an obstruction so he had Robin hospitalized and examined by a pediatric chest specialist. The chest specialist used a bronchoscope, a long flexible tube inserted into her lung via mouth and windpipe, to look into the lung where he saw and retrieved the peanut without having to do surgery.

Summary

This introductory chapter provides a brief introduction to a few selected topics central to the understanding of asthma, a huge, complex, and not fully understood disease. In it we sketch the disease's prevalence, negative and positive features, usual symptoms, causes, and triggers, and forms, types, and levels of severity with which it turns up.

The chapter refers the reader to later sections of the book that cover the topic more fully and will help the asthma sufferer or caregiver to understand and to deal competently and confidently with the disease.

In Chapter 1 we highlight and try to lessen the severe emotional impact the disease exerts on its victims or those who look after them. To emphasize the importance of a careful, informed differential diagnosis of symptoms, we conclude by enumerating and describing other respiratory diseases or conditions that sometimes pass for asthma.

Finally, here as well as throughout the book, we offer brief accounts—patient histories drawn from our experiences that illustrate or enlarge on the topic under discussion.

2

The Onset and Course of Asthmatic Disease

Asthma and Age

In Chapter 1 we used a venerable but still useful pair of categories to talk about what causes asthma. Intrinsic or internal asthma *(nonatopic)* traces to unknown factors, often viral infections, that lead to wheezing. Extrinsic or external *(atopic)* asthma follows exposure to triggers outside of the body and requires Immunoglobulin E (IgE) involvement (see Chapter 3, pages 42–45, for more on IgE). Both forms of asthma can be inherited. The age at which asthma first turns up offers a clue to its type.

This if-then typology works provided one has stayed in the same general geographic area. If you moved from Chicago to Sacramento at age twenty, and then developed asthma for the first time, one of the many California pollens probably triggered your symptoms.

Asthma can turn up at any age. When asthma surfaces in the very young and in adults, it most likely has a genetic or hereditary basis; from ages five to twenty, environmental triggers—dusts, pollens, and so on—usually evoke the symptoms.

Whether the cause relates to allergies or not, all asthmatics owe their symptoms to hypersensitive airways that can go into spasm with exposure to exercise, infection, irritants, or medications. The susceptibility of airways to spasm depends on age; the younger the individual the more vulnerable. As children (and their airways) mature, their asthma symptoms

TABLE 2.1   How to Tell If Asthma Is Atopic or Nonatopic

If the first asthma attack occurs	*then*	*its likely type is*
before the age of five		nonatopic (intrinsic asthma)
from age five to twenty		atopic (antigen-caused, IgE-linked or extrinsic asthma)
over age twenty		nonatopic (intrinsic asthma)

tend to moderate and may seem to disappear altogether. Regardless of age, though, a one-time asthmatic has airways that, under certain conditions, will go into spasm yet again.

The Course of Childhood Asthma

Just before his second birthday Sean, an obliging, cheerful, fun baby, came down with a cold and his parents noticed he had trouble with his breathing. They took him to the doctor, who prescribed some medications that relieved some of the cold symptoms and the breathing problem eventually faded away. However, both parents had allergy problems as children and they rightly feared that trouble lay ahead.

Thereafter, every time Sean had a cold it would slip into an asthma attack, and the attacks kept getting worse and worse. Finally, at the onset of even the slightest sniffle the parents knew there would come a time when they would have to rush him to the ER for treatment. Without that aid Sean would struggle for each breath, his color gradually changing, his lips going blue as his body got less and less of the oxygen it needed. The attacks made the parents feel helpless, frightened them, and filled them with dread. Then, Sean started wheezing even when he didn't have a cold. His mother noticed that his wheezing coincided with her ragweed-induced attacks of hay fever. She mentioned it to the doctor, who agreed that ragweed probably made matters worse for Sean.

The family talked things over and decided to move to a ragweed-free part of the country. The father, a salesman, had the freedom to transfer to another office of the company he worked for. They chose Nevada, where Sean's and his mother's ragweed allergies vanished immediately. Sean's bouts with asthma continued for a time whenever he had a cold but became milder and less frequent as he grew older. He had his last severe attack at the age of seven and his last ever at ten. Sean was lucky in that it was only ragweed; for many asthma sufferers, moving may only delay their symptoms—until they become allergic to new pollens such as sage in Nevada.

Now in his mid-teens, Sean seems free of symptoms although he does wheeze a little, coughs, and produces a lot of mucus whenever he mows the lawn and disturbs one of the large, pollen-dusted rice-paper plants that ring the patio. He also wheezes slightly following vigorous exercise.

Asthma is most often seen in children because asthma affects smaller airways more drastically than larger ones. When larger airways constrict, enough room remains for air to move, but when child-size airways go into spasm they may completely block the passage of air. In children, especially children under six, more than 80 percent of the airways are anatomically small. From the age of six and progressively thereafter the percentage of small airways decreases until it reaches 20 percent. Because of that simple fact, asthma is always worse, more frightening, in very small children.

During early childhood more boys than girls have asthma. However, as they age, boys more often show improvement so that by puberty (twelve to thirteen years) the percentages level out.

Parents of asthmatic kids often hear the reassuring message, "He (or she) will grow out of it." Not so. Childhood asthma often improves as the lung anatomy changes to contain a larger percentage of bigger airways. Because most children have mild, intermittent asthma they become relatively free of visible and audible symptoms as they mature. Even so, they still have spastic airways and if they run into enough of the aggravating factors we listed in Chapter 1, they may once again start wheezing. This can happen years down the road—even after they reach adulthood.

The hyperirritability of the airways also eases with age. We do not know why this occurs but it may have something to do with the maturing of the smooth muscle that surrounds the airways.

Henry had his first of many asthma attacks at the age of three. The episodes caused major problems in the family. Henry's father blamed the asthma on weakness or flaws in Henry's character, contending that Henry could master the symptoms if he just "grew up" and "fought" and "stopped being weak." Henry's mother thought of him as an invalid who needed protection and sheltering from everything in sight. These opposing views fueled some fine arguments.

Despite his well-intentioned if misguided parents, Henry's symptoms eased as he got older so that by the time he reached 12 his symptoms had largely vanished, even when he neglected to take his medication. Naturally his mother attributed his improvement to her protectiveness; the father rejoiced that the kid had finally grown up.

Henry went on to college and then to medical school. One of his lecturers, an allergist, said flatly that children do not outgrow asthma. "When properly challenged, asthmatics will wheeze," he declared, somewhat pompously, Henry thought. After the lecture Henry cornered the professor. "I had asthma as a kid," he said, "but I don't have it any more."

"You've still got it," the prof said. "You just don't know it. Come on, I'll prove it to you."

They went off to the pulmonary function clinic in the hospital where Henry, nonplussed, learned that his air flow fell somewhat below normal values. Worse, after a 15-minute session on a treadmill, even though he felt fine, further measurements showed even more reduction in air flow and a slight tendency to wheeze.

"You've still got it, just like I said. It just doesn't bother you any more," the allergist said.

Henry agreed grudgingly. He didn't mention it to his parents.

One should not conclude that, because the symptoms have gone away, the asthmatic predisposition has gone with them. Older individuals who had childhood asthma often find, when stressed by exercise or encounters with certain irritant materials, that the asthmatic tendency lingers on. Sometimes the frequency and severity of symptoms will decline in individuals who, when young, had wheezed following viral infections. Their asthma got better as they grew older partly because the number of viral infections we catch decreases as we age. We develop immunity to many of these infections, an immunity that grows out of prior exposure, and as the number of colds falls off, so does the number of asthmatic episodes. In fact, some of these asthma-triggering infections like respiratory synctial virus infection—a condition caused by synctium, a complex form of virus—occur almost exclusively in very young children. If you or your child tend to wheeze following respiratory infection, the frequency of the attacks will likely tail off as the susceptibility to colds diminishes or the cold season passes.

On the other hand, as you get older you may also begin to wheeze for other reasons. Extrinsic factors—allergies—may begin to provoke reactions in the airways. Medical researchers disagree over whether the asthmatic child's viral infections predispose the development of allergies or the later-appearing symptoms merely represent a different manifestation of the same underlying cause. Despite this inconclusiveness on the parts of the researchers, as the parent of a child with asthma you can look for both good and bad tidings. On the plus side, you can reasonably expect that your child's and your life will become considerably easier as the child becomes older and the severity of the asthma episodes eases. Even so, try not to forget that your child does have asthma. As your child grows older—sometimes much older—he or she may encounter conditions or substances that trigger the quiescent but underlying genetic predisposition to wheeze. Always remember to tell your doctor, whatever your age, if you had asthma. For example, some drugs (beta blockers) that are used to combat high blood pressure can reactivate latent asthma. Also, there are many cases of allergies showing up as asthma that trace to new substances in the workplace.

Sue, an Intensive Care Unit nurse at a Chicago hospital, enjoyed radiant good health despite her seasonal hay fever. She jogged regularly, looked after her three daughters, and worked hard at and loved her job in the hospital's newborn nursery. Then she began noticing an itchy rash that developed on her hands. At first she ignored the rash, blaming it on the anti-bacterial soap she used, but the rash persisted even after she changed soaps. Then she started wheezing so she took her problems to the Employee Health Department. The specialists there quickly established that Sue was allergic to the latex protein in her gloves, her symptoms made worse because she favored the more comfortable and easier to shed powdered type. The people at the Employee Health Unit advised her to use non-latex gloves but Sue found that she started to wheeze whenever she set foot in the hospital. Sensitized now, the minute amounts of latex in the hospital's air were still enough to have her hypersensitive airways go into spasm. She had to leave the hospital; she no longer works in the health care field, wears a Medic-Alert bracelet, and must carry an Epi-Pen for use in an emergency.

We discuss the epidemic of latex allergy as well as other workplace associated triggers in Chapter 8.

Myths About Childhood Asthma

So many misconceptions and so much folklore surround childhood asthma that it will serve you well to note the points that appear in the accompanying sidebar.

The Usual Course of Adult-Onset Asthma

As the population of the United States grows and ages, the number of asthmatics in that population grows and ages. In fact, the number and incidence of patients with adult-onset asthma grows; over a period of years an estimated 3 to 4 percent of adults will have a first-time-ever diagnosis of asthma.

A physician treating a patient with adult-onset asthma symptoms will first look for the cause in the patient's workplace. Indeed, triggers encountered on the job account for the bulk of adult-onset cases. We cover the many triggering agents and the ways to respond to occupational asthma in Chapter 8.

The number of elderly—people approaching or past retirement age—who turn up with first-time asthma has also grown, and the incidence of asthma-related deaths in this late-onset group exceeds that found in any other age group.

The physician called on to treat a case of adult-onset asthma will first look for its cause in the patient's environment, and particularly any recent changes in job, locale, or dwelling.

The Dos and Don'ts, Cans and Can'ts of Childhood Asthma

- Emotional disorders *do not* cause asthma. Rather, having asthma can precipitate emotional problems.

- Children with asthma *can* and *should* participate in sports and athletic activities. They *can* and *should* play musical instruments; in fact, playing wind instruments builds up respiratory reserve.

- Asthmatic children *can* grow up and pursue any type of career or hobby desired, providing their asthma is adequately controlled and their environment or activities do not carry the triggers that set them to wheezing.

- Children with asthma *can* safely undergo surgery.

- Asthma may cause remodeling or reshaping of the lung but, unlike emphysema, if treated regularly, it will *not* destroy the lung; it is usually a reversible process where, between asthma attacks, the lungs return to their normal state.

- Children with asthma *should* experience normal growth and *will not* develop chest deformities unless given medications like cortisone, and then only rarely.

- Asthmatic children *can* attend birthday and slumber parties provided they keep alert to and avoid possible triggers and the party givers know of the child's susceptibility and what to do if exposure happens.

- Asthmatic children *should not* go to special care facilities unless their asthma resists control and demands constant, direct medical attention.

- *No one* with a record of asthma in adolescence qualifies for military service.

- If your first child has asthma, that *does not* mean that children who follow will also be asthmatic.

- Most asthmatic children *will* significantly improve if they follow a regular program of medication.

- Tonsillectomies and adenoidectomies *do not* cure asthma and should not be done on account of asthma.

- *Not* every child with asthma wheezes. Sometimes the only symptom amounts to a persistent dry cough.

Ernie, a lifelong resident of San Francisco, had never had trouble with allergies. However, he bought a house and a few months after he moved into it he began to cough at night. The cough kept getting worse and then the wheezing started.

Things eventually got so bad that Ernie consulted an allergist who put him through a series of skin tests. Ernie reacted violently to the test for cat dander. Ernie had no pets but the allergist asked if the home's previous owner had had cats. Ernie checked with the previous owner and learned they had indeed had cats, three of them, all longhairs that never went outside. Even though Ernie had vacuumed and cleaned the house top-to-bottom and redecorated before moving in, cat dander filled the wall-to-wall carpets. Ernie had the old carpet torn out and replaced with a new, low-pile covering after first vacuuming the floors carefully. He also had the drapes dry-cleaned.

Ernie's wheezing stopped immediately but it started showing up under extremely windy weather conditions or sometimes when Ernie caught a cold. It also flared up again when his girlfriend adopted a kitten.

But the search should not end with the environment.

Tree pollens had given Trudy problems for years. She treated her symptoms successfully with over-the-counter metered dose inhalers but one spring, following a particularly wet winter, the pollen count skyrocketed, her hay fever symptoms intensified, and her physician, saying she had developed bronchitis, prescribed a brief course of antibiotics. The antibiotics did not help and the respiratory symptoms not only worsened but changed so that Trudy found herself coughing and wheezing day and night. The doctor said that the problem had gone into asthma and prescribed a battery of medications that gave some temporary relief but did not ease the problems. At that point, however, Trudy's HMO insurance carrier pulled out of California and, through her former employer's continuing coverage, Trudy opted for a non-HMO plan, one of several alternatives available as part of her retirement package. Her new primary care physician (personal care provider) spent considerable time with her during a physical examination, took a careful history, and referred her to a specialist who ordered a CT scan of Trudy's sinuses (see Chapter 4, pages 59–62). The scan showed the sinuses to be widely infected so the physician prescribed treatment with antibiotics. Trudy took the medication faithfully and, after several weeks, the sinus infection cleared and the cough and wheeze abated. Her sensitivity to pollens persisted but Trudy's new doctor prescribed use of a nasal steroid to anticipate and manage the hay fever. While Trudy is asthmatic, her asthma symptoms are in remission and, with care, will remain so although she will need to be careful about respiratory infections that could bring back the sinus infection and the associated respiratory problems.

Asthma-like symptoms can arise from a variety of causes so misdiagnoses—wrongly attributing a set of symptoms to asthma or wrongly blaming another disease for truly asthma-caused symptoms—occur frequently, especially in the elderly. Seniors may have special need for respiratory and cardiac investigation to nail the diagnosis and this leads to complications.

- Patients with Medicare coverage may receive perfunctory care at some hands.
- Physicians reluctantly use spirometry (measurement of respiratory function) in the elderly, oftentimes because the patients have trouble carrying out the procedures or the procedures frighten or confuse them.
- HMOs may not pay for pulmonary testing; they generally put off carrying out sinus CT scans and methacholine challenge testing. They hope that by delaying you will decide to forget it. Learning how to be your own advocate is essential in today's "medical marketplace." Remember, it may not be your doctor who is delaying diagnosis; it more likely is a nonphysician playing the role of bean counter to maximize the company's profits.

Sally, age 60, saw her doctor for her persistent wheezing. Her doctor knew she had asthma but couldn't seem to get the symptoms under control. Sally's other complaint was that she had lost her sense of smell. Suspecting that Sally had chronic sinusitis, her doctor ordered a 4-way CT of the sinuses. It took three phone calls and six weeks before her HMO finally approved this five-minute X ray. The results showed that Sally had severe and widespread infection of her sinuses. Treated with antibiotics for over two months, she showed some but not sustained improvement. After an additional eight-week delay, Sally finally got approval to see an ENT specialist located an hour's drive from where she lived. The ENT specialist recommended sinus surgery. This procedure likewise required a six-week approval process and two additional weeks to schedule. Finally, Sally's sinuses were cleared out and her asthma has gotten much better. Sally wrongly blames her primary doctor for the delay, the confusion, and her prolonged suffering; in reality she should have complained to her HMO and especially her employer who makes the monthly HMO payments.

And even after arriving at a firm diagnosis of asthma, management or treatment may fail because the elderly:

- Often do not notice their breathing difficulties readily and, accordingly may underestimate the severity of their symptoms.
- Have trouble using peak-flow meters appropriately, thus getting unreliable readings of respiratory status.
- Under- or overmedicate because they cannot use metered-dose inhalers efficiently. (Several studies reveal that this melancholy fact applies to as many as 60 percent of elderly asthma sufferers.)
- May not adhere to medication or management procedures because of simple forgetting, failure to understand or carry out instructions, or (for the uninsured, low-income patients found disproportionately in this older group) the ruinous cost of medications not covered by insurance.

Asthma, at any time of life, is a burden; when it turns up for the first time in adults, especially older adults, it can be demoralizing. We make suggestions elsewhere in this book about strategies to follow in the choice of a physician or a specialist (see Chapter 13, pages 171–180) and the importance of faithfully recording and monitoring symptoms and the conditions surrounding them (see Chapter 5, pages 66–74). Beyond those suggestions we encourage "seniors" said to have asthma (or their in-home caregivers) to study and answer the following questions and discuss their responses with their physician.

- Did you change your job or residence before your symptoms began? If so, specify.

- Have you experienced any lifestyle changes such as diet, activities, illnesses, recreation, new pets, new venues, and so forth? If so, specify.
- If the doctor says you have asthma, do you accept the diagnosis? Have you seen another physician or specialist? If in doubt, discuss with your physician.

If medications or other treatment or management measures have been prescribed, answer the following questions.

- Do you know what effects they will have and how they will work on your symptoms? (If the answer is no, find out by asking your doctor or nurse practitioner.)
- Do you know what side effects they may carry? (If you answer no, talk to a doctor, a nurse practitioner, a pharmacist, consult the *Physician's Desk Reference,* or go to the web; see Appendix A.)
- Do you know exactly when, why, and how you need to take your medications? (If you do not know, get clarification from a doctor or pharmacist.)
- Do you have trouble taking medications or carrying out preventive procedures (such as difficulty swallowing pills, using your inhaler effectively, keeping track of your medications)? (If yes, tell your in-home caregiver, doctor, nurse practitioner, or pharmacist about the problem and ask for help.)
- Do you have a list of questions to ask your doctor, questions written out before the visit so that you don't forget? (If no, prepare the list if you do have questions.)

Asthma represents a serious—indeed potentially lethal—problem. Asthma, at its worst, means discomfort, debility, and even death, so it demands unfailing care and respect. It also deserves careful, effective, and solicitous treatment, treatment that does not fall easily into the lap of the elderly, but such treatment is available. Good care is possible when the older person—any person—insists on having proper care and then follows through faithfully on the care prescription given.

Why You Should Pay Attention to Your (or Your Child's) Asthma

The number of people who have asthma who wind up intensely ill with it or who die from it continues to rise. Those facts constitute reason enough to take the disease seriously. Despite the fact that your or your child's asthma responds quickly and easily to countermeasures should not lull you into making the mistake of not taking the disease seriously. Be prepared for a worst possible case scenario, even though that possibility might seem as remote to you as a trip to Mars. Asthma can turn ugly in a matter of minutes.

Judy had severe asthma during infancy. Her symptoms most often started with a cold. As she got older she found she needed medication only occasionally. During adolescence she had no problems at all with her asthma apart from mild wheezing during gym class. She generally carried a metered dose inhaler with her but almost never used it and didn't waste a lot of time thinking about it. Then Judy went on a field trip with her class and visited a candle-making shop. The strong odor and fumes from the shop set Judy to coughing. The coughing gave way to a wheeze that had her fighting for breath. She exited the shop thinking to get the inhaler out of her handbag. She scrabbled in it desperately until it dawned on her that she'd stopped carrying her medication a couple of years back and right now it probably sat at the back of her dresser drawer. Meanwhile her wheezing and shortness of breath became severe enough to send her to the ER while the rest of her classmates went on with their outing. Oxygen and a breathing treatment with Albuterol by the respiratory therapist brought Judy around and the experience taught her not to get careless about her symptoms nor to take them for granted.

Although it pays to be prepared for an asthmatic emergency, you should not think of yourself as an invalid, sentenced to a life of suffering and hardship on account of your asthma. There are millions of fellow sufferers out there. Simply figure out what might go wrong for you, get fully ready for an emergency, and hope that it never shows up.

Summary

Asthma can appear at any point during a lifetime. When it shows up in childhood, blame genetic—intrinsic—factors. From ages five to twenty the symptoms usually can be traced to irritants that trigger the asthmatic reaction. Asthma that turns up in adults may have genetic or environmental causes.

In children, the severity of the symptoms decreases as the child matures and the airways enlarge, but the susceptibility to the disease remains. Even though the symptoms can go dormant for years, once an asthmatic, always an asthmatic.

Like most common and troublesome diseases, a multitude of myths surround asthma, its course, its causes, and its treatment. We consider these beliefs and strategies and offer a primer for asthmatics, especially older asthmatics and their caregivers, on how to develop treatment strategies. We close the chapter by reminding readers of asthma's sometimes astonishing speed of onset and its potential deadliness.

3

Allergies and Asthma

The word *allergies* conjures up a host of meanings. To those of us who suffer from them, allergies can represent anything from a minor nuisance to a frightening, ever-present threat to life. Causes of allergies are becoming much better understood than those for many other medical conditions and treatment has improved and carries fewer side effects. Indeed, Eric Gershwin tells his students that if they cannot successfully treat an allergy case, then they have made the wrong diagnosis.

Bob, a 53-year-old hospital radiologist, has been treated for allergies most of his life. His symptoms worsen on windy days, when the pollution count is high, or when he ventures outside on cold, crisp days. He has tried just about every drug in the book—over-the-counter medications, prescription antihistamines, intranasal steroids. Sometimes they helped, sometimes they didn't, with no discernable pattern of success—or failure. Finally, an allergist reacted to Bob's off-handed complaint about having an itchy soft palate, figured that a hay fever masquerader, vasomotor rhinitis, might be responsible for Bob's symptoms, and prescribed a prescription nasal spray, Atrovent. Atrovent blocks the airway's cholinergic nerves. It has no direct or specific application to allergic complaints but its faithful use cleared up Bob's symptoms miraculously.

To many, the word *allergy* seems strange and exotic, which may help to explain its careless and widespread application. It has even taken on nonmedical connotations: "Maybe I'm allergic to my desk," muses Peppermint Patty, the cartoon strip character, to explain her poor grades.

Those fortunate enough to be free of allergies are inclined to regard an allergic person as an enigma, a crank, a hypochondriac, a malingerer, or a pitiable weakling. They have little understanding of the misery wrought by allergies and cannot sympathize with the millions who suffer from a staggering variety of allergic complaints. They cannot fully comprehend the anxiety and dread of a mother who does not know the cause of her child's allergy or even if allergy is involved; the acute discomfort and self-consciousness of an adult who endures hives and chronic itching; the agony of a teenager trying to live through the maddening discomfort and disfigurement of persistent eczema; the sense of failure experienced by a student with severe hay fever whose grades suffer because of the sedation produced by antihistamines; the athlete disqualified from competition because the medication she took to control her asthma showed up and had her flunk the drug test.

Even people who treat people with allergies differ in their views of allergy. The more medically conservative practitioner regards it as a specific set of conditions verified by rigorous laboratory tests. Others think of it as any of a broad and ill-defined series of reactions that almost everyone experiences at one time or another.

Medical authorities generally use the word *allergy* to refer to the hypersensitivity of the body to a specific substance, usually termed an *allergen* or *antigen*, that results in any of a wide variety of reactions. Allergic reactions include eczema, hives, hay fever, drug reactions, and, most important to us here, the wheezing, shortness of breath, and mucus production that attend asthmatic attacks.

Your asthma more than likely results from, or is made worse by, allergies. Out of a population of roughly 280 million in the United States, an estimated 50 million (17 percent) have some sort of allergic disease; about 18 million (7 percent of the total population and well over 25 percent of all allergy sufferers) have asthma. If you live in some states, like California or Texas, the incidence runs even higher.

What Is an Allergy?

Many authorities believe allergies originated millennia ago with the human body's evolution of mechanisms to rid itself of invading worms and parasites. The body fights these invaders by producing a special antibody called immunoglobulin E—IgE, for short. This antibody, a chemical released into the blood, helps the body attack and destroy foreign materials, especially those in the gut or lung.

Most parasites enter and live either in the lung or in the intestines of the host. Special groups of lymph nodes line the interior surface of the lung and the intestine and these lymphoid tissues harbor the cells that have the machinery to make IgE.

Probably production of IgE was once essential to man's struggle to survive the threat of parasites. However, as civilization (and hygiene) advanced, the prevalence of human parasites declined and the need to fight worms with IgE became less important. Most of us in the Western world no longer need these special IgE-producing cells.

Nonetheless, these redundant cells continue to exist, and, although they are not ordinarily called on to fight parasites, they remain in the body and continue to react to invasive foreign substances. Because they occur in the lung and the gut, things that enter the body from the outside world encounter these IgE-producing cells first; they monitor everything inhaled and eaten. Some people have the predisposition, probably inherited, to manufacture large quantities of IgE. This higher level of IgE does no apparent good; worse, it correlates with most forms of allergic disease. Individuals with this genetic tendency are often called *atopic*, a word used to characterize people with allergies.

An allergy, then, reflects nothing more than an individual's level of production of IgE. Those who make lots of it generally have allergies; everyone else puts out levels that are either irrelevant or too low to provoke an allergic reaction. Accurate diagnosis and efficient management of allergic symptoms rest on the detection and measurement of IgE.

What Happens in the Body to Trigger an Allergic Reaction?

The air we breathe and the food we swallow contain pollens and chemicals—antigens or allergens—considered foreign by the body. Our bodies process these foreign materials in one of two ways—either by routinely processing and degrading the substance and excreting it or by degrading the antigen but also producing IgE that reacts against it. Production of IgE evidently aims to accelerate the elimination of the allergen. Unfortunately, the process of manufacturing this antibody also unleashes an entire new array of body-immune machinery.

The process goes as follows: The IgE antibody produced binds onto certain specialized white blood cells in the body known as mast cells and basophils. The IgE antibodies attached to these white cells stand guard, like sentries looking out for foreign bodies or chemicals (allergens). If the allergen enters the body, as when a grass pollen is inhaled or a particular food eaten, these sentry IgE antibodies quickly detect it. As soon as the allergen touches them, the sentries shoot holes in the white cells. The white cells, because they now have holes in their walls, release stored chemicals, the most important of which is histamine. The release of histamine and the other stored chemicals cause allergic symptoms such as flushing, wheezing, and hives. Unhappily, the white cells do not quit at that point. Once breached, white blood cells begin to synthesize a whole new group of chemicals in the body. Some of these chemicals include substances known as prostaglandins and leukotrienes. The white cells may require from several hours to as long as several days to produce these substances. However, once manufactured and released, they may cause persistent, severe, and stubborn allergic symptoms. This delay in production of the prostaglandins and leukotrienes contributes significantly to some forms of asthma, especially occupational asthma. Thus, the elements that combine to produce allergic symptoms include the presence of the allergen (a substance you are allergic to), IgE antibodies, and white cells.

The Danger of Allergies

Sometimes the appearance or the severity of an allergic reaction defies prediction. For example, two young men, each eighteen years of age, may see the same doctor for a strep throat. Each man has received penicillin many times before and both men are given the same prescription for penicillin. One takes the penicillin for ten days, clears the strep infection, and goes his merry way. The other takes the penicillin and, within a few minutes of swallowing the first pill, breaks out in hives, begins to wheeze, has acute shortness of breath, and experiences a serious drop in blood pressure. Without immediate emergency treatment this man could die.

Fortunately, of the millions of Americans who suffer from allergies, most experience only minor inconveniences. They endure the annoyance and discomfort of hay fever during the pollen season, or they may have an occasional bout of hives or eczema as a child. For most of these individuals, antihistamines, coupled with an occasional visit to a physician, enable them to manage their symptoms comfortably.

How Repeated Exposure Makes Allergies Worse

Most children get immunized against diphtheria, whooping cough, tetanus, polio, and measles. These vaccinations are extremely effective.

The process of immunization usually involves a series of injections, or shots. Pediatricians know immunization works, but must take place at certain ages and when certain intervals between shots are observed. For example, a child may require several doses of a polio virus before developing adequate immunity. With each successive dose of the vaccine the body makes a better antibody response. This process is known as sensitization; when adequately sensitized, the child has sufficient antibodies to ward off the disease.

Essentially, the same process of sensitization applies to the appearance of IgE antibodies. The body must encounter allergens over a sufficiently long period of time before they set off an adequate IgE response. Many people have to be exposed to an allergen scores of times before even small amounts of IgE are seen. To seriously atopic people, IgE antibodies may develop after brief or casual exposure.

Dr. Pierce is an oral surgeon. An active jogger who stays in good shape, he neither smokes nor drinks. During childhood he had scarlet fever and was given an injection of penicillin. The scarlet fever improved, but Dr. Pierce remembers that for several weeks after the injection he had hives. It has been more than 25 years since the scarlet fever, and Dr. Pierce has not had to take penicillin since. One morning he wakes up with a severe sore throat. His doctor diagnoses a strep infection, and gives Dr. Pierce a prescription for penicillin. Dr. Pierce reminds the family physician of the hives he suffered from as a child. The physician, rightly concerned that Dr. Pierce might be allergic to penicillin, prescribes an antibiotic known as Keflex. Dr. Pierce takes the Keflex and within minutes collapses, covered with hives, wheezing and desperately short of breath—an anaphylactic shock reaction. He is rushed to the emergency room and immediately given an injection of adrenalin. He recovers without incident. Dr. Pierce is severely allergic to penicillin; his family doctor forgot that a small percentage of patients allergic to penicillin also have a cross-reactivity to other antibiotics, among them Keflex.

It is important to know not only what you are allergic to but whether there are other substances that share enough characteristics with the offender to produce a cross-reaction. Peaches, for example, are in the same food family as almonds. If you are allergic to peaches you will likely react allergically to almonds (Chapter 7, page 111, lists food families).

If a person lives in the same area for a long time, the sensitization process occurs every season. As the seasons roll around, the amount of IgE produced by the atopic person may continue to go up. In fact, if you measure the quantity of IgE in the blood of a hay fever sufferer regularly over a period of twelve months, you will find that the level rises with the onset of the pollen season and stands at its lowest before the beginning of the next season.

One common treatment for allergies—perhaps the most popular medically administered one—is to deliver injections that introduce the offending antigen into the body in a series of gradually increasing dosages. This procedure, if appropriate for your condition and if it works, desensitizes you to the offending substance. In effect, it modifies—checkmates—the process by which your allergy established itself in the first place. Chapter 4 discusses the allergies commonly associated with asthma; Chapter 15 critically evaluates the use (and abuse) of allergy shots.

Summary

Allergies and asthma go hand in hand. This chapter explores that relationship. Allergies, an evolutionary holdover, result from the body's reaction to invasion by foreign substances. The invasion results in the production of an antibody, Immunoglobulin E—IgE—that, in its turn, triggers a range of symptoms that can cause anything from minor, temporary, and localized discomfort to persistent, severe, and even lethal respiratory or vascular failure.

Asthma is one major product of an allergic reaction. Ordinarily, the allergic (and asthmatic) reaction needs time and repeated exposure to the offending substance—the allergen or antigen—to develop. So it is with asthma.

To treat an allergy you need to know what triggers your symptoms and to stay clear of it. Where your symptoms persist stubbornly and exposure to their cause cannot be avoided, desensitization—immunization or allergy shots—can sometimes control allergies; otherwise, an array of medications can usually manage allergies (and asthma) comfortably.

4

Allergic Complications Associated with Asthma

Asthmatics whose symptoms are the result of an allergic reaction (these people are called *atopic*) can develop any of a number of other troublesome medical problems as well. These fellow travelers of asthma include eczema, hay fever, allergic conjunctivitis, ear infections, sinusitis, and acute bronchopulmonary aspergillosis. As an asthmatic or an asthmatic caregiver, you should know of and be prepared to address these conditions.

Eczema

Eczema (*atopic dermatitis*, or AD), the most tenacious and disturbing of the allergic skin disorders, usually shows up between the second and sixth months of life. It may persist for years or, rarely, for an entire lifetime. It affects about 4 children in 100 and is somewhat more prevalent among females; seen more often in urban and industrialized areas, it plays no ethnic or racial favorites. Like many allergic conditions, its incidence grows.

Eczema's most prominent feature is the intense itching it provokes, an itch so fierce that scratching becomes irresistible and brings on the ugly and disfiguring sores that are the hallmark of the disorder. It is often referred to as "the itch that rashes."

Charles had a severe case of eczema, which the doctor suspected he was making worse by scratching, even though Charles denied this vehemently. He permitted the doctor to put a plaster cast over his lesions, then went home and scratched right through the cast. The same doctor treated another patient, Paul, in the same way. Paul did not scratch and when the cast came off, his skin was clear.

Work through the decision chart in Figure 4.1 to decide if a skin disorder is eczema. Note, however, that the character and location of the disorder varies with the age of the victim: *infant* eczema starts after the second month, and most sufferers lose their symptoms by the second year. The "moist" or "wet" form of the disease is most common at this stage with the face, and especially the cheeks of the baby, the favorite sites for the lesions. *Childhood* eczema shows up after the second year and usually vanishes by the tenth birthday. Generally these children have "dry" eczema, which characteristically shows scaling. Distinct, flat, dry elevations on the skin predominate; lesions occur at the insides of the elbows and knees, on the neck, and on the skin behind the ears. *Adolescent* and *adult* eczema appear at adolescence or later. The "dry" type of lesion, often confined to the hands, is prevalent in this stage.

The cause or causes of eczema remain a mystery. Its sufferers, when tested in the laboratory, sometimes show elevated levels of specific Immunoglobulin E, and they will often display asthma or hay fever symptoms as well. Parents and physicians report that the condition may break out or grow worse during peak pollen seasons or after eating certain foods.

Carefully conducted experiments using skin tests that tried to tie hypersensitivity to specific foods to eczema have proved inconclusive. We do not recommend routine skin testing for individuals suffering from eczema because of the risk of triggering a reaction or worsening an existing one. Thus, all that we can say about eczema symptoms is that they are associated or linked with other bodily signs and exposure to allergy-producing substances to which the individual is susceptible—foods, dust and pollens, animal dander, and molds may make them worse. Consequently, eczema sufferers or their parents must rely on elimination diets (see Chapter 7,

48

FIGURE 4.1   Decision Chart for Eczema

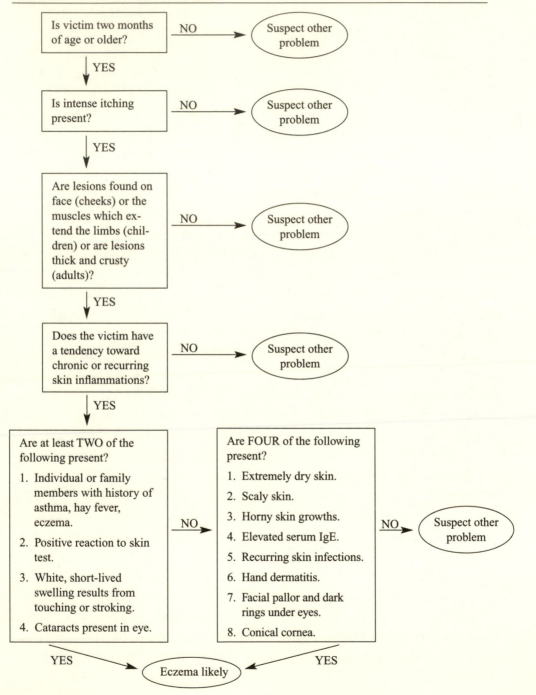

page 114) or careful, critical observations to identify the agents that appear to produce or worsen the symptoms. Because of the possible role of foods in producing eczema, newborn children, especially those with allergic parents, should be breast-fed for at least their first six months. This will delay the need to feed babies' formula, cow's milk, and other foods until later in the first year of life. Breast-fed babies have less eczema (indeed, fewer allergies of *all* kinds) than bottle-fed babies. We recommend that pregnant women not eat any peanuts and we discourage children under four years of age from eating peanuts or any nut products. Although this may be an extreme position, a growing body of evidence suggests that nut allergy can begin even *in utero*. Further, the infant's immature gut tract allows potential allergens, like nuts, to penetrate the body early in life when the susceptibility to allergies is greatest.

The treatment of eczema has to take into account a number of factors—type and extent of the disease, age and occupation of the victim, presence or absence of infection. Figure 4.2 sketches the steps and strategies for home treatment of eczema.

To the eczema sufferer, the disease's most disturbing features are unbearable itching, the unsightliness of the lesions, and how others react to them. It is almost impossible to keep from scratching, an impulse that may have caused the lesions in the first place, may make it worse, or may even bring on a secondary infection. Figure 4.2 lists various means of overcoming this powerful urge to scratch; controlling allergic skin disorders hinges on suppressing the impulse to scratch. Given a chance, these methods, backed up by the firm resolve not to scratch, will work.

Because society places such a high value on clear skin, eczema's unsightly lesions often set in motion a chain of events that only make a bad situation worse. Most eczemas eventually go away and leave no scars; however, the temptation to disguise or mask the lesions with cosmetics often proves irresistible. This compounds the problem because many cosmetics, allergens in their own right, aggravate the symptoms; scratching introduces the cosmetic into the lesion and this invasion spreads and worsens the lesion. Moreover, consumers often choose beauty preparations on the strength of what their manufacturers say about their properties; these claims can mislead. For instance, so-called "gentle" Ivory soap,

FIGURE 4.2   First Aid and Home Treatment for Eczema

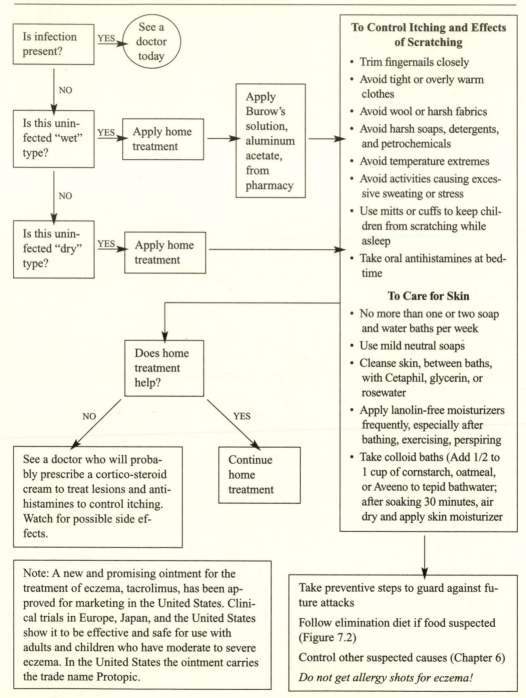

Is infection present? — YES → See a doctor today

NO ↓

Is this uninfected "wet" type? — YES → Apply home treatment → Apply Burow's solution, aluminum acetate, from pharmacy

NO ↓

Is this uninfected "dry" type? — YES → Apply home treatment

Does home treatment help?

NO → See a doctor who will probably prescribe a cortico-steroid cream to treat lesions and antihistamines to control itching. Watch for possible side effects.

YES → Continue home treatment

To Control Itching and Effects of Scratching

- Trim fingernails closely
- Avoid tight or overly warm clothes
- Avoid wool or harsh fabrics
- Avoid harsh soaps, detergents, and petrochemicals
- Avoid temperature extremes
- Avoid activities causing excessive sweating or stress
- Use mitts or cuffs to keep children from scratching while asleep
- Take oral antihistamines at bedtime

To Care for Skin

- No more than one or two soap and water baths per week
- Use mild neutral soaps
- Cleanse skin, between baths, with Cetaphil, glycerin, or rosewater
- Apply lanolin-free moisturizers frequently, especially after bathing, exercising, perspiring
- Take colloid baths (Add 1/2 to 1 cup of cornstarch, oatmeal, or Aveeno to tepid bathwater; after soaking 30 minutes, air dry and apply skin moisturizer

Note: A new and promising ointment for the treatment of eczema, tacrolimus, has been approved for marketing in the United States. Clinical trials in Europe, Japan, and the United States show it to be effective and safe for use with adults and children who have moderate to severe eczema. In the United States the ointment carries the trade name Protopic.

Take preventive steps to guard against future attacks

Follow elimination diet if food suspected (Figure 7.2)

Control other suspected causes (Chapter 6)

Do not get allergy shots for eczema!

harsh and irritating according to many medical authorities, should be scrupulously avoided by anyone with eczema. After weighing the trivial advantages of a cosmetic coverup against its potential risks, we strongly counsel patience and a small measure of self-denial.

Lucy had flawless skin from the day she was born. During her first two years of life she could have starred in an Ivory soap commercial. Indeed, her mother loved to lather Lucy up with the soap "safe enough for baby skin." At age 2, Lucy began to show signs of eczema. Her skin became so dry, it began cracking. Lucy's mother had trouble believing that Ivory was so very caustic. The pediatrician said that Lucy should be considered "allergic" to soap. "Bathe her as little as possible; use as little soap as possible; use Neutragena or Dove," she advised. Lucy, now 9, is six years past her eczema.

The support and understanding of others aids the treatment of eczema immeasurably, since anxiety and stress are a component of and a known contributor to these complaints. Friends and family can help if they realize:

- Apart from the skin disorder, the sufferer (unless troubled with asthma or hay fever) enjoys excellent health.
- The condition is diagnosable, curable, and controllable, and will have no serious aftereffects, even though the allergist may not know its underlying cause.
- Allergic skin disorders do *not* go from person to person; people who have them can handle food and socialize freely with *no* danger of transmitting their complaint to or infecting others.
- Allergic skin disorders are not the fault of those who have them.
- The vast majority of children with eczema will outgrow it by age sixteen.

The actions below will aid and support the eczema sufferer:

- Establish a stress-free environment that avoids criticism, nagging, picking on, harping at, or making fun of the sufferer.

- Confer with the doctor and family members to bring about a full understanding of the nature of the disorder, to plan management steps, to determine responsibility for the steps, and to show how others can help carry them out.
- Locate other victims of the same disorder to put the sufferer in touch with them. Your hospital or doctor can help with this. In some places throughout the country support groups ("eczema clubs," for example) exist to help sufferers and their families.
- Develop an "action plan" for prevention and one for treatment.

Allergic Rhinitis (Hay Fever)

Almost 35 million Americans have hay fever (allergic rhinitis) with or without asthma. Next to dandruff it is probably America's most common chronic condition.

An astonishingly long and diffuse list of inhaled substances—house dust, molds, pollens, insect parts, animal dander, and, increasingly often nowadays, airborne chemicals and irritants encountered in the workplace can trigger atopic dermatitis. Plant products, vegetable gums (present in denture adhesives and tooth powders), insecticides, hairsprays, and many other inhaled substances have all been found to cause "hay" fever.

Hay fever differs from asthma and eczema, the other two members of the so-called allergic triad, in a number of ways. It usually shows up somewhat later in life, after sensitization has occurred; it generally does not clear up or relent as you grow older; and shots often control it comfortably and safely. Fortunately, hay fever is usually mild and seasonal, and, for most sufferers, represents nothing more than a brief period of discomfort that the newer prescription nonsedative antihistamines or intranasal corticosteroids manage effectively. We do *not* recommend use of over-the-counter antihistamines; they cause drowsiness, increase the risk of falls, burns, and accidents on the job or in an automobile, and impair school and work performance.

The symptoms of hay fever, so familiar that they almost need no description or elaboration, include:

1. Recurrent sneezing, often five to ten times consecutively; worse in the morning.
2. Itchy, smarting, watery eyes.
3. An "itch" in the roof of the mouth, ear canals, or throat (you want to "scratch" your throat with your tongue).
4. Allergic "shiners," or circles under the eyes.
5. Chronic mucus discharge from the nose.
6. Chronic nasal stuffiness, often forcing mouth-breathing.
7. Wrinkling and scratching of the nose.
8. Rubbing of the nose, particularly in an upward direction.
9. Unexplained nosebleeds.
10. Loss of the senses of taste or smell.

Distinguishing a nasal cold from hay fever is sometimes difficult, but the character of the nasal discharge can be revealing. Generally, hay fever's mucus is thin and colorless; a cold's mucus is often very thick and yellow or green in color. If fever accompanies the symptoms, an infection, not hay fever, accounts for them.

Hay fever's symptoms result from breathing in an allergen or irrittant to which one is sensitive. These particulate "aeroallergens," not visible to the naked eye, range from two to sixty microns in diameter—thousands of them would be needed to cover this dot (.).

Hay fever usually begins with sneezing and a runny nose. As it intensifies, the eyes may tear and smart, the nasal discharge becomes more copious, and the sneezing worsens to the point where it becomes incessant. This persistent sneezing can cause intense soreness and pain in the muscles of the chest and diaphragm. At this point asthmatic symptoms may appear—wheezing, difficulty in breathing, and mucus production in the airways. If not treated—or if the source is not avoided—these asthmatic symptoms can intensify to a point where they require drastic treatment.

Hay fever symptoms are at their worst when the sufferer is directly exposed to high concentrations of the allergen responsible, but once the reaction starts, relatively low dosages of the allergen can keep it going. The result? Fitful, interrupted sleep and the attendant discomfort and stress.

Hay fever is no fun. Worse, individuals who do not have it have no way of knowing the acute discomfort and the real danger it represents. One cross every hay fever sufferer has to bear is the well-meaning friend who says "bless you" and laughs with every last one of your sneezes.

Home Treatment of Hay Fever

You can fit hay fever into any one of a number of categories according to its cause. The resulting method of treatment will vary according to the triggering agent; in all cases, environmental control of the responsible allergens is vital. To treat your hay fever, first find out what you are allergic to by referring to your history and by having a physical exam and, if indicated, allergy testing (see Chapter 5, page 74). Once you know the cause, certain actions follow. If you are severely allergic to pollens, for instance, work to avoid the pollens that are responsible for your discomfort. Find someone else to mow the lawn, keep your window closed at night, install an air purifier, if possible vacation far, far away during the peak allergy season. If you react to animal dander, find another home for Spot or Puss; if feathers in your pillow, down sleeping bag, or comforter have you sniffling or sneezing, get them out of your bed. Where house dust or dust mites bring on your symptoms, clean up and control them aggressively.

Chapter 6 covers simple preventive measures that are certainly easier, and often more successful, than drug therapy. Beyond appropriate avoidance measures, the type of treatment depends on the type of symptoms you show (see Table 4.1).

Drug Treatment of Hay Fever

Antihistamines have long been the standard treatment for most people with mild hay fever. Relatively inexpensive, some antihistamines carry a decongestant supposedly designed to help clear mucus in the nose. While these over-the-counter (OTC) antihistamines work well enough for most hay fever sufferers, their side effects, as noted earlier, are unacceptable. Although many doctors still recommend these antihistamines and millions spend billions buying them or similar drugs, they are outdated and should give way to

TABLE 4.1   Home Treatment for Hay Fever

Type of Symptoms	Treatment	Comment
Mild, seasonal	Establish and avoid cause	Asthma Finder (Figure 5.1) may help; review Chapters 5, 6
	Use over-the-counter antihistamines as necessary and if tolerated; otherwise use prescription nonsedating antihistamine	Be alert to possible side effects; beware of dangerous interactions with alcohol, other drugs; if asthma is also present, beware of sedation. Usually no activity limitation necessary
Mild, chronic (year-round)	Establish and avoid cause	See above
	Impose any necessary environmental controls	Air purifiers or conditioners can help greatly; other measures to block out or minimize exposure to allergens also useful
	Use newer prescription antihistamines like Allegra, Claritin, or Zyrtec	See above
	If symptoms persist and not helped by OTC remedies, ask physician for prescription intranasal steroids (Nasacort, Rhinocort, Vancenase)	Must be started at least one week before they affect symptoms; establish and use only minimally effective dose
		Avoid activities or environments that make symptoms worse
Moderate to severe, seasonal or chronic	Establish and avoid cause	See above
	Impose any necessary environmental controls	See above
	Use prescription medications if necessary	See above
	Get allergy shots	If allergen positively identified and the procedure otherwise indicated
		Reduce exposure by limiting activities appropriately

the newer antihistamines, available only with a prescription. Three good antihistamines are now available: Allegra, Claritin, and Zyrtec. Zyrtec, the most potent, has the fastest speed of onset but causes sedation in around 12 percent of users. Taken at night, though, Zyrtec causes sedation in less than 1 percent of users, no worse than that for a placebo. Both Claritin and Zyrtec come in a syrup form and both are now available with a built-in decongestant. More important, it appears that these drugs may someday be available over the counter. Antihistamines address mild to moderate hay fever symptoms but do not relieve severe symptoms unless a nasal corticosteroid supplements them. An intranasal antihistamine spray (Astelin®) proves effective and convenient for some patients, but can irritate the nasal passages and does not address the eye symptoms that frequently accompany hay fever. Astelin may also cause lethargy and drowsiness.

We have long known that cortisone significantly relieves severe hay fever. It used to come in only two ways—orally in the form of Prednisone (a form of cortisone) taken four to seven days or more prior to the start of the pollen season or by a cortisone injection once or twice during the season. Both methods carry severe toxic side effects that we cover in Chapter 14, page 191.

Chemists have worked to reduce cortisone toxicity for the past two decades; about twenty-four years ago a number of breakthroughs occurred. Researchers discovered that they could synthesize a drug like cortisone that, if sprayed in the nose, does not survive in the body for more than a few minutes and will be metabolized (destroyed) before being absorbed. With these new synthetic versions, you get the benefit of cortisone and its hay fever–controlling virtues, without its nasty side effects in your nose.

We routinely recommend these intranasal steroids, or cortisonelike materials, for moderate to severe hay fever sufferers whose symptoms do not respond to, or who simply cannot tolerate, antihistamines.

Sylvia, a law student, has had hay fever for the past eight years. Allerest, an antihistamine, helps her symptoms but makes her so sleepy she just cannot do her studies. Her doctor prescribed intranasal steroids. Two weeks later she was back at her doctor's to celebrate. She had never before felt so symptom-free during pollen season.

These medications are so effective that many physicians believe that if they do not work, the diagnosis of hay fever probably errs. One word of advice—these preventives need several days to take effect. Don't expect your symptoms to stop immediately after a spray; relief will come along five to seven days after you start taking the medication. Because of this delayed action, intranasal steroids must be taken regularly and in advance of need. Start them a week or two before the season commences and discontinue them as soon as the season ends.

Intranasal steroids currently on the market include Beconase, Vancenase, Rhinocort, Nasonex, Flonase, and Nasacort. They carry different price tags that run from $15–$35 per canister. A canister lasts approximately three to five weeks, depending on frequency of use. The initial dosage usually amounts to two sprays in each nostril once or twice a day. As noted, the medication needs at least five days to take hold. Once the medication works, cut back the dosage until you establish the minimum amount that will continue to control your symptoms. After two or three weeks only one spray in each nostril daily ought to suffice for many people. Aqueous forms are less irritating. We recommend choosing the cheapest product as they do not differ in efficacy if properly taken. Children as young as six can safely use some of these sprays.

Another development in the treatment of hay fever is an over-the-counter nasal spray called Nasalcrom. Available only by prescription until several years ago, this spray contains a solution of cromolyn sodium, the same medication once widely used for the treatment of chronic severe asthma. Not a steroid, it has to be taken more frequently than intranasal steroids, up to four to six times daily. While not as potent as intranasal steroids, Nasalcrom works for most people. It is a useful alternative to intranasal steroids; it hardly ever burns or irritates the nose (one disadvantage of steroids). Accordingly, children accept and use Nasalcrom more readily.

Allergic Conjunctivitis

Allergic conjunctivitis, inflammation of the eyes, usually accompanies hay fever or allergic rhinitis. In fact, before skin testing was done, physicians would check for allergies by putting a crude extract of allergen in the white of the eye, the conjunctiva area. They would then rub the eye and see if it became red. This was obviously a very crude test but illustrated that if the eye reddened after exposure to an allergen, other accompanying symptoms could be traced to the allergens. A large number of conditions can produce conjunctivitis. If the eyes are extremely itchy, both eyes are involved, and the sufferer also has underlying hay fever, blame allergic conjunctivitis. The treatment of allergic conjunctivitis resembles that for allergic rhinitis. In many cases, a systemic or orally taken antihistamine will relieve the inflammation. In others, a topical or local eye drop is needed. The agents used include vasoconstrictors, antihistamines, mast cell stabilizers, and anti-inflammatories. The agents used depend on the severity of the symptoms, the cost of the medicine, and whether the person wears contact lenses. Usually a combination of antihistamine and decongestant are recommended—Vasocon A and Naphcon A. Both of these drugs are now sold over the counter. They act rapidly but like most topical antihistamines, they can be very irritating when applied to the eye. In some instances, a topical nonsteroidal anti-inflammatory drug, Ketorolac (Accular®) is used but it has some drawbacks. Relatively expensive, it may also produce burning and stinging and should not be used if one wears contact lenses. In severe cases, topical agents that prevent the degranulation of mast cells are sometimes used. These include cromolyn sodium, nedocromil, and olopatadine (Patanol®). The last works particularly well. Topical corticosteroids are also used for severe cases, but they increase the likelihood of an eye infection, cataracts, corneal perforation, glaucoma, and even loss of vision. We recommend that they be used only on the advice of an ophthalmologist or an allergist.

Recurrent Ear Infections

Many a parent knows the anguish of nights spent with a youngster with an earache. The symptoms and history vary little from child to child: an infant or toddler has had a cold and a runny nose for one or two days. Suddenly, often without warning, the child's temperature shoots up and an excruciatingly painful earache develops. Nothing the parent does pacifies the child, who becomes restless and irritable, cannot be put down, and will not sleep. The episodes last from eight to twenty-four hours and generally respond to a mixture of antibiotics and decongestant therapy. Children who develop ear infections of this nature should be seen immediately by their doctor, who will look in the ear to determine if the infection stems from a virus or bacteria; if bacterial, antibiotics are given.

Children with recurrent ear infections often have a history of allergic rhinitis, or hay fever, and many also have asthma.

Blame the child's anatomy for these infections. The Eustachian tube, a thin tube that runs between the nose and the ear, is extremely small in young children and it only takes a small amount of mucus or thickening to clog or block the tube. The clogging causes the pain and swelling of the eardrum that accompanies the infection.

Regardless of the cause, the treatment of children with recurring infections is the same. Tiny plastic tubes are inserted in the eardrum to allow movement of air in the middle part of the ear. The procedure, by improving air supply and circulation, helps out the blocked Eustachian tube and reduces the likelihood of ear infection.

These air tubes, relatively easy to install, have some disadvantages. In very young children (less than one year old) the tubes tend to fall out. They can be reinserted in the ear, but if it happens frequently the eardrum becomes too thin and flexible to support the tube. Implanting ear tubes requires a minor operation, so that the children must be anesthetized, and that can upset both child and parent. In addition, once implanted, the tubes need care to avoid complications. Water must be kept out of the ears, which means that swimming and taking showers are out, and washing hair requires care.

Sinusitis

The sinuses, a network of hollow spaces behind the nose, occupy most of the front of the head and drain upper airway mucus. They also act as a generalized cleanser of facial and nasal tissue. These caves are connected by narrow holes or orifices. If these connectors become blocked, as happens all too often, the cavities behind them also become clogged and inflamed. The common and debilitating chronic inflammation that occurs in these caves, or sinuses, often accompanies asthma and hay fever.

Individuals with sinusitis complain of a heaviness, a feeling of stuffiness behind the nose and below the eyes. The feeling can grow so severe that it leads to a characteristic sinus headache. If the sinus becomes infected, a fever accompanied by a purulent (pussy) nasal discharge may occur. The headache and the pain of sinusitis produce acute discomfort.

Sinusitis in asthmatics occurs much more frequently than it does in the general population, and when it does, the asthma may be much more difficult to treat. This does not mean that sinusitis induces asthma; it only makes it less responsive to treatment. Moreover, the sinusitis may be chronic and silent (indolent); in existence for so long that it goes unnoticed. Where asthma symptoms persist for no other apparent reason, the possibility of sinusitis should be carefully and thoroughly considered.

The Diagnosis of Indolent Sinusitis

One of the most underutilized diagnostic procedures in the management of patients with asthma is a four-way CT scan of the sinuses. Compared to a sinus X ray, a CT scan provides more information, involves less radiation, and costs less. The scan reveals all the sinuses in the body, shows the size of the sinus, and indicates whether the tissue is swollen or inflamed. It may even reveal the presence of fluid within the sinus.

If your asthma becomes difficult to control or if you have had asthma for some time seemingly without problems, and then suddenly go through a prolonged bout (often following a viral illness), and your symptoms become stubborn, consider a CT scan. If you have a puslike nasal discharge, a CT scan is strongly indicated. We recommend that you mention this possibility to your doctor; some practioners still use an older sinus test called a Waters view of the sinus. Although the Waters view can be helpful, it is *not* as good as a four-way CT scan.

The Treatment of Sinusitis

Allergists and ENT (ear, nose, and throat) specialists disagree about the best way to treat sinusitis. Allergists advocate treating bacterial infections of the sinuses with a minimum of four to six weeks of antibiotic therapy. Sinus infections can be chronic and are resistant to therapy. That is why we allergists prescribe a several-week course of antibiotics and admonish patients to complete the full course. Note, however, that many bacteria have become resistant to antibiotics. Note, too, that we do not indiscriminately recommend antiobiotics if the sinusitis is acute and perhaps caused by a virus. In any event, just a few days of antibiotics directed at sinusitis accomplishes little—other than to encourage the emergence of antibiotic-resistant strains.

ENT physicians contend that sinus irrigation—flushing out the sinuses—should happen relatively early in treating patients with sinusitis. Although they may prescribe a course of antibiotics at the outset, they will resort to irrigation quickly if improvement does not occur. Since approximately 50 percent of the cases do not respond to a prolonged course of antibiotics, irrigation may be required anyway, and neither allergists nor ENT specialists have little to shout about in the cure department.

The Use of Nasal Sprays in Sinusitis

If we could remove any single group of drugs from the pharmacy shelves, it would be over-the-counter nasal sprays such as Afrin, Neosynephrine, and 4-Way, designed to clear nose and sinus passages. A common head cold can clog sinuses and make a person acutely uncomfortable. In such circumstances a brief—no more than one- or two-day—course of these nasal sprays may produce significant relief. For the patient with allergies, however, use of these drugs may become habitual and addictive. We have seen scores of asthmatics become so hooked to these sprays that they end up using them three to ten times a day for years on end. This abuse results in a syndrome called *rhinitis medicamentosa,* a swelling and constriction of the nasal passages caused by the medicine itself. Although the medicine seems to work at first, as time passes adaptation occurs and larger and more frequent doses are required to produce an effect. A vicious cycle begins with the nose perpetually clogged unless (and sometimes even when) these nasal sprays are used. For that reason we strongly discourage their use. If you suspect that your symptoms come from overuse of nasal spray, have your physician confirm the diagnosis. Once identified, the condition can be treated readily with topical steroids. Note, too, that many sufferers from chronic nasal congestion can use "Ocean Spray" or similar products that contain only saline and water. Irrigating nasal passages with these products can have beneficial results with no troublesome side effects.

The Use of Antihistamines and Decongestants in Sinusitis

For many years antihistamines and decongestants were the treatment of choice in the management of sinusitis. However, recent studies have demonstrated that these remedies do little or no good. Antihistamines, in particular, may only dry up sinus secretions and make them harder for the patient to clear out. Decongestants may help a few individuals but are clearly not as efficacious as once believed for hay fever or sinusitis. When needed, antibiotics are the mainstay of and the key to successful treatment of sinusitis. Once controlled, you and your doctor should search to find out why you developed sinusitis in the first place.

Acute Bronchopulmonary Aspergillosis

Acute bronchopulmonary aspergillosis occurs exclusively in individuals who have asthma. In this syndrome patients develop extreme allergy to the mold *Aspergillus*, a fungus. When skin-tested with the mold *Aspergillus*, people who are sensitive to it react severely and IgE levels, if determined, are high. Finally, a special blood test for aspergillosis, called precipitating antibodies, will be positive. This condition is rare but can occur whether your asthma is recent or long-standing and regardless of your age.

Pauline has had asthma for about 15 years. Ordinarily, well-controlled with Albuterol, an inhaled steroid, and an occasional Prednisone burst, for the past two weeks she has noted a significant increase in cough and mucus production. The mucus, particularly thick, seems to be tinged with some greenish material. She also feels as if she has a fever, although the two times she took her temperature it read normal. The usual drugs she takes for asthma do not seem to work this time. Her doctor listened to her chest and thought she might have pneumonia. He ordered a chest xray, which showed an infiltrate—some inflammation within the lung. The doctor felt fairly confident about the diagnosis of pneumonia but he remembered mention of a syndrome called acute bronchopulmonary aspergillosis, so, to be on the safe side, he tested her and found she did have the condition. He treated her with a high dose of Prednisone and has maintained her on a higher dose of inhaled corticosteroids. Pauline took several days to respond but now feels much, much better. Six months later she is completely symptom-free and her asthma is under control.

If Pauline's doctor had not been aware of this syndrome, two serious conditions might have followed. First, acute hypersensitivity to *Aspergillus* can result in actual destruction of lung tissue. Second, it can produce abnormalities in the architecture of the air tubes, called bronchiectasis. Here the air tubes, in addition to being irritable, become tortuous, developing outpocketings and big sacs, subject to recurrent infections that make the asthma much more difficult to treat.

Although acute bronchopulmonary aspergillosis is rare, you should know of it. If your asthma becomes more difficult and more resistant to usual treatment or if you develop a more severe or stubborn cough and the mucus becomes thick and tenacious and looks different from that produced during prior bouts of asthma, you should alert your doctor to the possibility of acute bronchopulmonary aspergillosis.

Summary

This chapter, focusing as it does on allergic diseases, may appear to miss the point and the prime subject of this book—asthma. Not so. Allergies and asthma, like ham and eggs, tend to go together. Although some asthmatic reactions have nonallergic causes, a number of allergic diseases do provoke, coexist with, complicate, and intensify asthmatic reactions in millions of sufferers.

Here we name and discuss these fellow travelers of asthma; eczema and hay fever that, with asthma, make up the "allergic triad," along with their lesser companions, allergic conjunctivitis, ear infections, sinusitis, and acute bronchopulmonary aspergillosis. We describe the symptoms of these complaints, sketch their typical onset and course, indicate the ways they interact with asthma, tell how and with what they are treated, and assess the virtues and drawbacks of various remedies and treatment strategies directed at them.

As with asthma, control of the companion diseases rests fundamentally on the identification and avoidance of the substance or condition that triggers the symptoms. Also, as with asthma, we note that the symptoms of these cohorts will yield to prompt, informed, and aggressive treatment. Allergic diseases in general as well as asthma in particular are manageable individually or in consort.

5

Identifying the Cause of Asthma

Steps Toward Taking Charge of Asthma

To take charge of your asthma you need to:

- Identify the causal agents—the substances or conditions that bring on your asthma. (This chapter deals entirely with this fundamental aspect of asthma care.)
- Avoid the causal agents. (How you do this is covered in Chapter 6.)

Depending on the severity of your symptoms, you may also need to:

- Control or suppress the onset of symptoms with medication or, where appropriate, desensitization through allergy shots. (Chapters in Part 3 fill you in on the many aspects of care for and control of asthma.)
- Treat symptoms with medications. (Chapter 14 names, evaluates, and indicates the conditions and limits for use of the many asthma drugs and medicines available.)

What Are Asthma's Causal Agents and Which Ones Make Me Sick?

Finding its causal agent is the single most important step you can take toward controlling your asthma. Unless and until you know exactly what brings on your wheezes, you will have trouble treating them and you will always be troubled with them. A multitude of substances or bodily conditions precipitate asthma attacks. The most important ones are:

- Colds or upper respiratory infections, especially in children
- Allergens (dusts, pollen, molds, animal dander, and so on)
- Foods, especially food additives
- Vigorous exercise
- Hyperventilation (fast, shallow breathing often associated with emotional or stressful experiences)
- Certain drugs or medication, especially aspirin and ibuprofen (such as Advil and Nuprin)
- Air pollutants, including tobacco smoke, smoke from wood-burning stoves, and the by-products of automotive or industrial combustion like carbon monoxide, ozone, nitrogen dioxide, sulfur dioxide, and particulate matter

We deal with each of these causes individually a bit later on in this chapter. First, however, you need to know what to do to identify what triggers your symptoms. You may already know what brings on your asthma. If you do not, the surest way to pinpoint the cause of your asthma is to carefully and faithfully fill out and maintain the Asthma Finder (Figure 5.1). This is an easy routine to follow in learning what makes you wheeze, *provided* you do it without fail and over an adequate period of time.

Begin by photocopying the Asthma Finder and filling it out every night before going to bed. This should take you no more than ten minutes.

Use the Symptoms section (identified in the left margin of the form) to record the severity of your symptoms on a given day. If you had no symptoms at all, check 0. With mild symptoms that did not keep you from your regular daily activities, check 1. With moderate symptoms that kept you

FIGURE 5.1   Asthma Finder

		Mon	Tue	Wed	Thu	Fri	Sat	Sun	TOTAL
How severe were your symptoms?									
No wheezing	0								
Very mild wheezing	1								
Audible wheezing	2								
Loud wheezing	3								
Severe wheezing	4								
What were your PEF	AM								
readings? (G, Y, or R)?	PM								
When did your symptoms show?									
Morning									
Afternoon									
Evening									
During the night									
Did you have any respiratory symptoms?									
Cold (cough, sniffle, sore throat)									
Flu									
Sinusitis									
Other*									
Were you exposed to airborne irritants?									
Pollens									
House or other dust									
Animals/pets									
Mold									
Were you exposed to cigarette smoke?									
Were you exposed to asthma-triggering foods, beverages, or additives?									
Foods containing metabisulfite (see sidebar, page 71)									
Foods containing tartrazine, FD&C #5									
Other possible triggers (berries, fish, mollusks, crustaceans, nuts, peanuts, milk, eggs, wheat)*									
Were you exposed to asthma-triggering medications?									
Aspirin or salicylates									
Other pain or headache remedy									
Cold medications									
Nose drops									
Antibiotics									
Were you exposed to air pollution or automobile emissions?									

FOR _____ (Name) WEEK OF _____ TO _____ (Date)

* Specify

(continues)

FIGURE 5.1   *(continued)*

	Mon	Tue	Wed	Thu	Fri	Sat	Sun	TOTAL
Were you exposed to chemicals, fumes, or odors?								
Did you exercise vigorously?								
Did you experience any asthma-triggering climatic factors?								
Brisk wind								
Cold, dry air								
Rain/snow								
Did you experience any emotional triggers?								
Stress								
Anxiety								
Conflict								

from carrying out *some* activities, check 2. If you had symptoms severe enough to keep you away from work or school or confined to home or bed, check 3. Check 4 if you had symptoms so severe that you had to go to the emergency room or hospital.

The Symptoms section also provides a space for you to record twice-daily peak expiratory flow (PEF) readings. The PEF meter measures how much air you can blow out in one exhalation; asthma symptoms impair your ability to do this. PEF readings offer an objective measure of the status of your airways and the Asthma Finder provides a space to record them.

To use the PEF meter you must first establish your own personal best score by recording the highest score that you achieve on the device under conditions when your asthma symptoms are either totally absent or minimal. Then, each morning and evening, get a peak flow reading by noting the highest of three trials. Next, grade that value by comparing it to your personal best according to the following table:

TABLE 5.1   PEF Scores, Grades, and Suggested Responses

Score's Percent of Personal Best	*Grade*	*Suggested Response*
80–100%	G (Green: proceed)	No action needed
50–80%	Y (Yellow: caution)	Consider starting or increasing your medication
below 50%	R (Red: danger)	Medical alert! Follow emergency procedures and notify your physician.

The percentage boundaries of G, Y, and R given here are only suggestions; work out your own grading system with your physician. Note too that your physician can write a prescription for the relatively inexpensive PEF meter; with luck, your insurance company will pay for it. But make every effort to get one. If finances are a problem, tell your doctor, who may be able to get you a free one. Your pharmacy will carry several different makes and models of this relatively simple device and a web search for PEF meters will yield names and addresses of suppliers as will Appendix B. Take note that PEFs come in child and adult sizes so make sure you get the right one.

Under the Possible Causes section that takes up the rest of the Asthma Finder, enter a check mark for any item that drew a "yes" answer for that day. At the end of the week, count the check marks for each item and record the number in the "Total" column. To interpret the Allergy Finder, try to connect the severity of your symptoms to the possible causes you have checked. For instance, if you checked 0, *No wheezing*, in the symptoms column for the entire week, any possible causes you did check may not act as triggers for your symptoms. If you had a 2 or 3 on the symptoms scale and your PEF came up Y or R, what possible causes did you check on that day or the day before? If you had asthma symptoms all week, did any of the possible causes draw checks every day? Look for patterns, relationships between possible causes, and the appearance or worsening of symptoms and make note of these linkages.

You may have to keep the Asthma Finder for a number of weeks (photocopy the form) before a pattern emerges, but stick with it. It's your best tool for identifying what triggers your symptoms, although the seven tips that follow may help you in your search for the source of your asthma.

Colds or upper respiratory infections are by far the most common forerunners of asthmatic attacks in children. The cold symptoms—sneezing, sniffling, coughing, stuffy nose, sore throat, possibly a slight fever—usually appear before the asthma takes hold. Then the congestion gets worse, the chest feels constricted, and shortness of breath, deep coughing, and wheezing shows up. These asthmatic symptoms—asthma—may hang on well after the main infection has run its course.

Pat's asthma started in childhood and has never disappeared. Although she often goes for several months between episodes, her wheezing at the age of 43 comes on in exactly the same way that it did during her early years. Whenever she develops a cold, stuffy nose, or sore throat, with or without a fever, she knows that within a few hours to a couple of days her chest will tighten up. The pattern is so unchanging and predictable that she has learned to start her asthma medications at the first sign of a cold. This tactic often significantly reduces or totally prevents the wheezing that accompanies a cold. She also knows that she must continue to take her medications for two to three weeks following the onset of a cold. In fact, during the late fall and winter when colds and the flu are going around, Pat takes her medication even though she has no symptoms—a simple precaution, but one that works. Come spring, the medications get shelved.

Up to half of all asthmatics show allergies to *pollens, house dust and dust mites, animals, or molds,* but these allergies do not necessarily produce asthmatic reactions. They will, however, if you have a high level of IgE or if you have airways that go into spasm.

Gabe remembers his first summer at camp. That year his mother kept reminding the counselor that Gabe had allergies and needed to take his medication every day without fail. When asked what Gabe was allergic to, his mother said, "All living things." Gabe had a fine time that summer; he also learned that he was not allergic "to all living things." Grass pollens, he discovered, brought on his symptoms. Whenever he was exposed to grass pollens without the protective shield of his medications, the IgE response led to wheezing and shortness of breath. When away from pollen or appropriately medicated, Gabe had no problems at all.

Tracking down the specific substance or substances in this group that cause your symptoms will go more smoothly if you keep in mind that the symptoms often coincide with other happenings. They may come around at about the same time each year or they may get worse when aggravated by conditions that put particulate material into the air you breathe (stiff

FIGURE 5.2   Asthma-Causing Food Additives

Tartrazine

Tartrazine is a dye (FD&C yellow, #5) added to foods to "improve" their appearance. For many years, it was believed that it was a significant factor in exacerbating asthma in some patients. This was an overestimate, although there are still some patients who are tartrazine-susceptible. The list below only suggests the literally thousands of places it may turn up. Read labels carefully and without fail. A typical label may read:

"INGREDIENTS: Enriched wheat flour … whole wheat flour … oil shortening … sugar, corn syrup, malted barley flour, lecithin, FD&C yellow #5, and artificial flavor."

Baked goods, breads with food
   dyes added, sweet breads,
   whole wheat
Butter
Candies
Cereals, colored
Cheeses
Chips (potato, corn, taco)
Fish, frozen (some: check label)
Fruits, canned (some: check label)
Ice creams

Jello (gelatin)
Lozenges
Margarine
Meats, prepared
Mouthwash
Mustard
Pudding
Sauces and gravies, prepared
Toothpaste
Yogurt

Metabisulfite

Metabisulfite (sodium bisulfite), a food preservative and freshener, draws haphazard regulation from the Food and Drug Administration. For example, one bunch in four of sulfited fresh table grapes must be tagged with a label declaring that sulfite has been added. This misleads customers into believing the untagged clusters do not contain the chemical. In addition, imported preserved foods may contain sulfites that the overseas manufacturer is not required to list among the ingredients named on the package or container. Salad bars, nowadays, probably carry less risk; however, metabisulfite may turn up in many processed foods including beer and wine as well as show up unadvertised in certain foods especially prone to spoilage. Foods likely to contain sulfite include:

Beer
Cheeses
Cider
Cordials
Fruit juices
Glucose (syrup and solid)
Jell-O (gelatin)

Pickles
Potatoes, whole, peeled, or sliced (raw)
Salsa
Sausages and sausage meat
Vegetables, dehydrated, especially peas
Vinegar
Wines (red, white, or rosé)

winds; sweeping the garage; riding with the car windows open) or they invariably turn up after a visit to the same physical location. If you always get wheezy when you visit Aunt Grace and her houseful of cats, the felines likely have much to do with your symptoms.

Foods draw much unwarranted blame as causes of asthma. The popular idea that some mysterious, insidious food allergy causes your symptoms— "It must have been something I ate"—has little backing. Foods seldom cause asthma, although some people do react violently to specific foods. Food additives can and do, though, particularly metabisulfite, a food preservative. The accompanying sidebar lists foods likely to contain tartrazine or metabisulfite.

Alan has had asthma all his life although he controls it effectively with medications. However, on several special occasions he developed a cough and breathing problem so intense that he had to cut the evening short. These episodes happened when Alan and his wife had dined out; widely differing cuisines and menus were involved. Alan went back over what they had eaten on each of these evenings and noted that the cough usually appeared after he drank wine. He reported this to his allergist, who concluded that metabisulfite in the wine might have provoked the coughing and wheezing. He told Alan to give the wine a pass; Alan complied and has had no more metabisulfite-caused acute episodes of asthma (see also Kevin's case, Chapter 1, page 13).

If you believe that an allergic reaction to food triggers your asthma, Chapter 7 spells out the steps to take to track down the culprit.

Vigorous exercise is frequently implicated in bronchospasm. Interestingly, the form the exercise takes has much to do with it. Swimming, relatively benign, is unlikely to provoke airway collapse in asthmatics, whereas running or jogging often does. Whether exercise will cause you to wheeze also depends on the temperature and humidity of the air you breathe—the moister and warmer the air, the less the likelihood that you will have a bronchospasm. Chapter 9 discusses exercise and asthma in detail.

Emotional responses—anger and fear in particular—have long taken the blame for causing asthma. Emotional states do not *induce* asthma but they often cause rapid, shallow breathing or hyperventilation. This hyperventilation in individuals with sensitive airways can end in bronchospasm and wheezing. Other ways in which emotional reactions following conflict, stress, or danger induce bronchospasm may exist, but they remain unknown at this time.

Many drugs, particularly those classified as nonsteroidal anti-inflammatory drugs (aspirin, ibuprofen, Advil, Nuprin, Motrin, and their relatives) can provoke violent asthmatic reactions. If you have asthma, steer clear of aspirin and all other nonsteroidal drugs. The package label or your pharmacist will tell you whether your pain relief medicine falls in this category. Many common cold medicines contain either aspirin or ibuprofen, so be careful and read the label.

Grant has suffered from mild intermittent asthma all of his life. He has never identified its cause because most of the time it is not so bad. He did notice that when a fever came with the cold the asthma also turned up. This led Grant and his doctor to conclude that asthma occurred with more severe infections. However, Grant became suspicious of that conclusion after reading news stories about the possible role aspirin plays in inducing Reye's syndrome in children. Grant, an adult, could not get Reye's syndrome, but the story got him to thinking because he routinely took aspirin for bad colds. Grant talked to his doctor, who affirmed that aspirin could make asthma worse in some people. His suspicions aroused, the doctor had Grant take a small amount of aspirin after doing some pulmonary function tests. He then waited a short time and had Grant repeat the tests. On retrial, Grant's performance on the pulmonary function tests decreased slightly, although Grant did not notice any change in how he felt and had trouble believing he was having some collapse of his airways. The doctor explained that during a virus-caused cold the airways tend to collapse and the cumulative effect of the infection and the aspirin produced Grant's wheeze and shortness of breath. Grant now uses acetaminophen when he has a cold and fever.

Numerous notorious incidents of serious *air pollution* in industrial areas have caused epidemic respiratory illnesses and deaths. The dense smog in

London in 1952 was one such event. Air samples taken during this episode showed a tenfold increase in the concentration of sulfur dioxide and particulate matter. Studies done in London as well as later ones in France's Meuse Valley and in Donora, Pennsylvania, showed that 88 percent of asthmatic people develop respiratory symptoms during these air inversions. Apparently sulfur dioxide, ozone, and the particulate pollutants resulting from the combustion of fossil fuels cause airways to go into spasm. In fact, virtually anyone, asthmatic or not, will develop bronchospasm from sulfur dioxide. Asthmatics, because of the hypersensitivity of their airways, react severely and become quite sick at concentrations of sulfur dioxide too low to bother people without asthma. Some authorities believe that atmospheric pollution causes the epidemic rise in asthma cases

In addition to atmospheric pollutants, including the smoke from wood-stoves, tobacco smoke—first- or secondhand—is an important triggering agent for asthma and must be avoided at all costs.

> Brandon's asthma shows up when winter sets in. His symptoms are worse at home, even worse at night, and usually fade away in springtime. He also gets better when he is out of the house and away at school. Finally his mother put two and two together and suggested (correctly) that it was the smoke from their wood-burning heating stove that had Brandon wheezing.

Even though it was a tight, efficient stove, the small increase in particulates in the air tipped Brandon over the edge. The telltale clue? No symptoms away from home.

Allergy Tests

Using the Asthma Finder carefully and conscientiously should enable you to pick out what causes your wheezing. In the event that it fails to come up with the cause, you may want—or your doctor may recommend—a series of allergy tests in the doctor's office to identify the agent responsible for your illness.

Before submitting to a course of tests to try to pin down the source of your asthma,

- Be sure you have *honestly* and *unsuccessfully* tried, through the Asthma Finder or other diary or record-keeping process, to identify the source of your asthma.
- Be sure you know exactly what the allergist is going to do—what the tests are, how many, how drastic—and the risks you run in having them carried out.
- Be sure that while you are being tested, competent emergency medical attention is *immediately* ready if needed.

Allergy Skin Tests

Skin testing is a much-used and, unhappily, much-abused method for detecting what you are allergic to. It has long been known that introducing a dilute solution of an antigen—one capable of provoking an allergic reaction—can cause the skin to show a wheal and flare response in a person susceptible to it. Thus, if you are allergic to a given allergen, your skin, when the antigen comes in contact with it, will redden (flare) and a small hive (wheal) will form. Inhalation tests, a reliable alternative procedure that directly involves the respiratory system, can also be used but they carry the risk of a severe reaction, so skin tests represent a less risky alternative. They also permit the application of many antigens at one session, an additional advantage.

Positive reactions to skin tests appear and can be interpreted within twenty minutes. (The bodily processes underlying the appearance of the telltale hive in allergic people are as follows: The antigen binds IgE antibodies specific to it, triggering the release of histamine and other mediators from mast cells. The characteristic signs of sensitivity, the flare and wheal, follow.)

Use allergy tests only when all other reasonable means of detecting the cause of your symptoms have failed. Although carefully administered skin tests are generally safe and reliable, they can err and they do carry risk.

In the best of circumstances, skin tests confirm suspicions that symptoms trace to otherwise undetected allergens. They should follow a comprehensive medical history and a physical examination and be administered in full knowledge of the nature of the symptoms, especially their time and place of occurrence.

The mere suspicion of allergy should not in itself justify performing a battery of tests for all possible allergens. Good physicians will have solid hunches about what patients are sensitive to. Thus, skin tests usually nail down what the patient reacts to and, in some instances, how severe the sensitivity. Skin tests should only employ allergens that, according to the patient's history, have some clear possibility of causing the symptoms. (Since physicians base their fees on the number of skin tests they perform, the potential for abuse—needless overuse—of the procedure exists.)

The decision to do skin tests ultimately rests on the patient's history and environment and the physician's experience. Be wary if your allergist recommends wide-scale skin testing. Adequate evaluations, even in the most baffling cases, should require no more than 120 tests. Individuals subjected to 150, 250, or even 300 allergy skin tests should question the need for such a barrage, especially in light of the fact that some of the antigens used to test for rare or obscure causes, sometimes poorly standardized, may not reliably diagnose what brings on your allergy.

How Are Skin Tests Done?

A nurse or doctor usually administers skin tests. However, a physician should always be within immediate calling distance because generalized anaphylactic reactions (a potentially lethal form of shock) can and do sometimes follow skin tests. The two more common ones are the prick and the intradermal tests.

Prick tests are usually applied to the lower or upper arm or the back; if many tests are to be carried out, the back is the preferred site. First, the nurse or doctor cleans the skin at the site with alcohol. Next, she sketches a grid, usually with a marking pen, to indicate the sites of the various tests, spacing the sites one to two inches apart. She then applies a single drop of each suspected allergen to a square of the grid with a medicine dropper. Next, she inserts a sterile testing needle through the drop of antigen and into the skin. The procedure, merely a prick, should not hurt; the minute lesion should cause no bleeding. If you feel uneasy or apprehensive about the procedure, ask for a trial test to see exactly what is involved.

Approximately twenty minutes after making the prick, the nurse measures the wheal and flare and records a score based on the severity of the reaction to the substance. (Disposable standardized grids, more comfortable and convenient, especially when you must undergo a large number of tests, are now available.)

Prick tests usually come first, partly to identify individuals with extreme sensitivity to antigens and partly because they are safer, even when given to severely allergic patients. Skin tests rarely provoke an anaphylactic or life-threatening reaction.

If you do not react to the prick test, the intradermal test follows. In severely allergic people or in those where the prick test is positive, the intradermal test will not be carried out. In intradermal testing the test sites are first cleaned with alcohol. Then the doctor injects a minute amount of antigen solution under the skin. This creates a small bleb or blister-like mound of solution under the skin. The intradermal test, more sensitive than the prick test, can pick up mild or moderate allergies. It is always done on the arm because it presents heightened risk of severe, generalized allergic reactions. If such an allergic reaction develops, then a tourniquet placed above the site of the test will block the antigen's invasion of the rest of the body. Barring complications, the doctor examines the site twenty minutes after the injection and measures it for wheal and flare.

The grading systems used to evaluate the wheal and flare response will vary from one physician to another. To standardize observations, however, in addition to the suspected allergens, two comparison tests are made. One substance known to produce a strong response (usually histamine) and another that does not provoke a response (usually saline solution) are included in the battery. The responses to these two tests define the upper and lower limits of your reactions and assure their accurate interpretation.

Which allergens to test for depends in part on where you live. Test antigens fall into several categories or types. First and most common are those using pollens extracted from trees, grasses, and weeds. Even though your symptoms point to a particular pollen—sensitivity to grass, for instance—your allergist will probably screen with a full panel of tests in order to be thorough and to get an idea of how atopic you are. Second come the mold antigens; molds exist almost everywhere and many asthmatics react to them. Third come the environmental agents, allergens found in and around the home, such as house dust, animal dander, and insect parts. Finally, there are extracts available for skin testing that claim to detect sensitivity to certain foods. These last tests should rarely be used; they are crude and unlikely to yield useful information. If you or your doctor suspect that foods trigger your symptoms, you should have a special challenge test as described in Chapter 7, page XXX.

Interpreting Skin Tests

Interpreting the results of skin tests gets complicated. They can be extremely helpful and informative, especially when carefully chosen antigens are used and the results are carefully tied to your medical history. Skin tests do not always jibe with the way your symptoms play out in real life. Some special problems and circumstances make interpretation or evaluation of test results extremely difficult. Individuals who have dermatographism—a skin so sensitive that it turns red, even when lightly touched or stroked—react positively to everything, including the saline solution given as a negative control. Skin tests have no meaning for them. Likewise, people with skin diseases like eczema and psoriasis cannot provide interpretable results and the test itself may put them at risk (see Table 5.2). Some children cannot tolerate skin tests, whereas some adults, perhaps frightened by the process or dreading the needle, balk at doing the tests, even though they are painless, nondisfiguring, and, when properly done, carry little or no risk. Finally, you cannot be tested if you are taking

TABLE 5.2   When to Avoid Allergy Skin Tests

Condition	Reason
Infancy (two years or less)	Not likely to be positive
Where eczema or psoriasis is present	May irritate the skin severely
Dermatographism (a condition in which the skin reddens and swells following pressure)	Tests cannot be interpreted
Use of antihistamines	Antihistamines block the skin test

antihistamines—these drugs block skin tests from working. Then there is the cost. Although insurance will usually cover a panel of skin tests, the bill can run more than $500 to $1,000.

Eighteen-year-old Eric has had hay fever for the past 12 years. He takes Zyrtec for control. However, during a really bad allergy year, and especially on the windy days, he notices that he wheezes a bit. He sees his doctor about this. The doctor thinks Eric would be a good candidate for allergy shots. He knows from his history that Eric most likely has mild, intermittent, pollen-triggered asthma. Eric takes a battery of skin tests containing antigens from trees, grass, weeds, molds, dust, and animal dander. The results confirm why Eric's wheezing always peaked during the grass pollen season and single out the grasses to blame. The doctor considers advising Eric to have allergy shots to desensitize him to the offending pollen and discusses it with Eric and his dad. They finally decide that since Eric's discomfort lasts only about six weeks, it was foolish to have him undergo an expensive and prolonged series of allergy shots when Eric's problem was self-limiting and readily handled with medication.

Bronchial Challenge Testing for Asthma

If you believe you have allergy-induced asthma that skin testing failed to diagnose, you may be one of the very small number of individuals for whom a technique known as bronchial challenge is appropriate. The technique also applies if you have a special and unusual asthma history that suggests sensitivity to a chemical found only in your workplace. In the latter case, if you show no symptoms on vacations or days off from work, if you feel well when you wake up in the morning and feel okay at work but several hours after getting home you start to wheeze, an occupational irritant may be affecting you. In such instances, where disability and workers' compensation considerations apply or when workers may have to face retraining and even reemployment, bronchial challenge tests can pick out the offending allergen. These tests are given when you are symptom-free and not on medications. You would first inhale a saline mist solution to get a baseline measure of pulmonary function (see page 68 for more about PEF measurement). Then you inhale a nebulized spray, a fine mist containing a possible antigen. Following this you will provide another PEF reading. This procedure continues with graded doses of antigens alternating with PEF readings. The pulmonary function test establishes if a reduction in air flow correlates with the inhalation of a given antigen. Although it is accurate, this test is expensive and should be administered only by experienced physicians at either a clinic with immediate access to emergency room equipment or, preferably, by overnight admission to a hospital. The reason for these precautions? Although standardized procedures beginning with extremely dilute solutions of antigens have been worked out and serious reactions rarely occur, they do happen and when they do they require emergency treatment. There is also a similar test known as the methacholine challenge test. In this case your doctor is questioning whether your symptoms are even due to asthma at all. You will be asked to inhale either methacholine or saline in a blind manner (you won't know which you are inhaling) and pulmonary function will be measured. Asthma sufferers have a significant decrease in their air flows to methacholine but not to saline.

Fred struggled with a terrible nighttime cough for over 6 months. Nothing seemed to help. Finally, he went to his doctor. The doctor, also stumped, treated Fred for asthma even though unsure about the cause of the cough. Finally, he referred Fred to a pulmonary specialist who ordered a methacholine challenge test. The test came out positive affirming that asthma was indeed the culprit. The doctor put Fred on a course of high dose inhaled steroids. He had a great result and Fred's cough cleared up.

Laboratory Tests for Allergies

The alternatives to skin testing are radioallergoabsorbent (RAST) and fluorescence (FAST) tests of the blood. These tests directly measure IgE antibodies in the blood. Although reactions to skin tests vary in intensity according to individual responsiveness, type of skin, current use of antihistaminess, or hormonal state, RAST and FAST tests have little such individual variability. More expensive and much slower that skin tests, RAST and FAST involve drawing blood samples and subjecting the samples to laboratory analysis. The results allow for reliable statements about IgE concentration. Consequently, RAST tests with their ease, simplicity, and specificity are often preferred by patients. For others, because of speediness of results, skin tests remain the procedure of choice. RAST and FAST tests are still being researched and refined and these investigations will lead to more efficient and precise methods of detecting the presence of IgE antibodies.

Other blood tests are under development or being used for the diagnosis of allergies. On the development side is the experimental basophil degranulation test that entails isolating the white cells in a blood sample. The suspected antigen is then added to the white cells and they are observed to see if they release histamine. Largely under study in research centers or laboratories, it has little clinical use at this point.

Another and more frequently seen blood test is called total serum IgE. It has some limited value, but it often errs. Mistakes happen because many people with severe allergies have normal levels of IgE, whereas many other people with high IgE levels have no allergies at all. These discrepancies owe much to the fact that IgE levels fluctuate or vary for a variety of reasons other than allergies. For instance, individuals with parasitic infections such as worms may show extraordinarily high levels of IgE. However, physicians may order total serum IgE to help in their baseline evaluations or to aid in the diagnosis of a unique complication of asthma called acute bronchopulmonary aspergillosis, the rare but dangerous condition discussed in Chapter 4, page 62.

Unhappily, on the "advocacy" side, certain other blood "tests" have enjoyed some vogue. Prominent among these are the collection of so-called cytotoxic tests, also known as "cytotoxicity," "leukocyte antigen sensitivity," "leukocytotoxicity," "Bryan's," or simply "food sensitivity testing." These tests have been found to be useless—even dangerous—in diagnosis and treatment. They do not identify the hidden causes of allergic symptoms and, like the long list of unproven and ineffective "medical" tests offered by unscrupulous practitioners, should be shunned.

Summary

This chapter holds the key to successful and effective management of your asthma by spelling out the steps and procedures involved in identifying with certainty the agents or conditions that trigger your asthma. This crucial identification process precedes and enables the other steps that, altogether, add up to your taking charge of your symptoms.

We identify asthma's various causal agents and spell out strategies you can use to find out which of them causes your symptoms. Basic to this discovery process is the Asthma Finder. We provide it, instruct you how to use it, and give examples of it in action. Supplemented by medical advice, the Asthma Finder should give you a clear and definite idea about exactly what causes your symptoms—and once you know this you are well on the way to taking charge.

Where diagnosis is difficult or elusive there are tests available and we list, describe, and evaluate them—skin tests, laboratory tests, blood tests—as well as the tests you should take pains to avoid as ineffective or even dangerous.

Wherever appropriate we have provided accounts of the experiences of patients to enlarge or drive home a particular point and to make the narrative more immediate and personal.

PART TWO

Avoiding Asthma's Common and Uncommon Causes and Complications

Avoiding the Cause of
Your Asthma

Chapter 5 named the major asthma-causing agents. Once you have identified the one—or ones—responsible for your symptoms, you need to avoid them. This chapter tells you what steps to take to eliminate or reduce your exposure to the conditions or substances that make you sick. The key to smart, aggressive, effective control of your symptoms depends on knowing what triggers your asthma and knowing exactly what you need to do to avoid or reduce exposure to those triggers. In the sections that follow we spell out specific avoidance tactics you can adopt if your asthma is traced to:

- Airborne allergens
- Food or food additives
- Respiratory infections
- Exercise
- Emotional stress
- Drugs and chemicals
- Atmospheric polluters

None of these antigens offers an easy target; some, like exposure to colds and flu or to certain food additives, simply cannot be avoided. But for many allergens, near complete avoidance can happen and even limiting exposure pays off in fewer days absent from work or school or dollars spent on medical care.

General Strategies

The agent that causes your symptoms will determine your avoidance tactics. For instance, if your asthma follows respiratory infections it makes considerable sense to stay away from and avoid making hand-to-hand contact with people with colds or the flu. When drugs, foods, or food additives trigger your wheezes, work to know exactly what you are ingesting. Look for the name of the allergen in the ingredients listed on container labels, ask what goes into restaurant dishes before ordering, keep up with the pollution standards index (PSI) or air quality index (AQI) forecasts. Put yourself in charge.

This unfailing vigilance has a downside. It can make you conspicuous, make you into a minor nuisance, make you vulnerable to social pressures. If distancing yourself from somebody with the sniffles causes raised eyebrows, if wearing a mask on bad pollen days makes you stand out, if your waiter gets irked at your questions, accept these thoughtless actions as part of the price you have to pay to stay healthy. *Put your own needs and condition first!* If you know that hard exercise outdoors on a cool autumn day in PE class will have you fighting for your breath, explain your situation and ask for a suitable alternative activity. Increase your medications when needed. If somebody should offer you salsa on your chips, eat it—after reading the package's list of ingredients so you know that the snack contains none of the sulfites that will make you ill.

Appendix B will help you to find products and suppliers catering to the special needs of people with asthma. These suppliers and many of the products they vend also occupy sites on the web. Check them out on your home computer or the ones at your school or your local library.

The bottom line? Avoiding or minimizing exposure to asthma-producing agents calls for everlasting, unfailing vigilance as well as a healthy helping of discomfort and sacrifice. The dividend? A less debilitating, less aggressive, more tractable disease.

Airborne Allergens—The Big Five

The Big Five airborne allergens—pollens, dust, animal dander, insect residues, molds—can provoke asthma. Keeping these triggers out of your environment and out of your body adds up to your first and most important line of defense. At one time surgical masks or uncomfortable, painful sterling silver screens inserted into the nostrils barred entry to dust or pollens. Today, air purifiers do the work and an effective air filtration system can work wonders in how well you manage your symptoms. The market offers a large number and variety of these systems. They may use any one or a combination of filtering devices and may range in size from tiny, wearable, "personal" units to ones designed for use in automobiles or small or large indoor spaces to centralized, whole-house systems like the one Merle, below, installed. By no means perfect, they can help.

> Merle, an active, lively man well up in his seventies, used to spend a lot of his time each spring at the hospital, getting emergency treatment for acute asthma attacks caused by pollens. He reacted to many of the wild grasses that flourished in the area where he lived. Allergy shots did not help him and medications did not keep him out of the ER when conditions got bad. A few years ago Merle and his wife decided to build a new home and his physician suggested he have a central air purifier and special window screens installed. This did not add much to the cost of the house because the plans already called for it to have central air conditioning. The results, then and ever since? Nothing but sensational! Merle still has some seasonal problems, symptoms, but controls them effectively with metered dose inhalers. The air filtration system paid for itself in its first year alone, just in saved emergency room bills.

Table 6.1 summarizes the filtration systems available for room-type purifiers, their approximate costs, and other relevant data. If you and your doctor decide that you ought to use an air purifier, keep the following points in mind.

TABLE 6.1   Type, Operation, and Costs of Room-Size Air Purifying Devices

Filter Type	Operating Principle	Purchase Price	Annual Filter Costs	Comment
Electrostatic or electronic	Precipitates particles on electrostatically charged filter	$350 and up	Up to $70	Some noise; generate ozone, an irritant
HEPA (high efficiency particulate arresting)	Traps particles in an extremely fine screen	$150 to $600	$75 to $200	
ULPA (ultra low penetration air)	Traps particles in an ultrafine screen	$175 and up	$100 to $250	
Fiber or fiberglass	Traps particles in fine screen	$100 and up	$5 to $20	Will not catch smaller particles: some noise; some models of little or no use
Ionizing	Gives particles a negative charge, which causes them to attach to positively charged surfaces	Up to $100	N/A	Quiet; units small; larger spaces may require more than one unit

NOTE: Increasingly, purifiers incorporate multistage combinations of filters with an ionization feature commonplace as well. Other units designed to control particular pollutants like smoke, microorganisms, radon or other gases, or formaldehyde emissions may incorporate HEGA (high efficiency gas arresting), EMF (enhanced media filtration), or ultraviolet (UV) technologies.

- Many air purifiers now combine two or more technologies so that the devices will screen out pollens, dust, and vapors. Some go so far as to eliminate household odors.
- Some Medical Equipment and Supply (so listed in the Yellow Pages) firms allow customers to try out units before rental or purchase. Ask if this is possible; if not, rent for a period. Keep in mind that insurance may cover rental or purchase costs or, if uninsured, these outlays qualify as a tax-deductible medical expense.
- To work effectively a purifier should completely recirculate the air *at least* four times an hour or have a clean air delivery rate (CADR) about two-thirds the room's volume. (The Association of Home Appliance Manufacturers tests and labels air purifiers for CADRs for dust, smoke, and pollen and certifies that the unit will clear the air a

stated number of times in a room of a given size. This information will help you choose a purifier that will fit the cause of your asthma and the size of the space it will need to clear. Note that the CADR assigned comes from operation of the unit at top speed.)

- Tight-fitting window filters that screen out larger airborne particles give air conditioning or purifying devices a boost.
- Make sure that your purchase from either a medical equipment specialist or a large chain retailer has specifications that meet or exceed the ones of the unit you successfully tried out. The medical supply field has manufacturers and vendors who misrepresent their products.
- See the January and September 2000 issues of *Consumer Reports* for a useful evaluation of several popular brands of air cleaners. You will find these reports in your local library.

Additional Ways to Avoid Exposure to Airborne Allergens

Air purifiers clean the air but have no effect on airborne antigens—dust, dust mites, animal dander, insect residue, mold—that have already colonized your space. To control these resident triggers:

- Use furniture and surfaces that do not attract or hold particles. Avoid overstuffed furniture or irritant-holding fabrics like plush. If necessary, use hypoallergenic covers over the pillow and mattress (Appendix B tells you how to find suppliers). Steer clear of feather or down pillows or coverings.
- Books catch dust or mold. Keep them dusted and dry. Where mold is the culprit, take pains to keep living and sleeping areas dry. Use a dehumidifier if necessary (see Appendix B) and eliminate patches of damp in basement or closet areas. (A low-wattage bulb left burning in closets will often control mold or mildew.) Silica gel or exposed crystals of dichlorobenzene will rid the house of fungi, but use them with caution and air the area completely before inhabiting it again.

- With regard to animal dander (saliva, sloughed-off skin, or pelt), cleanliness rules. Asthmatics should keep only the kinds of pets that do not produce dander—tropical fish, for example. (Even then, be sure the fish tank does not put a crop of mold into the air!) Birds, dogs, cats, rodents, and horses can and do provoke severe reactions in susceptible individuals. If you must own a pet, keep it out of the house. And even then you could be in trouble.

Dr. Mercer was invited to take the Dean's job at West Coast College. He had no sooner arrived at his new location in a small California city when he fell seriously ill with a violent reaction to horse dander. The whole area was "horse country" and he could find no place to live that kept him free of exposure to the dander. His acute sensitivity forced him to turn down the offer and return to his former position which offered neither the salary nor the prestige of the new job but at least it did not have him struggling for breath all of the time.

Avoiding House Dust

Avoiding the mix of substances that make up house dust—probably the most pervasive and the most stubborn of asthma's many triggers—calls for hard, unrelenting work. House dust allergen consists primarily of the house dust mite, a multilegged microscopic spider that loves to eat your sloughed wet skin after you shower. Hundreds of thousands of them live on your pillow alone and it is nearly impossible to eradicate them. The following suggestions will help you deal with this menace.

In General

- Do not use upholstered or ornately carved furniture, bed canopies, rugs, hanging plants, fabric wall hangings or tapestries, knickknack shelves, fabric lamp shades, stuffed animals, flocked wallpaper, or other examples of dust-catching decor.
- Dust collects on electrical or electronic equipment—light fixtures, radios, TVs, sound reproducing equipment, computers—and on radiators and in heating vents. Clean them regularly.

- Use hard-finished, nonretentive surfaces—bare wood, glass, metal, plastic, synthetics, fiberglass.
- Dust surfaces daily with a damp mop or sponge. If you vacuum, use only canister or tank-type models or a central vacuum cleaning system with the collection tank well away from the living and sleeping quarters. An asthmatic should not run a vacuum cleaner or should wear a mask while doing so.

In the Bedroom

- Remove all carpeting, wall hangings or decorations, books, and other dust collectors; store clothing in cleaned, closed closet or chest of drawers.
- Replace curtains, drapes, and venetian blinds with roll-down window shades.
- Use an air purification system (see above).
- Install a Breathe-right® (or similar brand) encased pillow cover. Costing about $7, it will lasts several years. It goes over your pillow and under your pillowcase and denies access to the mites that would ordinarily live in your pillow. Also use only synthetic pillows; avoid down or feather comforters and wool blankets.
- Wash blankets frequently (every two to four weeks).
- Air condition if possible; keep relative humidity below 50 percent (low humidity kills dust mites).
- Note well that antigens can turn up in odd, unexpected, and innocent-seeming places.

Four-year-old Kathy's asthma traces to dust and dust mites. Kathy's room, as dust free as you could ever make it, has no shelves, rugs, or curtains. A hypoallergenic cover encloses the mattress but Kathy still wheezes at night. Kathy absolutely insists on having her stuffed teddy bear in bed with her every night. Her mother has long suspected that that disreputable, tattered, soiled specimen carries the antigens Kathy reacts to and causes the nighttime wheezes. The mother tells the pediatrician about her hunch who suggests that Kathy get a new bear, a washable one, one that will not pick up dust and can be wiped clean. At first Kathy spurns the new, hard-edged Teddy but her mother stays with the idea, gets Kathy to the point where she plays with the newcomer and eventually accepts the substitute. At that point the dear old bear leaves on a long vacation.

Avoiding Asthma-Causing Food and Food Additives

The advice here is simple and obvious; do not eat the foods—or much more likely, the food additives or contaminants—that you know will bring on your asthma. So long as you exercise a certain amount of vigilance and caution you should manage to stay clear of the offending item or items. Know exactly what you will eat by studying labels thoroughly and carefully. Ask questions. Resist the temptation to try new or unfamiliar foods or to see if you can get away with eating something that you have every reason to believe will give you trouble. Know and watch out for complicating factors you may encounter.

- The offending food or substance may appear in unexpected places. Milk, responsible for asthmatic symptoms in susceptible individuals, turns up in everything from bologna to zabaglione; tartrazine (yellow food dye no. 5) seemingly goes into nearly everything processed or prepared; as we have already noted, alcoholic beverages and foods susceptible to spoilage can carry a load of metabisulfite. (See Chapter 5, page 71 for likely sources of these additives.)
- The offender can belong to a big family whose relatives can trigger symptoms. This cross-sensitivity happens frequently in food intolerances. Thus, if peanut butter (a pea) makes you wheeze, all the other members of the pea family—the many species of peas and beans as well as acacia, licorice, and tragacanth, a plant-based gum used as a vehicle in many medicines—might also make you sick. Chapter 7 identifies the food families and their members.
- People allergic to latex often cannot eat kiwi, mango, melons, avocado, Brazil nuts, and other fruits and vegetables because the latex proteins often cross-react with these foods.

- In addition to the food itself or to additives intended to enhance its appearance or reduce spoilage, food contaminants may also trigger asthmatic reactions. Insecticides and herbicides often turn up in fresh or processed fruits and vegetables; steroids and antibiotics appear in almost all commercially produced meats and fowl; fish taken from polluted or contaminated sources may contain a concentration of heavy metals such as insecticides high enough to provoke an asthmatic reaction in sensitive people. Avoiding these threats is especially difficult, although increasing numbers of markets carry certified organically grown, pesticide- and herbicide-free produce, and offer meats free of additives—all at premium prices. Carefully washing fresh fruits and vegetables will reduce some of the risk; environmental health agencies do issue warnings about eating fish taken from contaminated or polluted sources.

Identifying these food-based asthma-provokers is tricky, but here again a carefully-maintained Asthma Finder (Figure 5.1, Chapter 5) represents your best resource. Keep a systematic, comprehensive record of what you consume and relate that record to your symptoms. See also Chapter 7 for a more detailed discussion of diet and asthma.

Reducing Colds and Respiratory Infections

Unless you live in a bubble you cannot avoid exposure to colds and respiratory infections. To the parents of asthmatic children it seems as if the kids keep coming down with one cold after another, colds that slip into yet another asthma attack. Between the ages of two and four, children typically have an average of ten to fifteen colds a year but these repeated infections may have a good side by helping to develop resistance to them. You may manage to reduce the number and severity of your or your children's colds or make the body more able to combat them by taking these precautions:

- Maintain good health habits: plenty of sleep, adequate, balanced diet, and so on.

- Stay in good physical shape. Follow a regular program of exercise and control your weight.
- Avoid contact with people with coughs or sneezes.
- Do not get overheated; avoid drafts.
- Wash your hands frequently during the day and keep them away from your mouth and eyes. Don't shake the hands of people with colds.
- Drink plenty of fluids, two quarts per day minimum, preferably water.
- Ask your doctor if you should have flu or pneumovax shots.
- Help children to follow these guidelines. In addition, teach them not to share eating utensils or glasses, to avoid using public drinking fountains, and to cover their mouths when they cough or sneeze.

If a virus causes your or your child's respiratory infection (and this is most often the case), stay away from antibiotics unless you have a secondary bacterial infection. Antibiotics will not help the cold and they can carry troublesome side effects, including the development of more serious antibiotic resistant strains of the virus in your body.

Using Home Vaporizers Effectively

Pediatricians often recommend the use of vaporizers at home to treat colds and croupy coughs. Croupy coughs, typically deep, sharp, and insistent, respond well to vaporizers, devices that blow air over a water-filled reservoir, thus generating a vapor mist. Inhaling this moist and, with some appliances, heated air relieves the cough. Inexpensive and durable, home vaporizers enjoy popularity but they carry drawbacks you should know about.

- The cough of patients with asthma differs markedly from the one seen in a child who has croup. An asthma cough reflects collapse of airways or bronchospasm and vapor alone will not relieve it.
- The repeated addition of water to vaporizers almost always results in the formation of a thick coating of mold and bacteria in the reservoir and especially in the tubes and equipment that vaporize

the air. The fine mist put out by such a machine will carry a cargo of mold and germs, the last thing you want to breathe because the mix may trigger an allergic reaction and make your asthma worse.

Alice's cold-linked asthma attacks started at 18 months of age. Over the years her mother took her to a succession of doctors, all of whom prescribed medication to be started at the onset of a cold and to continue for as much as two weeks. Recurrent sinusitis now troubles Alice. Virtually every cold ends with a sinus infection and her doctor cannot figure out why this invariably happens. Referred to an allergist at a nearby medical school, Alice and her mother were asked if they used a vaporizer. They did, unfailingly, whenever a cold hit. The allergist had the vaporizer brought in to the clinic and examined despite the mother's insistence that that was unnecessary, that she cleaned the unit carefully with vinegar every week. The ugly mold residue clogging the metal tubes over the reservoir astounded her. Acting on the allergist's advice Alice's mother discontinued use of the vaporizer. Now, although Alice continues to catch colds, the bouts of sinusitis rarely occur. Alice does wheeze after exposure to damp, dank environments, and she can never go into the basement of their home without becoming quite uncomfortable. Allergy skin tests revealed acute sensitivity to molds.

We recommend judicious use of a vaporizer for very small children (below the age of six) who have croupy coughs. Clean all parts daily using a diluted solution of vinegar. Discontinue its use if it doesn't work.

People often ask us if warm vapor is better than cold. Cold or warm vaporizers do not differ in their clinical effects but burns, some of them serious, can be traced to use of the hot mist type. Accordingly we recommend the cool mist models.

Avoiding Exercise-Induced Asthma Attacks

If vigorous exercise pushes you into an asthmatic attack, you have three choices: exercise anyway and suffer the consequences, take up another activity that does not have you ill when you finish it, or take preventive medication beforehand.

Matthew has had asthma most of his 15 years. PE at school, and even fast walking, causes him to wheeze so severely he can't keep up with the other kids, and this inability bothers him almost as much as the asthma. His doctor says he has exercise-induced asthma and has recommended that he take albuterol, which usually works in situations like this. Unfortunately, Matthew finds the albuterol makes his heart race distressingly. Matthew's parents consulted another physician who recommended the daily use of Singulaire, a leukotriene inhibitor. (We discuss these drugs in Chapter 14.) Since starting this regimen, Matthew's stamina has improved greatly and, to his immense satisfaction, his athletic skills have picked up markedly too.

As we noted in Chapter 5, not exercising in cold, dry conditions or ones that require sustained, breath-taking exertion helps to keep asthmatics from becoming symptomatic. Exercise is important, however, and we cannot emphasize too strongly the value of every asthmatic learning to swim and to swim often in the uniquely favorable conditions that the activity/sport offers to them.

Avoiding or Managing Emotional Stress

Asthmatics, because their disease is chronic and sometimes severe, suffer inordinately from emotional stress. The gravity of the symptoms and the way in which they turn the ordinary, unattended act of breathing into a laborious struggle for breath is enough to trigger hyperventilation that originates with fear and panic. Added to that, however, are the myriad emotional upsets that plague the families of asthmatics. Asthmatics and their families needlessly experience frustration, feelings of helplessness, and self-blame over the attack; the symptoms terrify children who spend a lot of time wondering if, this time with this attack, they will die. Children, and adults too, need solicitous and understanding care and reassurance to overcome this private dread. Sometimes parents and nonasthmatic siblings actively resent the attention, care, and expense that the asthmatic requires. Explaining the nature of the disease and the reasons for the intensive and time-demanding treatment openly and straightforwardly goes a long way toward easing this source of tension and friction.

At the same time, parents may increase a child's insecurity and anxiety by being oversolicitous and overprotective. As a result, they discourage their offspring from participating in and enjoying ordinary activities and pleasures and thereby keep them from developing normally. In doing this, they forge an undesirably close dependency that may persist and prove hard to break in later life. At the same time they make it possible for the ailing child to learn to use his or her condition to have his or her own way in the family or elsewhere. Maintaining a proper balance of effective care of asthma symptoms on the one hand and fostering the closest to normal development of the child on the other requires patience, understanding, and the willingness to take some risks. The following suggestions will help you or your child to avoid some of the major difficulties that arise from emotional responses to asthma.

- Keep the lines of communication open. Discuss problems frankly and directly as they arise. Do not let them fester.
- Do not think of yourself as an invalid. With thought and care you can do just about anything anyone else can.
- Do not treat your asthmatic children as invalids. If you do, they may start believing you.
- If your job—or school or home environment—carries the kind of stress or tension that makes your asthma worse, try to identify the cause and work with the other people involved to reduce or eliminate it.
- Control stress or tension by slowing yourself down. Yoga, exercise, imagery, meditation, or other tension-reducing activities may work for you.
- Seek outside help if your illness consistently has you feeling unhappy, depressed, or anxious. Your friends, your minister or priest, social workers, psychologists, counselors, your physician—any one of them can give you a hand.
- If your child or lover or friend has asthma, work to create a laid-back atmosphere with easy give and take. Work consciously to avoid stress, conflict, and anger.

- Under absolutely *no* circumstances should you, an asthmatic, take sedatives, sleeping pills, or tranquilizers to reduce stress, nor should you provide them to an asthmatic child or friend.

Most allergists will tell you that emotional reactions in and of themselves do not cause asthma but they do provoke rapid shallow breathing that prompts the sensitive airways to go into spasm.

Avoiding Asthma-Causing Drugs and Chemicals

Drugs can endanger the life of the asthmatic.

Louis, 54, has had exercise-induced asthma since childhood. A few months ago he started having chest pains, went to his doctor for a checkup, learned that he had angina, coronary artery disease. The doctor prescribed propanolol (Inderol) to reduce the severity of the chest pains. Within hours of taking his first dose of propranolol, Louis began wheezing and his chest tightened and started to heave. Fearing he was having a heart attack, he went to the ER; the doctors there hospitalized him, gave him oxygen, and hooked him up to the usual monitoring devices, all of which put out "normal" readings. One doctor, puzzled by the disagreement between symptoms and electronic readouts, guessed that Louis' symptoms might trace to the propranolol because she knew that it, along with other heart medications, elevates the muscle tone in the airways, and especially so for asthmatics. That proved to be the case for Louis, who had an effective alternative medication prescribed.

Louis learned the hard way what every asthmatic should know and practice religiously. Every time you get or fill a prescription, remind your physician, dentist, or pharmacist *without fail* that you have asthma. Propranolol is one of a class of drugs called beta-antagonists that are widely used for high blood pressure and certain forms of heart disease. In fact, people with recurring chest pains, heart disease, and hypertension or high blood pressure may routinely be prescribed beta blocking drugs. In Table 6.2 we have listed the names of the beta blockers that keep metered-dose asthma medications like Alupent and Ventolin from doing their job.

Sedatives and tranquilizers fall in a second class of drugs you, the asthmatic, should scrupulously avoid. Stay away from Buspar, Ambium, Sonata, and any drugs that are classed as benzodiazepines. Although asthma often produces anxiety, its symptoms should *never* be treated with tranquilizers. Previous administration of sedative agents to control anxiety frequently catches the blame for the death of asthmatics. If your doctor, knowing that you are an asthmatic, prescribes sedatives or tranquilizers for you, find yourself another doctor *immediately*. Alcohol, also a potent respiratory depressant, must not be drunk when you are having problems with your asthma.

As many as 60 percent of asthmatics will wheeze after taking aspirin or other nonsteroidal inflammatory drugs. The symptoms these drugs produce, often low-level, may only show with pulmonary function testing (or with your peak flow meter) and this may encourage you to dismiss them as no big deal. However, suppose you come down with a cold that has you short of breath and wheezing slightly. If you take an aspirin or other nonsteroidal anti-inflammatory drug, the small effect it exerts on the underlying condition may push you over the edge into an acute attack and a trip to the ER. Because of this risk as well as other side reactions connected with these drugs, we advocate use of acetaminophen (Tylenol or a generic equivalent) that does does not provoke or intensify asthma's symptoms.

If you have arthritis or any other condition that demands the use of nonsteroidal anti-inflammatory drugs, your doctor should "challenge" you with these drugs to find a safe alternative. The challenge goes like this: First, you take a pulmonary function test. You then take the drug by mouth with repeat pulmonary function tests following twenty minutes, one, two, and even four hours later. By looking at the before and after pulmonary function test scores, the doctor can tell if the drug is potentially dangerous for you. On the good news front, there is some preliminary evidence that suggests that the new antiarthritis drug, Celebrex, may help your arthritis but may spare your asthma. More data are needed, however, before Celebrex can be recommended for use by asthmatics.

Do not take any drug without first letting your doctor know about your asthma. Consult the *Physician's Desk Reference* (available in your doctor's office or local library) for possible side effects. If even the possibility of an asthmatic reaction exists, do not take the drug; ask your doctor to pre-scribe a safer alternative.

A Special Word on ACE Inhibitors

A major improvement in the treatment of hypertension was the develop-ment of a new class of drugs called ACE inhibitors. (ACE is an enzyme in the body that constricts arteries and thereby elevates blood pressure.) These drugs are very useful in the treatment of high blood pressure but they can produce a very bad cough and angioedema (swelling of your face and even your airway).

> Geri had high blood pressure all her life and hated the side effects from some of the drugs that she had previously been given. But she had a great response when she was prescribed Enalapril (Vasotec) for her pressure. However, four months later she developed a bad, dry hacking cough. She saw her doctor who thought she had developed adult onset asthma. The doctor prescribed inhalers but the cough persisted. Finally, her doctor stopped the Enalapril and the cough went away. Geri had suffered a well known complication of ACE inhibitors called angioneurotic edema. Left untreated it can be fatal!

We name two classes of ACE inhibitors, ACE 1 and ACE 2 in the side-bar; at this time ACE 2 drugs, newer and more expensive, seem not to carry the unpleasant and dangerous side effects.

Chemicals

Countless dyes, preservatives, stabilizers, and other chemicals are added routinely to food; some chemicals even masquerade as food. For the most part their impact on the body or their relationship to asthma remains un-clear. However, metabisulfite, a preservative, causes asthma and tartrazine, a food dye, has a place on the list of suspected triggers. We believe that many chemical additives may harm asthmatics but proof of our suspicions awaits scientific study. The case for metabisulfite is well proved; for tar-

TABLE 6.2   Drugs or Medications Asthmatics Should Avoid

Type of Drug	Effect	Generic (Brand) Names
Beta blockers	Elevate muscle tone in airways	Betapace, Blocaderm, Brevibloc, Cartrol, Inderal, Kerlone, Nadolol, Sectral, Tenormin, Toprol-XL, Zebeta
Sedatives, tranquilizers, depressants	Depress or inhibit respiratory status	Alcohol, Mebaral, Nembutal, Ativan, Halcion, ProSom, Valium, Versed, Ambien, Bevitamel, Diprivan, Mepergan, Phenergan, Propofol, Simply sleep, Sonata, Unisom
Nonsteroidal anti-inflammatory drugs	Trigger respiratory spasms	Anaprox, Arthrotec, Cataflam, Celebrex, Clinoril, Daypro, Disalcid, Dolobid, EC-Naprosyn, Ecotrin, Feldene, Indocin, Lodine, Mobic, Motrin, Nalfon, Naprelan, Naprosyn, Orudis, Oruvail, Ponstel, Relafen, Tolectin, Toradol, Trilisate, Vioxx, Voltaren
ACE inhibitors (to treat high blood pressure)	Triggers asthma-like cough, swelling of face and in airways	ACE 1: Accupril, Aceon, Altace, Captopril, Lotensin, Mavik, Monopril, Prinivil, Univasc, Vasotec, Zestril
		ACE 2: Atacand, Avapro, Cozaar, Diovan, Micardis, Teveten

trazine the possibility remains but the data have lost some credibility. For other preservatives the data are mostly anecdotal but persuasive in individual cases. Chapter 5, page 71 discusses metabisulfite and tartrazine and tells you where these substances occur.

Carol's asthma symptoms worsen whenever she eats anything containing FD&C #5, a yellow food dye. Junk food brims with this chemical, tartrazine—fast-food taco places dish it out by the barrel! Carol scrupulously avoided these foods, but she still had low-level but persistent problems with her asthma. She took faithfully the medication her doctor had prescribed but she still wheezed most of the time. Often her wheezing seemed to worsen not long after she took her medication. She mentioned this to her doctor who determined that her medication contained tartrazine to make it appear more palatable. He was surprised as many doctors are not as sure anymore of tartrazine's connection to asthma but, he switched Carol to another manufacturer's brand of medicine and she got better almost immediately.

Companies that market asthma drugs have learned from such cases not to put food dyes in asthma remedies. However, antibiotics, birth control pills, and hormones, among many medications, do contain food dyes. Whenever you start on *any* new medication, monitor your reactions to it carefully to see if it induces or intensifies your asthma symptoms.

Ellen finds that her face swells up and her asthma gets worse when she eats red licorice and other foods and pills that contain red dye. In her case there is no doubt that red dye makes her sick; if she avoids it, she stays much healthier.

Avoiding Air Pollution (Especially Tobacco)

Tobacco smoke is the most common and most serious *air pollutant. Asthmatics and members of their households should not smoke tobacco.*

Asthmatics have long known that tobacco smoke makes their symptoms worse but the nature of the influence tobacco and cigarette smoking exerts on lung and heart disease has only recently come to light. For asthmatics, tobacco carries additional bad news.

Tobacco smoke, basically a poison gas, paralyzes the lining of the airways, preventing them from clearing out normal mucus and the debris that accumulates every day in the lungs. The uncleared mucus thickens and may become infected after contact with tobacco smoke. The smoke also contains carbon monoxide, which can cause significant pulmonary irritation and even collapse of the lungs. The irritation also weakens the already fragile air sacs and makes them more vulnerable to infection or spasm.

If you smoke, in addition to the damage tobacco exerts on you directly, the secondhand smoke that you produce can harm those close to you. Secondhand smoke definitely irritates lungs and children who live in homes where a parent or parents smoke have more frequent and longer hospitalizations for acute asthma episodes than children who live in nonsmoking environments.

From our standpoint, one of the more agreeable developments in the United States during the past decade has been the demonization of cigarette smoking. Most public spaces like workplaces, restaurants, airplanes, cinemas, concert halls, theaters, and so on forbid smoking and those places that do permit smoking provide nonsmoking areas. The asthmatic has the right to breathe clean air, can reasonably expect to have it, and can take steps to avoid exposure. The most important avoidance measure? Declaring the home a smoke-free zone and outlawing smoking anywhere on the premises. Beyond that, seek out smoke-free areas and insist on nonsmoker rooms in hotels or motels. Remember that foreign countries and some foreign airlines are not as progressive so don't forget that when you travel.

Smokers have their problems, too. As noted, tobacco smoke can do serious damage to the nonasthmatic and most smokers want to break the habit. Mark Twain wryly noted that "Anyone can quit smoking. I've done it myself twenty times."

Twain recognized the stubbornness of addiction to nicotine. A variety of programs exist to free smokers from that form of bondage. None of them work without fail. Organizations that offer smoking cessation programs can be found in the list of resources given in Appendix A. Your doctor can offer suggestions and advice, many HMOs sponsor programs or clinics, and support groups do help addicted smokers kick the habit.

The air also carries pollutants other than tobacco smoke and some contaminants—ozone and sulfur dioxide in particular—are potent causes of asthma. High concentrations of these triggers result from a conspiracy of climatic conditions—usually an inversion layer of air trapped by a high pressure system that permits a buildup of polluters arising from automobile emissions and combustion of other fossil fuels. These gases give asthmatics lots of trouble.

Most cities with significant "smog" problems—and more and more cities have smog problems these days—forecast air quality, putting the projected air quality on the newspaper's weather page or reporting it on the broadcast news. The report usually consists of a number that translates to an adjective like "low" or "moderate" or "high." When the Pollution Standards Index

(PSI) or Air Quality Index (AQI) peaks, some communities will declare an air quality alert that warns people with respiratory problems or otherwise at risk to stay indoors, avoid strenuous activities, and take other precautionary measures. The indexes relate to normal people, people without respiratory problems, so a predicted reading of "moderate" will have asthmatics showing symptoms. If you are asthmatic and bothered by smog, keep close track of the PSI readings and when a forecast of "moderate pollution" turns up, stay inside, keep your windows closed, and relax. Keep indoors until the smog clears. If you absolutely must go out, wear a disposable paper mask like the ones physicians or dentists—or carpenters—wear. You will find them at the pharmacy or the hardware store. The masks will not filter out the gases but they will take care of particulate matter. In addition, take it easy, don't hurry or exercise, and avoid exposure to obvious triggers in the environment like automobile exhaust, smoke, and dust.

Other Asthma Triggers

Myriad other substances—substances we have not mentioned—can cause an asthmatic episode. Many household cleaning products, especially detergents and aerosol cleaners, can set you to wheezing; so can solvents, glues, cosmetics, perfumes, and powders as well as smoke from a fireplace or candles or fumes from kerosene lamps.

With all of these antigens, following the procedures spelled out in Chapter 5 will permit easy detection and point the way to simple and straightforward avoidance. All of the products have nonallergenic substitutes—possibly excepting the candle on the birthday cake. When the birthday rolls around, limit yourself to one symbolic candle, and get it out of the room swiftly and discreetly as soon as it is blown out. Not as much fun as a veritable bonfire atop the cake but better than bronchospasm.

Avoiding by Relocating

Years ago, before most of the medications now available for the treatment of asthma came into use, physicians often recommended that sufferers move to warm, dry climates—Arizona and New Mexico especially.

This advice probably thrived on anecdotes about individuals whose asthma—or allergies generally—improved significantly following relocation. Such improvements doubtless did happen when the cause of the symptoms was definitely established and the site chosen for relocation permitted its complete avoidance. But the incidence of asthma plays no geographical favorites. The incidence of asthma among southwesterners matches that of folks who live in regions of the country that have harsher climates. Uprooting and moving a family to another location to escape asthma or other allergic disease can end in crushing, cruel disappointment. Taking determined steps to control asthma in the home territory makes much more sense—logistically, economically, and medically.

Summary

Chapter 6 deals comprehensively with the absolute key to successful management of your asthma—avoiding the cause of your symptoms. After outlining general strategies we tell you how to stay away from or manage:

- Airborne antigens (pollen, dust, dust mites, animal dander, insect residue, and molds)
- Food, food additives, and contaminants
- Respiratory infections
- Exercise and cold air
- Emotional stress
- Drugs and chemicals
- Atmospheric pollutants

that may bring on or worsen an asthma attack. We direct you to other sections of the book that elaborate on these topics and we offer critiques of strategies and devices that come into play in this element so vital to the effective care of asthma.

7

Diet and Asthma

Reactions to Food: Allergy or Sensitivity?

Virtually any food or drink can trigger an asthmatic reaction in a susceptible person. In some instances the asthmatic symptoms represent a true allergic (atopic or IgE-related) response. However, in most cases the reaction merely represents an intolerance or hypersensitivity, not a true
allergy. The difference matters because it may distinguish potentially life-
threatening reactions from minor inconveniences.

A wide variety of foods, food colors, and food preservatives or preexisting conditions in the individual can also produce symptoms that closely
mimic asthmatic reactions and, in fact, account for most negative reactions to "food." This mimicry makes precise diagnosis extremely difficult.
However, find comfort in the knowledge that, although diagnosis of the
reasons for food intolerances on hypersensitivity is complicated and un-
certain, its treatment is extremely easy—simply stay away from whatever
you know causes your problem. Finding out what causes the mischief and
steering clear of it matters more than diagnosing your symptoms as allergic
or hypersensitive.

Even allergists disagree on the definition of what constitutes a food allergy. The more cautious ones diagnose food-linked asthma as allergic only
in instances where tests detect the presence of the antibody IgE. Others
believe that when classic asthmatic symptoms appear—wheezing, shortness of breath, and mucus production—the diagnosis of allergic or atopic
asthma is likely, even if no antibody accompanies the symptoms. Whether

allergy or hypersensitivity, sufferers know that to keep symptom-free they need to avoid the offending agent.

The Usual Course of a Hypersensitive Asthmatic Reaction to Food

Food hypersensitivity can cause wheezing and shortness of breath. However, it has no "usual" course, and its symptoms can vary dramatically in their severity (see Tables 7.1 and 7.2). What happens depends on a host of factors, including the degree of sensitivity or vulnerability of the individual and the amount and form in which the irritant is ingested. Sometimes an asthmatic reaction to food occurs with unbelievable speed and severity.

> Kim, a 17-year-old girl, has a sleepover with a group of her girlfriends. She prepares a snack for herself: a tuna sandwich and soda. After a few minutes she complains that she doesn't feel well, breaks out in hives, starts having severe breathing difficulties, becomes confused, and comes close to passing out. The parents of the hostess rush her to the emergency room of a nearby hospital where she is treated for anaphylaxis (or an acute allergic reaction). Fortunately, Kim recovers quickly. It turns out that Kim is violently allergic to peanuts. Kim knows that and scrupulously avoids contact with peanuts or foods containing peanuts. What she did not know is that the knife that she picked up and used to make her sandwich carried a small amount of peanut butter left by its previous user—a microscopic amount, but enough to produce Kim's near-fatal reaction.

In most instances, happily, the sequence of events is more leisurely and the symptoms less grave.

Medical Evaluation for Food-Hypersensitive Asthmatic Reactions

Sometimes identifying an asthmatic reaction to a particular food or substance doesn't add up to a problem or need a doctor.

TABLE 7.1   Symptoms of Food Hypersensitivity

Location of Reaction	Symptoms in	
	Children	Adults
Gastrointestinal	Colic, vomiting, diarrhea	Diarrhea, cramps, constipation
Pulmonary	Wheezing, shortness of breath, cough	Wheezing, shortness of breath
Ear, nose, and throat	Runny nose, nasal congestion, ear inflammation	Runny nose, nasal congestion
Central nervous system	Headache	Headache
Skin	Eczema, hives, itching	Eczema, hives, itching
Vascular	Faintness, drop in blood pressure, loss of consciousness (rare in infants); irregular heartbeat	Faintness, drop in blood pressure, loss of consciousness, irregular heartbeat
Psychological	Irritability, hyperactivity*	Irritability, depression, psychosis
Other		Tension-fatigue syndrome

  * Hyperactivity or hyperkinesis. Despite widespread popular belief to the contrary, little credible evidence links this troublesome syndrome to particular foods.

TABLE 7.2   Types of Food-Hypersensitive Reactions and Symptoms

Type of Reaction	Symptoms
Anaphylactic (within seconds to 30 minutes)	Pallor, shock, intense and widespread itchiness, wheezing, shortness of breath, hives
Immediate (3 to 60 minutes)	Vomiting, diarrhea, wheezing, shortness of breath, itching, hives
Intermediate (1 to 12 hours)	Vomiting, diarrhea, hives, wheezing, shortness of breath, nasal congestion or runniness, flaring of eczema, headache, cough
Delayed (after 12 hours)	Tension-fatigue syndrome, "allergic" manifestations, respiratory discomfort, depression

For years Ted had followed the custom of having a glass of robust red wine with dinner. Just about the time he turned 60 he began having a dull, throbbing headache and a slight wheeze most evenings. He had his blood pressure checked but that seemed to be fine. He didn't have any other problems and during the day at work he felt well. Away on a pack trip with a couple of friends, Ted didn't have anything alcoholic to drink for three days. No headaches or shortness of breath either. "Aha," he thought. When he got home from the camping trip he followed the simple expedient of drinking, as usual, some nights, and not drinking other nights, and recorded his reaction. The results: If he drank, he had a headache and a wheeze, but with no alcohol, no symptoms.

It is probably safe not to see a doctor when you absolutely know what the offending food is, it does not provoke a life-threatening reaction, it is easily avoided, and if you stay away from it, your symptoms vanish. In all other cases, seek medical advice to get help in establishing what causes your problem and what you need to do to deal with it effectively. See the doctor, because some instances of what appear to be food intolerance actually result from organic deficiencies or chronic illnesses that, if not recognized and treated appropriately, can threaten life. In the case of anaphylactic reactions, you absolutely must get medical advice to put together comprehensive avoidance strategies and to develop familiarity with and competence in carrying out emergency procedures.

The Leading Causes of Asthmatic Reactions to Food

As we noted at the outset of this chapter, any food—and many of the substances found in it or added to it to enhance its appearance or growth, ward off insects, improve its flavor, or preserve its freshness—can set off a reaction in a susceptible person. The condition or state of the individual—illness, enzyme deficiencies, thyroid malfunctions—can also interact with foods to cause reactions.

Foods that appear on any list of leading causes of food hypersensitivity depend on the expert doing the listing. Cow's milk, eggs, shellfish, nuts, and wheat provoke reactions, but the unanimity stops there. Legumes (peanuts and soybeans) are mentioned frequently, as well as fish and mollusks. However, authorities disagree on the role of tomatoes, chocolate, and citrus fruits, which are often labeled as allergens, although strict laboratory experiments fail to support this charge. (Chocolate can make one sick, but it is not borne out that the sickness is allergic.) The nomination of other substances such as cola apparently owes as much to subjective bias as to scientific study.

To make matters more confusing, parents often label certain foods like strawberries, other berries, and tomatoes, foods that certainly cause rashes, especially in young children, as allergens. In fact, no evidence exists that IgE mediates "strawberry rash." Some people are hypersensitive to strawberries but not "allergic" to them. Table 7.3 illustrates the wide range of symptoms that foods and additives can trigger. And, to add to the complexity, people who react to a given food may react to other foods that belong to the same food family. Table 7.4 lists food families and members.

TABLE 7.3   Causes of Hypersensitivity Reactions and Their Characteristic Symptoms

Causal Agent	Symptoms
Foods such as strawberries, tomatoes, citrus fruits, shellfish	Rash, itching
Mold that is often found in cheeses, fermented meats like salami, fermented beverages like beer, dried fruits, yogurt	Rash, itching, respiratory problems
Antibiotic contaminants (bacitracin, penicillin, tetracycline) found in meats, poultry, or milk	Rash, itching, respiratory, gastrointestinal (GI) problems
Insect residues in spices	Rash, itching, respiratory, GI problems
Chemical food additives	
Monosodium glutamate (MSG)	"Chinese restaurant syndrome" (flushing, headache, chest pain)
Metabisulfite, Tartrazine	GI symptoms, headache, rash, itching, respiratory problems
Bacteria and bacterial toxins	GI symptoms—pain, gas, diarrhea
Enzyme deficiencies	GI symptoms, colic (in infants)
GI tract diseases including gastric and duodenal ulcers, hiatal hernia	Gastric distress (pain, burning, gas)

TABLE 7.4   Food Families

Family	Members
Apple	Apple, pear, quince
Aster	Lettuce, chicory, endive, escarole, artichoke, dandelion, sunflower seeds
Beet	Beet, spinach, chard
Blueberry	Blueberry, huckleberry, cranberry
Buckwheat	Buckwheat, rhubarb, garden sorrel
Cashew	Cashew, pistachio, mango
Chocolate	Chocolate (cocoa), cola
Citrus	Orange, lemon, grapefruit, lime, tangerine, kumquat, citron
Fungus	Mushroom, yeast
Ginger	Ginger, cardamom, turmeric
Gooseberry	Currant, gooseberry
Grains	Wheat, corn, rice, oats, barley, rye, wildrice, cane, millet, sorghum, bamboo shoots
Laurel	Avocado, cinnamon, bay leaves, sassafras
Mallow	Cottonseen, okra
Melon	Watermelon, cucumber, cantaloupe, pumpkin, squash, other melons
Mint	Mint, peppermint, spearmint, thyme, sage, basil, savory, rosemary, catnip
Mustard	Turnip, radish, horseradish, watercress, cabbage, kraut, chinese cabbage, broccoli, cauliflower, brussels sprouts, collards, kale, kohlrabi, rutabaga
Myrtle	Allspice, guava, clove, pimiento, (not the red pepper form of pimiento)
Onion	Onion, garlic, asparagus, chives, leeks, sasaparilla
Palm	Coconut, date
Parsley	Carrot, parsnip, celery, parsley, celeriac, anise, dill, fennel, angelica, celery seed, cumin, coriander, caraway
Pea	Peanuts, peas (green, field, blackeyed), beans (navy, lima, pinto, string, soy, etc.), licorice, acacia, tragacanth
Plum	Plum, cherry, peach, apricot, nectarine, almond
Potato	Potato, tomato, eggplant, green pepper, red pepper, chili pepper, paprika, cayenne
Rose	Strawberry, raspberry, blackberry, dewberry, loganberry, youngberry, boysenberry
Walnut	English walnut, black walnut, pecan, hickory nut, butternut

NOTE: A person senstive to any one member of a given food family *may* react to other members of that family.

Identifying the Causes of Food-Related Asthma

The disagreement about what a "food allergy" is or what brings it on has made the study and treatment of food intolerance one of the most difficult areas in the field of clinical allergy. Even so, identifying the cause of a reaction and developing successful tactics for avoiding it, although tricky, can be accomplished if you pay close attention to your symptoms and keep careful records.

Figure 7.1 sketches a strategy to follow in identifying the food (or the myriad of additives, contaminants, or other conditions) responsible for a hypersensitive asthmatic reaction. The figure takes you through a conservative and minimally risky series of steps to follow to identify the cause of your hypersensitive reaction to food. Careful observance of an elimination diet is the key to finding out the information you need. The accompanying sidebar presents a general elimination diet, together with the steps you will need to follow to see it through to a successful conclusion. Also provided is a list of food families that help you to avoid and offer clues to foods that possibly contribute to your reaction. Following the procedures outlined in Figure 7.2 and sticking faithfully to the elimination diet, if called for, should point to whatever causes your wheezes. The hardest part of the process? Forcing yourself to stay on the seriously monotonous diet.

When you have isolated the source of your reaction, your problems are over—almost. Along the way:

- *Do not* allow skin tests or challenges if your food intolerance is severe or life-threatening.
- Note that challenge tests are the key to dead-sure identification of specific causes of food hypersensitivity. If done, they should be conducted "double blind." In double-blind tests, your doctor prepares a number of gelatin capsules, some filled with glucose (sugar), others with different quantities of the suspected food. The capsules are mixed, so neither you nor your doctor knows what capsule holds what, although they are coded for later identification. Your reactions to each capsule are recorded, and that record becomes the basis for deciding whether you are hypersensitive to a specific food.

FIGURE 7.1   Identifying Food Hypersensitivity

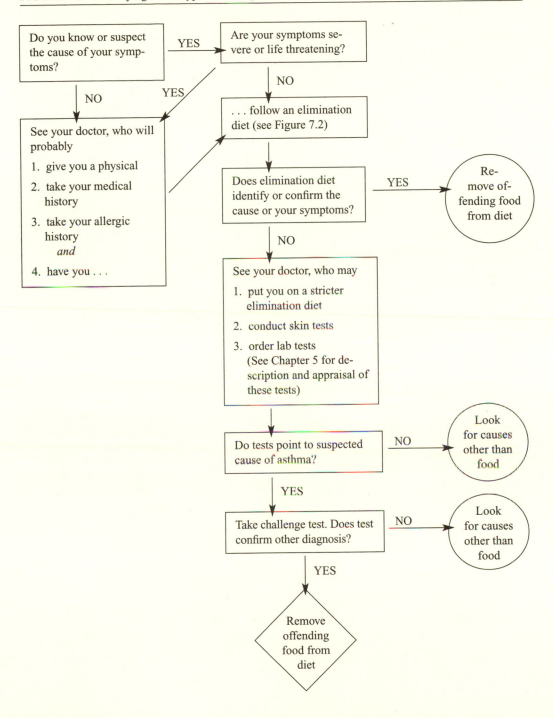

FIGURE 7.2 An Elimination Diet to Detect Foods Causing Asthmatic or Hypersensitive Reactions

Foods Allowed

Beverages	*Fruits and Juices	Oils
Water	Apricots	Crisco, Spray
	Cranberries	Olive oil
	Peaches	Any vegetable oil *except*
	Pears	oleomargarine

Grains and Cereals	Seasonings	*Vegetables
Rice	Acetic acid vinegar (white)	Beets
Rice flakes, Rice Crispies	Salt	Carrots
Puffed rice	Vanilla extract (synthetic)	Chard
Rice wafers		Lettuce
		Oyster plant
		Sweet potato

Meats	Sweetners	Dessert
Lamb	Sugar (cane or beet)	Tapioca

* All fruits and vegetables, except lettuce, must be cooked or canned.

Eat and drink only the foods listed. Avoid coffee, tea, soft drinks, chewing gum, all medications except those ordered by your physician.

Suggested Menu

Breakfast	Lunch	Dinner
Rice Crispies	Lamp chop	Lamb pattie
Rice wafers	Sweet potato	Boiled rice
Peaches	Beets	Carrots
Apricot juice	Rice wafers	Lettuce with acetic acid
Peach jam	Cranberry juice	Peaches
Water	Pears	Apricot juice

Instructions: Stay on this basic diet for ten days. Then on the eleventh day add, all by itself, first thing in the morning, the one food you believe is most likely responsible for your asthma symptoms. Eat in large amounts several times a day for three days and keep track of your reaction. If a reaction (wheezing, cough, shortness of breath) occurs, *stop*. Return to basic diet and after five days, try again. If reaction reappears, avoid this food henceforth. Go on in this same way to test other foods suspected of causing symptoms. Foods not triggering asthma symptoms may be retained in the diet.

- A suspect food may not lead to a reaction, when put to the test, because of the method of preparation, the amount consumed, the presence of other foods, or the state of the sample. If you have a good circumstantial case against a particular food, do not give up testing it too quickly.

- Skin tests (scratch or prick) for food hypersensitivity are crude, cover only a small fraction of the possibilities, are potentially dangerous, and are useful mainly in their ability to identify *lack* of sensitivity to a substance. They will rule out potential offenders—but the potential offenders, alas, far outnumber the specific tests available. A course of skin testing will likely eliminate some suspect foods, turn up a few false leads (false positive reactions), and, rarely, the real culprit.

The Role of Food in
Individuals with Multiple Allergies

Many allergy sufferers produce high levels of IgE when they are exposed to a number, sometimes a multitude, of foreign proteins. They may display any number of a raft of allergic symptoms ranging from hay fever to asthma, plus watery eyes, chest congestion, and skin reactions. Are these symptoms due entirely to things in the air, such as pollens, dust, or animal dander? Might food trigger some of them? At times food sensitivity can be an element in producing symptoms, yet not represent the entire problem. In these cases reliance on a patient's history and looking for a seasonal pattern of symptoms is extremely important; faithfully keeping the Asthma Finder (Figure 5.1 in Chapter 5) will help to resolve matters. Do your symptoms get worse certain seasons of the year? Are they worse after meals? Do they occur more or less frequently when traveling or eating away from home?

Some special associations also occur in people who have hay fever and coincidental sensitivity to certain foods. Individuals with hay fever may develop severe itching of the mouth, swelling of the throat, and breathing problems when they eat peaches, avocados, or melons. These reactions tend to show up primarily during the hay fever season; at other times these foods produce negligible problems.

Another special problem with multiple allergies occurs in young children who often absorb small quantities of food that remain undigested. The body recognizes these undigested foods as foreign, makes IgE antibodies, and food allergy symptoms result. As children grow older, however, their gastrointestinal tracts mature, their food is digested completely, and absorption of small quantities of undigested food no longer occurs. With this maturation of the intestine and proper food digestion, the symptoms of food allergy generally disappear. However, if these children later develop pollen sensitivity, their allergies to certain foods may return.

Mysterious Hidden Food Allergies

The fact that some individuals complain of a variety of food-linked nonspecific complaints, such as tension fatigue and headache, and the added fact that it is very difficult to diagnose food allergy using blood or skin tests, has made the entire subject of food sensitivity a hotbed of controversy. Many people (and many physicians too) wrongly believe that a firm diagnosis of food allergy cannot be confidently made. Rather, they contend that some hidden insidious sensitivity to food causes a form of asthma (and hay fever or eczema or both) that responds poorly to treatment. This view of the role of food in asthma, never borne out by rigorous scientific testing, errs gravely. Given a proper history, a carefully kept diary, and appropriate laboratory tests, your physician can determine exactly what foods you cannot tolerate and what part they play in your symptoms.

Nonallergic Asthmatic Reactions to Foods

As we have said, the diagnosis of a *true* allergy requires the presence of IgE, which binds onto special white cells and under the right condions (such as eating the food you are allergic to)—causes those cells to release histamine and the other chemicals that set you to wheezing. To complicate matters, allergens can directly cause your white cells to release histamine and the wheeze-triggering chemicals without IgE involvement. A large number of foods and drugs can do this. The best example? Sensitivity to berries, especially strawberries, in children. Sensitive children, if they eat berries, may develop itching, hives, breathing problems, or even a full-blown anaphylactic reaction. This sensitivity to berries often disappears as the child gets older.

Another well-known syndrome is "allergy" to shrimp, clams, oysters, lobster, or other crustaceans.

> Vickie has enjoyed good health all of her life but knows that after eating shrimp she will break out in hives and, if she gets enough of them, will wheeze too. She carefully avoids eating shrimp at home. However, as part of Vickie's job she often appears at meetings and banquets. She has found that a large number of hors d'oeuvres contain minced shrimp. Vickie has encountered shrimp stuffed in mushrooms or tomatoes, camouflaged in dips, mixed in large Caesar salads, and everywhere in Chinese and Japanese restaurants. She even reacts if the pan used to cook her dinner previously contained shrimp. Since she is often called on to speak—and her reaction to shrimp affects her dramatically—she has learned to carry an antihistamine in her purse. Even when she does not suspect that shrimp is on the menu, as a precaution she takes an antihistamine about 20 minutes before dinner. This prevents her from developing symptoms unless she has unknowingly consumed large quantities of the crustacean.

Food dyes and preservatives cause the bulk of these peculiar non-IgE reactions. The principal offenders and their locales are named in Chapter 5, page 71. To give an idea of the baffling complexity of the relationship of foods to asthma, note this—some (rare) folks with aspirin-triggered asthma often have their symptoms blossom or worsen when they eat foods containing tartrazine, the yellow food dye.

Controlling Asthmatic Symptoms Caused by Food Intolerance

To control asthmatic symptoms stemming from food intolerance, avoid the food that brings on the symptoms. If complete avoidance is not possible (because the list of irritants is long and diffuse) and if the hypersensitivity has truly immunological or allergic roots, then suppressing symptoms through medication is sometimes a workable alternative. This control step should be taken only under medical supervision.

Sometimes recurring reactions are due to lack of willpower.

Arthur, truly hypersensitive to chocolate, slips into an attack of allergic rhinitis—a streaming nose and a nasty postnasal drip along with some minor asthmatic symptoms—whenever he eats any chocolate. Yet, despite the acute discomfort it causes him, he has never succeeded in putting aside his craving for chocolate. So, whenever he yields to the temptation to eat a candy bar, he follows it with an antihistamine chaser. He knows he would be better off if he never ate chocolate again, but wryly says his inability comes from his lack of character.

Diet Recommendations

There are several fad diets and any number of home remedies or patent medicines that claim to relieve asthma. None of them has proved effective in practice or has stood scientific testing, and some of them (nasal drops or sprays, for example) can actually make asthma symptoms worse.

On the other hand, a well-rounded diet can help to prevent asthma. Any time you become weak and run-down because of a vitamin-deficient, unbalanced, junk food-dominated diet, you set yourself up for infections. Since colds and infections represent the most important asthma-triggering agents, a poor diet can contribute directly and significantly to more frequent and more severe asthmatic attacks.

Common sense should guide you. Get enough foods in the major food groups to satisfy recommended minimum daily requirements for proteins, carbohydrates, fats, vitamins, and minerals. Avoid excesses, particularly of stimulants, salt, sugar, and alcohol (not more than 1.5 ounces daily—two 12-ounce cans of beer or two light cocktails or three 4-ounce glasses of wine at the max). Limit consumption of red meats (once every other day is plenty) and eat plenty of fresh fruits and vegetables, cooked or (preferably) raw. Wash fresh vegetables and fruits carefully, even ones billed as completely organic. (Foods described as "natural," a seriously slippery adjective, may still contain preservatives and chemicals; read the list of ingredients carefully.) Drink plenty of liquids and provide for some fiber either through breads, vegetable intake, or cereal brans. Do not overeat and after eating, take a few minutes before you resume stressful activities. Depending on your ability to tolerate it, be judicious in your use of milk and milk products—cheese, cottage cheese, ice cream, yogurt, and so on. Avoid "empty calorie" foods like snack foods, which provide calories but have no other food value. Limit the number of heavily salted, high fat, fried "fast foods." Eat at regular times and try not to eat "on the go." Provide adequate time to sit down and enjoy your meal.

Do not employ food as a lever or bribe for an asthmatic child. All too often worried parents try to coax a child into acting or appearing better by fixing favorite dishes; this tactic can promote or encourage the appearance or the claim of symptoms.

Foods to Relieve Asthma Symptoms

For a long time people have known that hot, strong, black coffee will make breathing easier, relieve wheezing, and help to get rid of mucus. Although coffee may relieve mild asthma symptoms, it should not replace your medication. It also helps to drink large quantities of liquid, for two reasons:

1. The labored mouth-breathing so characteristic of an asthma attack has the effect of expelling much more moisture and, over a period of time, may lead to dehydration.
2. Raising and getting rid of airway-blocking mucus needs a proper liquid balance.

Water is probably the best and safest liquid to drink, although "sports drinks" are sometimes recommended. Formulated to imitate the chemical composition of body fluid, these beverages are more readily assimilated by the body, their manufacturers claim.

Asthmatics should probably avoid some liquids said to contribute to asthmatic reactions: orange or other citrus juices, milk, chocolate milk, and soft drinks and punches that contain preservatives or food dyes.

Anecdotal accounts claim that chicken soup heavily laced with garlic helps asthmatics, but, unfortunately, no hard evidence is available. Apart from the abovementioned coffee (hot or cold) and other beverages that carry significant loads of caffeine, we know of no food or drink that will ease the symptoms of asthma.

Summary

Almost any food or drink can provoke a reaction in a person susceptible to it. Reactions to food or food additives can involve the gastrointestinal, pulmonary, nervous, or vascular systems and can vary greatly in speed of onset, severity, and duration.

Reactions that take the form typically seen in asthmatic attacks—wheezing and severe shortness of breath—can follow ingesting food or drink and can represent either an allergic (atopic) or a hypersensitive reaction. The experts quibble about this difference but, once the reaction shows, its treatment follows a predetermined course regardless of its allergic or hypersensitive origins.

While the authorities debate the nature and meaning of the underlying process, dealing with asthmalike symptoms associated with something eaten or imbibed is painfully simple; identify what causes your symptoms and stay away from it. We name and describe tests that exist to help identify triggers that elude ordinary detection. The need to involve these tests happens rarely. If the trigger tends to show up everywhere, take the trouble to learn how to look for it and be aggressive about avoiding it.

On the other side of the asthma/diet discussion, there is no credible evidence that certain foods or specialized diets ward off asthmatic attacks although strong, black coffee does provide some relief from wheezing. A sound, balanced diet coupled with a faithful program of exercise and careful control of body weight helps make asthmatics less vulnerable to the infections that cause asthmatic episodes.

8

Chemical and Occupational Asthma

Many of the substances you routinely encounter—dusts, vapors, gases, fumes—can bring on entirely new asthma symptoms or make preexisting ones worse. Indeed, for nearly three centuries we have known that materials other than pollen, animal dander, and dust can cause asthma. In 1713 the Italian physician Ramazzini described asthma-like symptoms that often occurred in flour mill workers. Since Ramazzini's time literally thousands of chemicals have exploded into the home, the workplace, and the environment. Chemicals, complex and sophisticated, turn up everywhere. We cannot avoid exposure to them; they get into our food, our apparel, the very air we breathe. Although by no means all of these chemicals cause or intensify asthmatic reactions, many of them do provoke allergic asthmatic (atopic) responses; thousands more of them can trigger nonallergic (nonatopic) sensitivity reactions—wheezing, coughing, and shortness of breath.

While it matters whether the reaction to a chemical is allergic or hypersensitive, the resulting symptoms do not differ qualitatively. Asthma—atopic or nonatopic—is asthma.

Reactions to Chemicals: Allergy or Sensitivity?

The antibody Immunoglobulin E mediates a true allergic reaction. Some physicians will interpret other types of responses in people as "allergic" when in fact they reflect a sensitivity. As we note in Sam's case below, this allergy sensitivity difference can carry important consequences.

Chemicals can make asthma worse in many ways:

- Exposure to some chemicals, like toluene, stimulates the production of IgE and may trigger a true allergic asthmatic reaction.
- Contact with other chemicals like IVP (the dye used to take X rays of the kidney) can cause body mast cells or white blood cells to degranulate and release histamine directly, even without IgE. Chemicals and drugs with this ability include codeine and polymyxin. (Codeine, an alkaloid drug derived from opium, relieves pain or suppresses coughing; polymyxin, an antibiotic, treats eye infections.)
- Contact or inhalation of the latex that goes into hospital type gloves can produce a very serious allergy that can affect your ability to work. Sensitivity to latex can make your asthma worse.
- Fumes or vapors from some harsh, pungent chemicals like plastics, gasoline, and glues can make bronchial muscles go directly into spasm without IgE mediation or any other bodily involvement.

Peter and Sam have worked as partners in a house-painting business for nearly 15 years. Peter likes the smell of fresh paint although he knows that the fumes and the paint itself contains chemicals that trouble some people. Sam, on the other hand, has always hated the smell of paint that made him nauseous and headachy almost from the start. But, with bills to pay, a family to care for, and no options he had to keep on working as a painter. Then, recently, his headaches worsened and he started having dizzy spells, bad news for anyone who spends a lot of time on a ladder. Sam went to his doctor with the hope that he, the doctor, would find Sam allergic to paint and that that diagnosis would qualify Sam for disability benefits. The doctor ran Sam through a series of tests, found no allergic basis for Sam's very real and troublesome symptoms, and advised him to get out of house painting. That put Sam on the horns of a dilemma. He solved it by leaving the partnership and going through some hard times before finding other work.

People develop nausea, giddiness, or headaches from many other materials that carry strong odors. Most of these agents will not cause asthma but certain ones, if breathed in, can trigger the disease or make it worse without IgE involvement. Table 8.1 lists some odor-producing substances that can provoke asthma without allergic (IgE) involvement.

By the same token, airborne particulate matter and smog can provoke chemical sensitivities and, along with sulfur dioxide and ozone, aggravate asthmatic symptoms by increasing the reactivity of the airways, again without involving IgE. Exposure to any of these triggers can occur virtually anywhere—at school, in the home, and outdoors as well as on the job.

Occupational Asthma

In a sense occupational asthma represents a special case of the chemically induced reactions we just discussed. Occupational asthma—asthma that occurs for the first time as the result of workplace exposure to a sensitizing agent—represents a significant public health problem. Occupational asthma is the most common work-related lung disease and a significant proportion of both new and exacerbated asthma in adults (up to 25 percent, according to some estimates) originate in occupational settings.

TABLE 8.1   Sources of Asthma-Provoking Odors or Fumes

aerosols	formaldehyde (formalin)
alcohol (rubbing)	incense
ammonia	ink
bubble bath or oils	insecticides and repellents
camphor	mothballs
candles	paints
castor beans (flour or oil)	perfumes
cleaning fluid	phenol
coal, gasoline, kerosene, oil	polyurethane
cosmetics	smoke
creosote	soaps
deodorants	tobacco
detergents	toluene
floor wax	turpentine

The workplace teems with materials or substances that can make asthma and allergies worse. Symptoms may include everything from hay fever with sneezing, nasal congestion, runny nose, watery eyes, and hives to asthma. Table 8.2 lists some of the industries that make heavy use of chemicals known to trigger asthma.

The histories of individuals having occupational asthma often resemble Joe's:

Joe shows up for work Monday morning at 8:00 feeling great. He quits work about 5:00, stops off at a local bar for a beer or two, then heads home. At 8:00 in the evening, so punctually Joe can set his watch by it, he begins coughing and wheezing. He coughs and wheezes throughout the evening and almost into the night, relieved only by medication. By morning the symptoms vanish and Joe returns to work.

At first Joe's doctor thought Joe might be allergic to something in the tavern or at home but numerous tests couldn't point to a probable cause. Joe then mentioned that nothing ailed him at home on weekends so the doctor concluded that something at the job triggered Joe's symptoms. Joe worked in a processing plant that converted whole milk to powder. He told the doctor that he dislikes milk and won't even eat ice cream because it gives him diarrhea. The doctor, intrigued, had Joe avoid all milk products for a few days and then had him drink a glass of milk. Nothing happened.

TABLE 8.2   Industries Linked to Chemically Induced Asthma

Communications and electronics

Detergent manufacturing and distribution

Dyeing and photocopying

Food production, processing, and packaging

Heath care workers

Lacquer and rubber manufacturing

Metal refining and plating

Oil production, refining, or distribution

Paint, plastics, and coatings, especially those using polyurethane

Pharmaceuticals and drugs

Printing

Textile weaving or printing (natural or synthetic fabrics)

The doctor concluded Joe didn't have an allergy to milk but he went on to ask if fumes or odors of powdered milk were present in the workplace. "Everywhere," Joe replied.

The family doctor referred Joe to an allergist who found that Joe had high levels of antibody directed at milk proteins. He also had Joe inhale a minute quantity of powdered milk. Four hours after this inhalation challenge test Joe began to wheeze.

Occupational asthma frequently follows this pattern of a delayed daily reaction with symptoms developing several hours after leaving work. Other common patterns include:

- Progressive worsening of symptoms as the workweek goes on with the worker rebounding as the symptoms vanish over the weekend, or, less often,
- A gradual decline, week by week, in pulmonary function

Specific Causes of Occupational Asthma

As Ramazzini pointed out centuries ago, millers and bakers often turned up with the symptoms now labeled as baker's asthma. Similarly, dust from coffee or castor beans can affect people who work in or live near to plants that disperse those materials into the air. Actually, more than 200 agents are known to induce asthma; Table 8.3 lists a few of the more common occupational asthma triggers and the occupations they affect.

Latex allergy has become epidemic, especially among health care workers—doctors, respiratory therapists, and nurses—but it also occurs in people who have undergone several surgical procedures (and their exposure to latex devices such as gloves). Latex, a protein derived from the rubber tree, goes into gloves used in hospitals, many other hospital products, and even balloons. A substance similar to latex protein turns up in many foods—melons, avocados, kiwi, Brazil nuts, and mangoes. Accordingly, people allergic to latex often cannot eat these and other fruits. The best way to establish the diagnosis of latex allergy is for your doctor to take

TABLE 8.3   Occupational Asthma Triggers and the Occupations Affected

Agent	Found In
Animal dander	Veterinarians, others who work with animals
Insects	Food handlers
Grain and flour	Bakers, millers, food handlers
Latex	Rubber workers, health workers, technicians
Metals (aluminum, cobalt, platinum, stainless steel, chromium, nickel, vanadium, zinc)	Metal workers, refiners, finishers
Metal fumes, welding fumes	Metal workers, welders
Organic chemicals, most notably*	
anhydrides	Those making or using plastics, epoxy resins, paints
formaldehyde	A major trigger affecting people who work with lumber, construction materials, furniture, home decorating
freon	Air conditioning, refrigeration workers
insecticides	Agricultural workers, food handlers or processors
isocyanates, including toluene	People who make or come into contact with polyurethane, insulation, paint, adhesives

* The symptoms provoked by these agents can show an acute, direct, and immediate response to the chemical itself. They should disappear after one leaves the contaminated environment.

a good history. Allergy testing for latex sensitivity is available but still not completely accurate. If you do have latex allergy, avoid it studiously, carry an Epi-Pen for emergencies, and wear a Medic-Alert bracelet.

In addition, individuals who work in "tight" buildings have turned up with asthma symptoms. These "efficient" buildings efficiently recirculate the degraded air and all that it holds—mold, fungi, microorganisms, emissions from building materials, dust mites, and a laundry list of vapors. Any one of these agents can provoke asthma in a susceptible worker who has the bad luck to occupy the space, regardless of the job performed—from the custodian to the CEO.

Do You Have Occupational Asthma?

To determine if you have occupational asthma, you should follow the steps you would take to nail down the cause of any other way in which the disease manifests itself (see Chapter 5). Maintain a careful and detailed history of the onset of the attacks and their relationship to other activities or events in your life. Then, if you come to suspect occupational asthma, consult a physician, either your own or the company's if it has one. The doctor should help you to determine if your asthma results from exposure to substances or conditions you encounter at work or if it can be traced to other causes. In the case of hard-to-diagnose symptoms you may face a lengthy process that would include a good physical examination and skin testing. Skin tests work particularly well in spotting occupational asthma caused by trimellitic anhydride, coffee beans, and enzymes or detergents. Pulmonary function tests administered before and after exposure to potential triggers may also apply and laboratory-based inhalation challenge tests can be prescribed, but you should submit to this last only under rigorous safeguards. Precise measures of the suspected trigger should be possible and administered in doses below the acute irritant level, no contraindications like heart disease should exist, and a physician should be in attendance because all respiratory challenges carry risk. On the downside, such tests require a preliminary period of preparation and may stretch out over a period of up to a week.

Hypersensitivity Pneumonitis and Occupational Asthma

If something on your job provokes persistent, recurring asthma, even mild, you have just one option—avoid the trigger by getting out of the worksite. The reason for this drastic action? Continued exposure can make the asthma much worse and may lead to the development of hypersensitivity pneumonitis, a serious syndrome.

This condition, a distant cousin of asthma, most often results from exposure to agents encountered at work. People with the disease almost always display sensitivity or allergy to chemicals or airborne allergens found in specific occupations. They may include farmers allergic to moldy hay, office workers sensitive to mold growing in office air conditioners, or lumber mill workers who react to redwood or maple dust. In addition to

TABLE 8.4   Causes and Conditions Associated with Hypersensitivity Pneumonitis

Causes	Conditions*
Bacteria (actinomyces) resulting from fermentation of organic matter	Farmer's lung, mushroom worker's lung, fog fever
Molds or fungi	Cheese-maker's lung, humidifier lung, sauna-taker's disease
Dusts or other airborne allergens or contaminants	Bird fancier's lung, wood dust disease, coffee worker's lung, ventilation system pneumonia

*The list of conditions is illustrative only and not meant to be complete or definitive.

wheezing, the symptoms, if left to continue unchecked, lead to severe and irreversible lung damage. Table 8.4 lists a few of the more common causes of this relatively rare lung inflammation and the occupations in which it occurs. If you suspect that something in your work environment causes your asthma, we strongly urge you to seek medical attention and have your situation reviewed carefully, while you try to avoid further exposure on the job until you know exactly what causes your symptoms.

The Treatment of Occupational Asthma

Occupational asthma usually follows exposure to triggers that invade the respiratory system. The key to successful treatment of occupational asthma—or any other asthma for that matter—rests on avoiding the agent that provokes the symptoms. Removing the worker from the worksite that holds the offending substance represents the surest avoidance tactic; shielding him or her from it also can work, although protective devices like face masks may prove awkward and uncomfortable, so cumbersome that workers neglect to use them as faithfully as they should.

Drug therapy for occupational asthma does not differ in any respect from drugs that are prescribed for other forms of the disease. However, medications do carry side effects and some asthma medications cause drowsiness or otherwise impair alertness. Around machinery or other industrial hazards this can spell danger, so this risk needs to be factored into the treatment regimen.

People with occupational asthma rarely receive a course of allergy shots designed to desensitize them to the triggering agent. This procedure, routine for pollen-triggered asthma, does not extend to the workplace because all too often the allergen or antigen remains unidentified, useful dosages or concentrations of the antigen have not been worked out, or the dosage endangers the recipient by carrying the risk of a severe reaction. Excepting veterinarians. Veterinarians with extreme sensitivity to animal dander do go through desensitization, unlike other occupational asthma sufferers.

How occupational asthma plays out depends on the length and the severity of the symptoms; its long-term prognosis can be gloomy. The growing intrusion of chemicals into all facets of life and their ability to provoke asthmatic and other sensitivity reactions has led some physicians and care providers to devise heroic procedures that keep people shielded from exposure to chemicals. One hears accounts of people with intractable, untreatable symptoms, or symptoms so severe that the sufferer cannot lead a normal life. The more extreme cases are labeled "universal reactors" and their condition is diagnosed as twentieth-century disease.

The drastic treatment regimens devised to address these symptoms originated with a group of practitioners who refer to themselves as clinical ecologists. The root causes of the diffuse symptoms most often prove to be psychosomatic in origin and the stringent environmental measures imposed by clinical ecologists are ineffectual in almost all cases and not recommended. Yet medicine bristles with practitioners who offer unproven, ineffectual, or dangerous cures and nostrums and you should know that asthma, occupational asthma, and chemical sensitivity is no stranger to this tendency. In our experience we do not recommend you see such doctors. Although there may be some fine practitioners in these groups, our general feeling is that they are more interested in your pocketbook than in you.

If you have asthma, occupational or other, or symptoms that stem from exposure to chemicals, your doctor should listen carefully and sympathetically to your complaint and pull out all of the stops in doing what is right and best for you. See an allergist, a pulmonologist, or a physician in occupational medicine.

Summary

Chemicals, a boon, a blessing, and a huge presence in contemporary life, also represent an abundant source of misery, triggering a bountiful crop of allergic and sensitivity reactions.

Over 200 chemicals and their odors or fumes are known triggers of asthmatic reactions. They may act through allergic (atopic) or nonallergic (nonatopic) mechanisms. Many of these agents, found in the workplace, trigger occupational asthma. This form of the disease occurs in a wide variety of industries; Chapter 8 lists the ones closely linked to chemically induced asthma.

We also describe the daily, weekly, and long-term patterns of onset that chemically induced occupational asthma can take, list causative agents, and sketch the steps needed to take to reach a firm diagnosis of occupational asthma. We stress the dangers of hypersensitivity pneumonitis, a rare but particularly nasty sequel to persistent occupational asthma and we spell out treatment measures for occupational asthma, measures that rely primarily on avoidance of triggers. Drug treatment procedures do not depart from those prescribed for other forms of the disease but, as a general rule, desensitization through administration of a graduated series of shots does not apply.

9

Exercise, Sports, and the Asthmatic

Exercise and Asthma

Exercise-induced asthma (EIA), a short-term narrowing or constriction of the airways that follows strenuous physical exertion, affects 90 percent of individuals with asthma. As many as 15 percent of the population, worldwide, experiences asthma symptoms after exercise. Exercise will trigger asthmatic symptoms in some people who do not otherwise show the disease; perhaps 10 percent of individuals with EIA have no history of asthma or allergy.

This commonplace complaint, given proper diagnosis and treatment, will not keep people with it from competing athletically, given the talent; an estimated one out of five of the athletes who competed in the 1996 Summer Olympics had EIA.

Despite its manageability, EIA can add up to big trouble.

Scott has had asthma most of his life. His mother says that virtually anything that changed Scott's life would have him wheezing—switching from formula to milk, going from warm indoors air to the outdoors, excitement, fever. So, it came as no surprise that Scott had to sit out routine childhood play activities during nursery school. The teacher commented that even when Scott sang too loudly she could hear him wheezing. Scott didn't take physical education in school; he had a doctor's excuse. As Scott grew older his asthma grew much less severe but he continued to believe and was told that he ought not participate in gym. Scott spent his whole school career on the sidelines. He did not join the Boy Scouts or school clubs, he did not date, he didn't attend sports activities and school events. He did make good grades. His parents, overprotective, constantly reminded him of the severity of his asthma. Scott, now a junior in college, has never really learned how to join in, to partici- pate, and blames his asthma for his social isolation. Lonely and ineffectual in his social endeavors, he calls asthma the curse of his life.

With help and encouragement Scott could have developed appropriate and manageable activities, ones that took account of his physical capabilities and limitations. Families with asthmatics need wide-ranging social and emo- tional support, support that physicians could provide. Unhappily, all too of- ten medical treatment stops with a physical exam and a handful of prescrip- tions. The long-term psychosocial fallout from the disease is ignored because the doctor does not have the time, the interest, or the skill to deal with it. We once asked ten mothers who had been referred to us because their chil- dren had severe persistent asthma if their physician had talked to them about exercise and physical activity for their child. The replies all came back the same: "Well, of course our doctor agrees that my child cannot participate in sports." For those mothers, and countless others like them, the fear of asthma, compounded by dubious medical advice, fostered the development of a needlessly overprotective and ultimately damaging approach to care.

Doctors must bring out into the open and help to dispel the crippling attitudes and negative feelings that asthma generates. Open, forthright discussion can counteract the guilt and the overwhelming and often mis- placed sense of dread that accompany the disease, as well as the overpro- tection with which families often smother their asthmatic members.

The Why, What, and How of Exercise for Those with EIA

Regular physical activity maintains both physical and psychological health, especially in children. The process of growing up and developing competence in and deriving satisfaction from peer interactions and relationships depends importantly on play. Children with asthma, including EIA, need encouragement and help to participate in physical activities to the fullest extent possible, consistent with health considerations; doing less carries the real risk of blunting their maturation, nourishing or compounding problems associated with low esteem, and creating other psychosocial problems. Avoiding exercise on account of asthma can ruin your health.

Typically EIA starts after a period of exercise, peaks anywhere from eight to fifteen minutes after quitting the activity, and stops in about sixty minutes. The severity of the symptoms—shortness of breath, wheezing, coughing—depends on the activity itself and the environmental conditions prevailing at the time.

In general, EIA will more likely follow activities that call for sustained periods of exertion—distance running, arduous cycling, aerobics. The severity of the bronchospasms also depends on the level of ventilation, how much heat and water loss has happened in the respiratory network (the more the worse), and the rate of rewarming and rehydration in the airway after the activity. Those susceptible to EIA can minimize risk or severity of attack by:

- Working out in warm, humid environments (or humidifying dry, cold ambient air by covering the mouth with a cold-weather mask or scarf)
- Warming up at the outset and cooling down at the end of any exercise period
- Avoiding poorly ventilated venues or conditions where a high pollution standards index (PSI) constitutes a threat
- Limiting workout periods to thirty- to forty-five-minute sessions

EIA victims will also find the following activities or pursuits less likely to cause them to wheeze:

- Aquatic sports and activities (swimming and diving), although we do not recommend scuba diving where other hazards associated with the manner of air delivery and its potential interaction with asthma exist. (We especially recommend swimming for asthmatic children and adults because of its merits as a physical conditioner and because of the warm, humid conditions that prevail. Your local American Lung Association or HMO will know of and may even sponsor swimming and other exercise programs in your locality specifically designed for asthmatic children and adults.)

- Short-burst activities (gymnastics, weight training, wrestling, jog-walk-jog, most racket sports)

Developing an interest in and some proficiency at sports has two pay-offs. The activity itself will help build up the respiratory reserve that is especially important to asthmatics, and the ability to compete at some level boosts confidence and self-esteem. Note well that when the proper preliminary precautions are taken—appropriate medication, warm-up, awareness of and informed adjustment to environmental and climatic conditions—individuals with EIA can participate safely and confidently at a level limited only by their talent in any sport or recreational activity.

Physical Training and Competitive Sports for Asthmatics

As we noted at the outset of this chapter, most asthmatics will show EIA following exercise or physical exertion. Quite understandably, this disposition encourages asthmatics to steer clear of activities that trigger their symptoms. This avoidance pattern has its consequences; by not exercising, asthmatics can see their physical respiratory condition deteriorate to the point where even the slightest bit of exercise brings on or worsens their symptoms. On the next level down this slippery slope, the threat of EIA serves as an excuse for avoiding exercise in any form—taking PE at school, walking to the store, the library, the post office, doing chores at home. This shackles asthmatics, keeps them from taking part in and enjoying many of life's pleasures, puts them on the shelf. To avoid this unhappy and destructive outcome we encourage asthmatics to pursue a regular program of exercise. It should follow a physical examination and testing of respiratory resources to confirm the diagnosis and severity of EIA. (In some instances vocal cord dysfunction can mimic asthma; in others, shortness of breath results from hyperventilation rather than bronchospasm. These EIA look-alikes call for different treatment.) An exercise challenge, free-run or laboratory, accompanied by staged monitoring of PEF or FEV measures ought to nail the diagnosis.

Specific elements in the program can vary according to individual needs and the available resources and facilities. Your doctor, a personal trainer, or a coach can fit you up with a program geared to your situation. Whatever its elements, it should:

- Take account of your needs, skills, and goals
- Be followed faithfully (daily, at the same time, with a diary record)
- Intersperse periods of activity with time for rest
- Be brief (thirty to forty-five minutes)
- Progress in easy stages from less to more demanding levels

You will likely find it easier to stick to the schedule if you choose activities you enjoy and do them with an exercise "pal." For individuals with EIA, participation in competitive team sports, a goal and an ideal for many, can create a conflict. On the downside, just doing the sport may bring on the symptoms, but doing the sport also provides an unmatchable experience of accomplishment and a sense of personal worth. Parents can help their asthmatic child to have this empowering experience by putting aside their own concerns about how participation might harm the child. Parents can help by making sure the competitor warms up, takes medication, when necessary, that will counteract the onset of symptoms, and provide support, especially in the form of reinforcing or encouraging comments.

Justin's persistent asthma with intense periods of wheezing started near his first birthday. At the age of three he knew that exercise would make him wheeze. As a kindergartner his parents signed him up for soccer. His initial excitement and eagerness peaked when he got his uniform but, as the time for the first match neared, he began inventing all sorts of excuses to get out of competing. His father encouraged him, said he could just show up and watch but Justin, mortified at the prospect of standing on the sidelines and sticking out like a sore thumb, did not want to suit up. Finally, about 20 minutes before the start of the match, Justin's dad persuaded Justin that it would be OK if he just played for the first few minutes and then told the coach he didn't feel well. Justin grudgingly agreed to this arrangement. However, once they got to the game, Justin got involved, got into it, forgot his fears, and enjoyed himself immensely. With the encouragement his parents patiently provided before each match, Justin learned to deal with his apprehension, to manage his symptoms, and to experience the pure enjoyment of participation and competition. Soccer and, later, other team sports did a tremendous amount to empower him and to build his morale and self-confidence.

On a precautionary note, asthmatics, EIA sufferers or not, should avoid exercise or competitive sports on days with high pollen counts or air pollution indexes or when battling a respiratory infection.

Exercise for Severe Asthmatics

A few children have such severe asthma that they simply cannot participate in regular competitive sports or training programs. Where the community does not have specialized resources to offer programs that would help such severely affected youngsters, the parents may have to step in. In these instances home-based programs involving parent-supervised breathing exercises, brief periods of physical activity, and, wherever possible, regular swimming sessions may help build up the respiratory reserve.

Even so, some children dependent on steroids or other heavy medications cannot perform these minimally demanding exercises. In their cases, taking part in special training may prove useful. Local lung associations and other health-related groups offer special summer camps for children with asthma and other conditions. We discuss these camps in Chapter 18 and one of the web sites given in Appendix A lists programs in your area. Your local American Lung Association will also know of nearby camps.

Adolescents, especially those who have had severe persistent symptoms in childhood, will often show poor muscle development and, rarely, chest deformities, sometimes accompanied by cardiac problems. These young-sters absolutely must participate in programs of physical activity that in-clude conditioning of the upper torso.

Managing EIA with Medication

EIA's bronchospasms do not differ in any way from those involved in other forms of asthma. We name, describe, and assess the medications used to control bronchospasms in Chapter 14. As we have already said, a physical examination with pulmonary function testing should precede treatment and development of a management plan for EIA. That examination should tell you, first, if exercise alone triggers wheezing. If not, the cause of your symptoms will determine the treatment and medication regimen you will follow. You should refer to the appropriate chapters in this section of the book to guide you in working out a blueprint for care.

Wheezing that traces exclusively to exercise or exertion simplifies treat-ment decisions greatly. You will need to decide whether to carry and use medications, and which ones to use, prior to exercise. We have listed be-low the medications commonly used to treat EIA along with their main advantages and drawbacks. We most often recommend the prodromal (be-fore exercise activity) use of handheld, metered-dose, $Beta_2$ agonists to control EIA because of their ease of administration, effectiveness, and economy.

Most of the drugs listed in Table 9.1 have short-term effects but, used appropriately, they will usually manage EIA. Some activities, sports, or in-dividuals do require longer-lasting medications. In those instances cro-molyn, inhaled corticosteroids, or long-lasting beta agonists (Serevent) will work.

Finally, the complications. Schools sometimes forbid students to have or use medication—particularly metered dose inhalers—on school prop-

TABLE 9.1   Advantages and Disadvantages of Common EIA Medications

Medication Type	Advantages	Disadvantages
Beta agonists (various metered dose inhalers, over-the-counter or prescription)	Quick-acting, effective, economical, convenient	Can cause rapid heart rate, tremors, muscle shaking
Inhaled corticosteroids	Effective, preventive	Must be taken in advance and on a regular basis
Cromolyn (Intal)	Effective, few side effects, especially useful with EIA	Slow to act, must be taken well in advance of need
Theophylline	Works adequately	Basically an adjunct to other medications; needs careful monitoring, carries side effects, stimulates central nervous system, requires large doses in advance of need, awkward to take; rarely used anymore
Leukotriene inhibitors (Acolade, Singulaire, Zileutin)	One pill once or twice per day	Must be taken regularly and in advance; expensive

NOTE: Several additional medications are sometimes directed at EIA, nedocromil sodium (Tilade) and furosemide. All of them can prevent EIA. Furosemide, a powerful diuretic, needs careful monitoring; leukotriene inhibitors have no therapeutic effect during the acute stage of the symptoms. Tilade evidently has no ill effects and works especially well with severe exercise-induced bronchostriction. One study hints that a daily dose of the unicellular *alga Dunaliella bardawil*, which contains high concentrations of beta carotene, may exert a protective effect against EIA.

erty. Help your child to work out an arrangement with school officials to carry and use needed medication according to agreed-on rules and procedures. At the same time work to convince the child that feeling awkward or embarassed at being observed taking the medication beats either not participating in an activity or having unprotected participation make him or her sick.

Summary

Almost all asthmatics will develop asthma symptoms following exertion or exercise. This exercise-induced asthma (EIA) discourages its victims from exercising regularly and vigorously, activities that asthmatics especially need to pursue. In this chapter we emphasize the special need asthmatics have for respiratory fitness. We sketch procedures and activities that will improve respiratory reserve, point out that with care, informed choice of activities, and appropriate medication EIA represents no bar to participation in any exercise or sport at any level consistent with the participant's abilities.

We emphasize the importance of the role parents play in developing effective strategies for coping with EIA and in supporting and encouraging their children to participate regularly in physical activities and, where feasible, competitive sports. We note that some limited exercise options exist and ought to be followed by severely asthmatic children and adolescents, and we conclude by reminding you that EIA, usually of short duration, responds quickly to a number of medications. We name the ones most often prescribed and list some of their advantages and drawbacks.

10

Surgery, Anesthesia, and Asthma

Presurgical Evaluation

Before undergoing surgery, asthmatics, like all other individuals, must undergo an intensive preoperative evaluation to make sure that their bodies can withstand the trauma of an operation. Because surgery often involves assisted ventilation and reduced respiratory capacity, the asthmatic may have added risk. Also, an alternative method of delivering medications must be found for any period of time in which the patient cannot take anything by mouth. The evaluation must pay careful attention to patient sensitivity to the presence of any underlying allergies to medications and other allergens found in hospitals or operating rooms, including latex.

Beyond the factors cited above, the presurgery evaluation needs to take a number of other factors into account. Although emotion does not cause asthma, emotional responses that cause the hyperventilation that makes asthma worse can occur. Apprehension experienced in the days prior to entering the hospital and in the hours immediately before the surgery can lead to fast, shallow breathing and trigger an asthmatic response and intense bronchospasm. To counter this tendency, you need to understand fully the nature of the surgery or procedure being done and the reasons for it. Knowing exactly the what and why of your surgery helps to dispel fear and insecurity. If you are apprehensive, do not understand, or need additional counsel or support, let your doctor know.

A number of agents can provoke an asthmatic attack either during the induction phase (the preliminary, preparatory, preoperative steps) or during the actual period of use of anesthetic agents. During the induction phase your physician may decide to administer diazepam or ketamine—relaxants that reduce preoperative stress. Alternatively, he or she may choose a gas anesthetic. Whatever the method for reducing preoperative stress, short-acting barbituratelike drugs such as thiopental should be avoided because they may trigger a cough and bronchospasm. You must routinely advise all doctors that you have asthma, even if it is very mild. Also make sure that everyone concerned knows what drugs you take and whether you have allergies. Do not assume that you can use your own medications freely in the hospitals because hospitals routinely confiscate medications and only allow staff to administer them.

Anesthetics

In pulmonary anesthesia, the most common form, the only agents that are routinely ruled out for asthmatics are cyclopropane and nitrous oxide. Cyclopropane is not used because it can produce irregularities in the heartbeat, which may be intensified in individuals taking beta agonists or theophylline for their asthma. Nitrous oxide, or laughing gas, a drug used for many years as an anesthetic agent, is avoided because it makes asthma worse. Other anesthetics routinely used such as isoflurane and propofol apparently do not produce an increase in wheezing during surgery. General anesthesia may produce some dilation of airways, which could actually help an asthmatic.

Injection or intravenous introduction of drugs that directly block nerves can anesthetize. Virtually all of the neuromuscular blocking agents, curare and succinylcholine among them, release histamine. In patients with asthma, this could represent a serious complication as histamine release may cause bronchospasm, even though it happens only rarely in surgery. As long as your surgeon and anesthesiologist know about your asthma and any prior bad reactions you have had to medications, you should have no problem. In any case, emergency plans worked out well in advance of the surgery should be in place and ready to roll.

Local anesthetics also come into the picture, especially for minor surgery treated on an outpatient basis. Dentists frequently employ such locals, especially drugs in the Novocain and lidocaine family. These drugs may provoke significant allergic reactions including everything from anaphylaxis (acute and intense collapse of the airways) to hives. There is no way of knowing in advance who will have such a reaction, but if you have shown *any* sensitivity to a local anesthetic in the past, tell your physician or dentist and have tests before surgery to determine if in fact you are allergic to the anesthetic slated for use. If you should test positive, alternatives exist.

The gravest problems involve patients who have accidents, are rendered unconscious, and must undergo emergency surgery. Comatose from an accident, you can do or say nothing in your own behalf. If you are an asthmatic and on daily medication, we urge you to wear a Medic-Alert bracelet so that medical workers will know of your medical problems.[1]

Harry, a lifelong asthmatic, controlled his symptoms efficiently with intermittent medication. Intensely allergic to penicillin, he had a serious generalized reaction to it several years ago. At the time his doctor advised Harry to get a Medic-Alert bracelet, but Harry didn't follow through, believing it wasn't worth the trouble and expense. Besides, he didn't want to wear a bracelet.

Five months ago an auto accident put Harry through the windshield and knocked him unconscious. Rushed to the hospital with a variety of fractures, cuts, and contusions, the attending doctor began him on antibiotics, including penicillin, to avoid infection. Within minutes Harry's respiration became labored and hives blossomed all over his body. The nurse saw the symptoms and alertly stopped the medication and called the doctor. He injected Epinephrine (Adrenalin) and got the symptoms under control in 15 minutes. However, during that quarter hour Harry turned cyanotic (blue) from lack of oxygen and has remained in a coma ever since. Nobody knows if the auto accident caused the prolonged coma—or if it resulted from the severe oxygen dehydration suffered during the adverse reaction to penicillin.

---

[1] Applications for Medic-Alert bracelets are available in physicians' offices or hospitals, or they may be secured from the Medic-Alert Foundation, P.O. Box 1009, Turlock, California 95381.

If you have serious allergies, carry warning identification. It may save your life!

The Interactions of Anesthetics and Surgical Drugs with Asthma Medications

The choice of anesthetic agents, as well as of any other medications administered during surgery, should take into account their potential interactions with asthma drugs. (A drug interaction means that the reaction to drug A, when taken by an individual who is already receiving drug B, may have a different or a more severe effect than usual.) Asthmatics on theophylline who also use high-dose beta agonists—both asthma medications—may experience irregularities of the heartbeat. An irregular heartbeat may also show up when theophylline is taken along with anesthetic agents.

Inform your surgeon without fail about *all* drugs, including herbals and dietary supplements, you have taken or are taking. Do not omit any. Some have long survival times and may remain present in the body for days. You should also name any illegal or addictive drugs you have taken. The doctor must have this information to treat you properly. The disclosure remains confidential, protected by doctor-patient privilege.

Other Dangers in Surgery

An operation produces a significant amount of stress for the body. It can and often does interfere with normal eating and drinking patterns. Nausea and vomiting commonly follow surgery. During the recovery phase, when you cannot take antiasthma drugs by mouth, you may still need to have their protection. Cutting out steroids, for instance, may bring about a catastrophic return of asthma symptoms. In addition, regular steroid users, stressed by surgery, may no longer have the capacity to produce enough cortisone of their own to meet the surgically produced challenge. If they fail to respond to the surgical trauma, their blood pressure may fall; they may then develop abnormalities in the electrolytic balance of their body fluids. That can lead to secondary failure of vital organs, including the kidney. Accordingly, physicians commonly provide asthmatics who take steroid medications with extra amounts of it, often intravenously, immediately prior to surgery and they may continue delivering steroids in this form for a few days after surgery. This standard, routine practice protects you.

Tim, fearing its side effects, has never liked to take cortisone. He preferred having a wheeze and tightness in his chest over taking this drug. Several years ago when inhaled metered-dose cortisone-like drugs appeared, he was elated. He did well on them, although he had to use the high dose inhaled forms because of the severity of his symptoms. The new drugs carried many of the benefits of cortisone with virtually none of its side effects. Thus it was with considerable consternation that Tim found out his doctor intended to give him intravenous steroids immediately before his disc operation. He flatly refused to take the steroids. The nurse tried and failed to contact the surgeon. The steroids were not given and the surgery had to be postponed. The doctor belatedly explained the need for the short-term steroids to Tim, who finally agreed to their use. Tim should have found out before surgery what to expect, but his doctor should also have explained beforehand and was negligent in failing to do so.

Asthmatics may also have some compromise of their lungs. This may grow out of long-standing persistent asthma or of asthmatic or bronchospastic problems experienced immediately prior to surgery. When you go into the operating room, you should take as much respiratory reserve as possible with you. This means that you should work seriously and faithfully on your asthma self-care in the weeks, days, and hours before your operation. In addition, your surgeon should test your respiratory reserve well in advance of surgery. If you have chronic problems with mucus production and secretions, see your doctor, or perhaps a respiratory therapist well before surgery, for advice on chest percussion that will make it easier for you to eliminate the troublesome mucus. If you will require respiratory therapy after surgery, find out beforehand exactly what will take place.

Where assistance in breathing may occur, ask what being on a respirator will be like, how it will feel, and what you can do to make the experience more comfortable and less threatening. You need to insist on trying it out *before* the surgery takes place. Most surgeons will not operate if you have smoked in the past eight weeks or you have had a recent upper respiratory infection.

Summary

Asthmatics need to take special care when undergoing any form of surgery, major or minor.

Anesthetics, local or general, can impair respiratory capacity; interact dangerously with ordinary asthma medications; provoke severe allergic respiratory reactions; and impede the progress of recovery because of inability to take medications ordinarily used to manage chronic asthma symptoms.

Recognized beforehand and planned for carefully by physician and patient who bear equal responsibility for advance preparation, these potential hazards and complications can be met and avoided. Asthmatics, with proper forethought and preparation, can undergo surgery uneventfully.

11

Pregnancy and Asthma

Pregnant women who have moderate to severe chronic asthma often express serious concerns about the adverse effects their disease and its treatment may have on them or their unborn child. Happily, by observing a few precautions, they have no reason to avoid or fear pregnancy on account of their disease. The asthmatic mother-to-be should know of and observe the same cautions that an asthmatic who is about to undergo a medical or surgical procedure would take (see preceding chapter).

If you are pregnant, your body must be ready to handle the physical and emotional strain of giving birth. Your asthma should be under firm control and your respiratory reserves at their best attainable level. During the pregnancy, you should work to improve your breathing to reduce mucus and increase your lung responses and airway capacity. Tell your obstetrician that you have asthma and ask what, if anything, you should do for it. In addition, keep the physician who looks after your asthma informed about your pregnancy and the medications you take.

You and your doctors' goals during pregnancy should include:

- Maintaining effective control of your asthma symptoms
- Achieving normal or as close as possible to normal pulmonary function coupled with regular use of your peak flow meter
- Continuing normal activities including exercise
- Preventing acute exacerbations of your asthma

- Avoiding side effects of medications that could put you or the baby at risk
- Delivering a healthy baby

Using Asthma Medications During Pregnancy

It is important both to you and to your baby that you know all you can about the drugs you may take. Unhappily, although millions of women have asthma, only a handful of scientific studies have looked at the effects on the fetus of drugs used to control asthma during pregnancy. The side effects of many new drugs are only evaluated in men, because the experimenters wish to avoid the risk of possibly having the drug cause abnormalities in the fetus; similarly, drug manufacturers do not want the complications and possible problems attending a woman becoming pregnant during drug trials. The precautions, though understandable, put asthmatic mothers and their physicians in a dilemma. Although physicians want to treat their asthmatic patients the best way they can, they also want to avoid harming the developing baby, and they simply do not have the information they need to make informed and risk-free decisions. A fair amount of data are available from animal studies, but a drug that appears safe in pregnant animals may not be safe for humans. Drug testing is so expensive and so chancy that all newer drugs for the treatment of asthma come with the warning that they have *not* been tested on pregnant women, and their effect on the fetus is therefore unknown.

Some drugs that are often prescribed for women with asthma can affect the fetus. Individuals who have asthma along with recurrent respiratory infections often take the antibiotic tetracycline. This antibiotic *should not* be used during pregnancy because it may affect the development of the baby's teeth and bones. Likewise, any drugs or compounds that contain iodine should also be discontinued, because iodine can affect the development of the thyroid gland in the baby. Too much iodine (iodine has been found in cough syrups) may even induce a goiter in the mother and the baby could be born with severely reduced thyroid function which, if undetected and untreated, could cause cretinism.

Several other drugs used in allergies have also been shown to be harmful to the fetus. They include the decongestant phenylephrine and the antihistamines phenylpropanolamine (recently removed from the market because of the risk of strokes), and brompheniramine. Some over-the-counter medications contain the latter three drugs. If you are pregnant or even think you might be pregnant, do not take medications containing these materials.

Beta agonists, theophyllines, cromolyn, and steroids are routinely used to treat chronic asthma. Theophyllines, chemically similar to caffeine, have been used for decades and taken by thousands if not millions of pregnant women. Although not studied rigorously, theophylline has *not* been associated with fetal abnormalities but as we note in Chapter 14, is less often prescribed for asthma nowadays because of its side effects. Beta agonists, including ephedrine, metaproternol, and terbutaline, have been neither studied nor approved for use during pregnancy; cromolyn, comparatively safe and free of side effects, has not had its effects on prospective mothers studied. Oral steroids, particularly if taken in the first trimester of pregnancy, have the potential for exerting significantly harmful effects on the fetus; topical inhaled steroids, safer than the oral variety, have not been well studied during pregnancy. Leukotriene inhibitors have not been studied for safety; avoid them during pregnancy. Table 11.1 lists the medications asthmatic women may take during their pregnancy, the standard dosage, and the level of risk they represent to the fetus according to the Food and Drug Administration.

We do not wish to alarm pregnant asthmatic women unnecessarily. Just because some drugs have not been studied does not mean they are harmful. Indeed, allergists and chest physicians often find it necessary to treat pregnant women with these drugs and have not observed and reported any obvious developmental defects in the babies. Limited studies in animals suggest that these drugs are probably safe.

Your best tactic? Try to determine the least amount of medication needed to control your asthma. At the time of delivery—or at any point during pregnancy for that matter—we would much prefer to treat a pregnant woman whose asthma is well controlled by drugs than a woman not on medication whose asthma is poorly controlled. The unmedicated woman runs greater risk of experiencing problems—including asthmatic ones—during delivery, including delivery complications (bleeding, infection, and prolonged labor due to blood oxygen insufficiency which reduces the muscle tone of the uterus).

TABLE 11.1 Drugs for Asthma Used During Pregnancy and Their Relative Risk to Fetus

Drugs	FDA Category	Dosage
Bronchodilators		
Epinephrine (systemic)	C	Used during acute exacerbation of asthma—0.3 mL 1:1000 solution given subcutaneously, and may be repeated in 20–30 min.
Terbutaline (subcutaneous and inhaled)	B	Subcutaneous injection: for acute exacerbation of asthma, 0.25 mg; may be repeated in 20 min. Inhaled: short-acting Beta$_2$ agonist. Two puffs every 4 hours as needed.
Albuterol (inhaled or PO)	C	Short acting Beta$_2$ agonist. Two puffs every 4 hours as needed.
Metaproterenol (inhaled or PO)	C	
Pirbuterol (inhaled)	C	
Salmeterol (inhaled)	C	Long acting Beta$_2$ agonist. Two puffs twice a day.
Ipratropium bromide (inhaled)	B	Anticholinergic. Two puffs. Usually not recommended for long-term care of asthma.
Theophylline (oral)	C	Methylxanthine. Adjust dose to keep serum concentration of 8–12 mcg/mL.
Anti-inflammatory drugs		
Cromolyn sodium (inhaled)	B	Nonsteroidal anti-inflammatory. Two puffs four times a day.
Nedocromil solution (inhaled)	B	Nonsteroidal anti-inflammatory. Not enough data about use during pregnancy.
Inhaled corticosteroids		
Beclomethasone	B	2–5 puffs two to four times a day
Budesonide	C	2 puffs two times a day
Fluticasone	C	1–2 puffs two times a day
Flunisolide	C	2 puffs two times a day
Tiamcinolone	C	2–4 puffs two to four times a day
Oral Corticosteroids		
Prednisone	C	For active symptoms, use burst 40–60 mg/d in single or divided dose for 1 week, and taper.
Prednisolone	C	

(continues)

(continued)

Drugs	FDA Category	Dosage
Leukotriene Modifiers		Not enough data for use in pregnancy
Montelukast	B	
Zafirlukast	B	
Zileuton	C	
Antihistamines		
Cetirizine	B	
Chlorpheniramine	B	
Diphenhydramine	B	
Fexofenadine	C	
Hydroxyzine		Contraindicated in early pregnancy
Loratidine		

A = Controlled studies in the pregnant woman. No risk to fetus demonstrated.

B = Animal studies have not demonstrated any fetal risk, but no controlled studies in the pregnant *or* animal studies have shown an adverse effect that has not been confirmed in women in the first trimester.

C = Animal studies have shown adverse effects on the fetus, and there are no controlled studies in pregnant women *or* studies in women and animals are not available. Drug should be administered if potential benefit outweighs the risk to the fetus.

D = Positive evidence of fetal risk exists. Benefits from use in the pregnant woman may make the drug acceptable.

X = Animal and human studies have demonstrated fetal abnormalities. Risk of the drug in the pregnant woman clearly outweighs any potential benefits.

The most dangerous drugs for the fetus are illicit recreational drugs such as cocaine and heroin. These drugs should never be used.

Some pregnant women elect to have a therapeutic abortion; such procedures sometimes use drugs that contain prostaglandinlike materials. These prostaglandins can induce severe bronchospasm and *should be avoided* in anybody with asthma. Before going through this procedure, find out its exact nature and the materials that accompany it.

Because asthma affects a significant proportion of pregnant women, most obstetricians know how to deal with asthma during pregnancy. On the plus side, a pregnant woman will experience some natural improvement in the anatomy of her respiratory system during pregnancy. In addition, the fetus manufactures a special form of hemoglobin that makes fetal red blood cells that are highly efficient in receiving oxygen from the mother. Accordingly, if the mother has chronic asthma during pregnancy, she may lose oxygen to her fetus and her asthma problem may worsen because the fetus, through its special hemoglobin, protects itself at the mother's expense. Even in women who have moderate to severe chronic asthma during pregnancy, the fetus usually receives enough oxygen.

This subject of oxygen delivered to the fetus may have special relevance to some women. Stress to your oxygen delivery capabilities, brought on by exercising too strenuously, climbing to extremely high altitudes, or flying in an aircraft without oxygen, may starve you of oxygen and therefore dangerously reduce the baby's oxygen supply. In addition to getting an ample supply of oxygen, you, the expectant mother, should also have adequate hemoglobin so that oxygen can be delivered effectively. During the first evaluation for pregnancy, have a complete blood count. If you are found to be anemic, the reason for the anemia must be diagnosed and corrected. Most often anemia traces to an iron deficiency. Because pregnant women encounter several extraordinary nutritional demands, they should take multivitamins with iron.

Joann, happily married for 16 years, has four healthy children. No one would suspect that she suffers from moderate persistent asthma. Her purse bulges with metered aerosols. She wears a Medic-Alert bracelet so that in an emergency doctors will know what drugs she takes, and she strictly avoids the causes of her asthma. At the onset of her first pregnancy her obstetrician told her that as an asthmatic she could forget about natural childbirth. When she asked for reasons her obstetrician simply disregarded her question, patted her on the shoulder, told her "now, now, don't worry." Joann, furious, immediately called her allergist, who recommended another obstetrician who had no qualms about natural childbirth in asthmatics. Joann's active participation in her own health care accounts for her successful management of her asthma as well as her trouble-free pregnancies.

Allergy Shots and Pregnancy

As we point out in Chapter 16, controversy surrounds the use of allergy shots for the treatment of asthma. Allergy shots do relieve allergic rhinitis (hay fever). However, allergy shots do not necessarily relieve the spastic airways of asthmatics.

Worse, allergy shots may also trigger an acute allergic reaction, an anaphylactic shock. Such an episode can seriously harm or even kill a pregnant woman; it may also induce a spontaneous abortion. For these reasons, allergy shots should *not* be started during pregnancy. Moreover, if you are already receiving allergy shots do *not* increase the dose. Maintain the same safe level you were receiving at the time your pregnancy was confirmed. That way you reap the benefits of the shots without running the risks attendant to increased concentrations and the possibility of an acute reaction to them.

After the Baby Comes

Most authorities agree that breast-feeding, if possible, returns maximum benefits to mother and child. Breast-fed babies show better rates of development and a lower incidence of infection and allergies than babies who are placed on formula early. With lactating asthmatic mothers, however, some of the drugs taken to combat the asthma may cross over to the infant and cause undesirable side effects. What drugs to take and the safe dosages should be worked out carefully with your pediatrician or family practitioner. We list some of the drugs likely to be taken by asthmatic mothers and the effects they can exert on their breast-fed children in Table 11.2.

TABLE 11.2   Drugs and Breast-Feeding

Drug	Possible Effects on Breast-Fed Child
Alcohol (beer is often recommended to help in production of milk; alcohol appears as a vehicle in many OTC medications)	Atypical development, drowsiness, deep sleep, weakness
Ephedrine (in decongestants and some beta agonists)	Irritability, excessive crying, disturbed sleep
Caffeine (in coffee, tea, cola, OTC cold medications)	Irritability, poor sleep patterns
Theophylline	Irritability, poor sleep patterns; rarely, vomiting, seizure, hemorrhaging
Theobromine (in coffee, tea, cocoa, or chocolate)	Said to cause irritability, colic; interacts with theophylline and heightens its side effects
Salicylates (aspirin)	Respiratory distress, very rapid breathing, restlessness
Iodine (may come from radioactive studies, cough medicines, decongestants)	Drowsiness, lethargy, goiter
Prednisone, other steroids	Lowered adrenal function
Heroin, cocaine, marijuana, methamphetamines	Retarded growth, addiction

Summary

Asthma complicates pregnancy. Like surgery, the delivery process, with its attendant medications, anesthetics, and hospital-based antigens, poses risks to the asthmatic mother and fetus. Asthma itself can impair the respiratory reserve the mother needs to sustain her developing fetus, represents a threat to her general health, and complicates childbirth. Some asthma drugs used by the mother during pregnancy or while nursing can endanger the fetus or newborn.

Notwithstanding these complications, asthmatic women who manage their symptoms faithfully and skillfully, maintain the health of their airways, and proceed with their pregnancy with full, informed consultation with their personal care-providers can, as have many before them, bear children without undue complications.

Perhaps the potential harm that asthma medications can visit on the developing fetus or neonate remains the single most common and studied concern. This chapter pays particular attention to that issue and offers information about possible medication-related symptoms and the degree of risk specific drugs represent to the child.

PART THREE

Caring for Your Asthma

12

Self-Help for People with Asthma

Usually asthmatics, at least the ones old enough to be out of their cribs, carry much of the responsibility for looking after their symptoms. All too often they fail to manage their symptoms competently.

If you have asthma and know what causes it, your self-care must begin with staying away from the trigger and thus avoiding symptoms, We devote Part 2 and especially Chapters 6 and 7 to the tactics that, if followed, will help you keep clear of many asthma-provoking irritants.

What you ought to do next in your self-help program depends on the persistence and severity of your symptoms. A national panel of experts on the treatment of asthma has recommended a step-wise approach to care. Your doctor should know about and apply that set of guidelines to your case. The Web address for those guidelines is http://www.nhlbi.nih.gov/guidelines/asthma/asthgdln.htm. The expert panel's recommendations rely heavily on pharmacological (drug) treatment. The level and type of drug use depends on the severity of symptoms and the individual's day-by-day respiratory status as evaluated by PEF or FEV measurements. (For more on PEF and FEV, see Chapter 5, page 68.) The panel also advocates the development of a team approach to treatment that involves patient, physician, nurse, and other caregivers who, as a group, will work together to inform and counsel you so that you can deal knowledgeably, efficiently, and competently with your symptoms. This management system, if followed, works nicely but it has its problems. Not all doctors know of or elect to stick with the guidelines, not all HMOs or insurers provide the recommended medications, and by no means do all asthmatics have a regular physician. For these reasons fewer than half of all asthmatics have a coherent care plan and, even if they do have one, many fail to follow it. In the sections that follow we outline the elements an individual self-care program ought to contain, how you can (with help) put your own plan together, and the things you need to do (and not do) in order to stay with it and make it work for you.

A Plan for Self-Management

A self management plan worked out in conjunction with your care provider should:

- Spell out your treatment goals
- Specify when and how to measure and record your respiratory status
- Tell you how to detect and respond to a respiratory emergency
- Instruct you on use of medications (when, how, and how much)
- Have you keep a daily record of your medication use, symptoms, and respiratory status measurements

Figures 12.1 and 12.2 offer a sample care plan and a daily diary record of preventive steps taken and status of symptoms. You will need to work out your own plan and diary with your physician, a plan tailored to your own situation and needs.

With help you will settle on the details of your care plan and the diary items to be monitored. We encourage you to copy, adapt, and apply Figures 12.1 and 12.2 if they fit your situation.

Your Team of Care Providers

A support network comprised of family, friends, health care professionals, and fellow sufferers will help you to take control of your asthma. You need

FIGURE 12.1   Asthma Self-Care Plan*
_____

Asthma Self-Care Plan for _____ Age _____ Today's Date _____

Personal Information

Symptoms (check appropriate boxes)   Respiratory Status   Known Triggers (check)

☐ Mild   ☐ Intermittent   Personal best FVC ____   ☐ Exercise   ☐ Dust

☐ Moderate   ☐ Persistent   FEV$_1$ ____   ☐ Colds, Flu ☐ Mold

☐ Severe   PEF ____   ☐ Pollens   ☐ Pets

☐ Insects/Cockroaches

☐ Other

Care Plan Goals

General (Check all that apply)   Personal (List in spaces provided)

☐ Be symptom free   _____

☐ Maintain best possible lung function   _____

☐ Not have limitations on activities   _____

☐ Not miss work/school oa/c asthma   _____

Your Daily Self-Care Actions (Record faithfully in your Asthma Diary)

Measure peak flow (specify when) _____

Record symptoms (which ones?) _____

_____

Use bronchodilator (when?) _____

Take daily medication, specifically

    Type and name _____ How much to take _____ When to take it _____

    Control 1. _____

             2. _____

             3. _____

    Quick   1. _____

    relief   2. _____

Plan for Management of Acute Symptoms

Conditions that may make symptoms worse (list) _____

Signs of distress: Elevated respiratory rate _____ Other indicators (list) _____

_____

Trouble signals	Response
PEF in yellow or red	Take beta agonist inhaler; repeat PEF
PEF remains in yellow or red	Repeat beta agonist in four hours
Low PEF persists	Talk to doctor. Take beta agonist, nebulize, go to oral steriod
No relief or easing of symptoms	Go to doctor or ER

* Suggested. Work out the exact content of your plan with your physician; its details will depend on the persistence and severity of your symptoms. Keep track of your daily status by maintaining an Asthma Diary. See Figure 12.2 and copy if desired.

Call 911 or go to the hospital if difficulty in walking due to respiratory distress occurs or lips or fingernails turn blue. The individual Action Plan must include information on how to assess the individual's status. Triggers should be named and the PEF zonal system should carry instructions on what to do when readings fall in each zone. Dosages should be indicated.

FIGURE 12.2   Asthma Diary

For (Name) _____

Week of _____ to _____ , 20 _____

	S	M	T	W	T	F	S	Comment
Preventive Actions								
PEF or FEV readings in Red (R) or Yellow (Y)								
Medications taken (name and check) Bronchodilator								
Inhaled Coricosteroid								
Other steriod								
Other medications								
Symptoms (check those experienced)								
Pulmonary								
Tightness of chest								
Shortness of breath								
Wheezing								
Cough								
Mucus production								
Other								
Cold or flu								
Low-grade fever								
Restless sleep								
Activities restricted								
Others (specify)								

See Chapter 5, page 68 for instruction on use of peak exploratory flow (PEF) or forced expiratory volume (FEV) meters.

For this individual, PEF or FEV readings < ___ define RED zone: between ___ and ___ define ___ YELLOW zone: over ___ define GREEN zone.

this informed, unconditional backing to manage your symptoms effectively.

The Role of Family and Friends

All too often family and friends do not know how the disease works. They may not understand asthma's severity or resent it because of its cost or the inconvenience it causes. They will sometimes attribute it to emotional or psychological shortcomings in you, flaws that you could overcome if you but tried. They may criticize the appropriateness or the necessity of the treatment procedures you follow. This attitude sticks out like a sore thumb and it may cause you to lose confidence in or even give up some or all of the elements in your care program. Most difficult and unhappiest of all, they may wrongly blame themselves for your troubles.

Counter these misunderstandings with direct and honest communication. Tell them that you do have asthma, help them to understand the nature of the disease, what causes it, its symptoms, the underlying physical processes, and how you go about treating it. Be forthright about your needs and your expectations of family and friends, at the same time paying attention to the consideration and the responsibility you owe to them.

Isaiah, 11, has moderate, persistent asthma with the constant production of mucus (and the unending struggle to raise and void it) its most prominent feature. Isaiah's mother finds his constant coughing, hawking, and spitting extremely upsetting; Isaiah's effort to get the mucus up and out actually make her physically ill and she continually rails, "Isaiah, stop your retching!" at him. She finally asked the family doctor to do something about Isaiah's problem; the doctor managed to mute the conflict by explaining the hyperproduction of mucus and the need to get rid of it as unavoidable features of asthma. He also managed to overcome some of her very real and upsetting disgust by showing her how to help her son expel the mucus by chest massage and physical therapy. At the same time he persuaded Isaiah to do his solo mucus-raising out of his mother's earshot.

The Role of Health-Care Professionals

Having the right family physician and, where necessary, specialist, is key to asthma care. Chapter 13, page 172, tells you what to look for in selecting a doctor. You will want to find someone who will work with other members of your support network and will help you and trust you to manage your symptoms. If he or she will not cooperate with your wishes, find someone else who will. (Some HMOs and most university medical school allergy departments, teaching hospitals, and your local American Lung Association promote asthma self-management vigorously and can point you toward physicians who support self-care.)

Apart from the MDs, other health professionals can help you to take charge of your symptoms. Nurses play a pivotal role in explaining the nature of the disease and teaching you how to take medications effectively. Psychologists, especially those interested in behavioral therapy, can provide training that addresses a range of symptoms that accompany asthma—anxiety, panic, and the like. In school settings, nurses, counselors, and sports medics offer help and useful advice. Occupational safety or health personnel and company doctors and nurses can help you locate causes of your complaint and suggest how to accommodate it effectively in a job setting.

The Role of Fellow Sufferers

Increasingly, outpatient clinics or hospital allergy departments sponsor asthma support groups. They bring together patients, professionals involved with asthma treatment, and, often, parents and other home caregivers. The groups meet periodically and in what most often amounts to an informal, round-table discussion format, provide information about the disease, discuss and exchange tips on treatment strategies, and give one another support and encouragement. These groups often prove to be informative and reassuring and encourage participants to stay with their self-care programs.

How to Stay with Your Asthma Self-Care Program

All too often asthma sufferers do not take care of their symptoms properly. Their failure happens because:

- They do not have a care plan in the first place, or
- The nature of the treatment, or
- The characteristics of the disease itself

encourage neglect of the management plan.

Putting an Asthma Care Plan Together

You will need medical advice to craft your asthma care plan. We devote Chapter 13 to telling you what to look for and how to locate a family doctor or specialist who will help you to take charge of your asthma. If you have insurance coverage or can afford to pay a doctor out of your own pocket you should have no trouble finding the right one. However, lack of insurance or low income puts adequate medical care beyond the reach of a significant slice of the American population. About one-third of poor people have no health insurance at all, and even with various governmental "safety net" programs 15 percent of all children (and up to one-third of ethnic minority kids) lack insurance coverage. Developing an asthma care program when uninsured or getting episodic treatment under emergency room or crowded, time-devouring, clinic conditions is next to impossible. If you have asthma, you absolutely need a care program; you need to know what causes your symptoms, how to avoid that cause, how to keep track of your condition, and what to do if symptoms develop or intensify. Unhappily, for low-income asthmatics, treatment all too often looks something like this:

> Maria Elena, 10, has had mild persistent asthma since she turned four. Her folks do the best they can but they both work at menial, seasonal jobs that

carry no fringe benefits and barely bring in enough money to keep the family going. Her symptoms occasionally flare up, especially when she has a respiratory infection. When that happens, she stays home from school and uses an over-the-counter inhaler to help her breathing. Once or twice a year she gets really sick, has to fight to breathe, and gets rushed to the ER at the county hospital. There the doctor checks her out, treats her with steroids, and sends her home with a prescription and instructions about taking the medication. The parents, not understanding them fully, have trouble carrying out these directions and do not have the resources to follow them in any case. The one bright note in this otherwise textbook example of how not to look after asthma is this—in the last couple of years the attacks have become less frequent and less severe as Maria Elena matures and her airways enlarge and become less constricted during bronchospasm.

This otherwise gloomy general picture has one positive aspect; low-income, uninsured asthmatics can find assistance in managing their disease if they know how and where to look for it. The help is out there. The available resources will vary from community to community; we have listed some of the more likely possibilities in the accompanying box.

For the uninsured population *not eligible* for participation in publicly supported programs, tapping into appropriate asthma treatment and care management services is difficult. Your local American Lung Association chapter, your best starting point, will know of and can direct you to resources available in your community. Apart from the American Lung Association, school nurses and counselors or social workers in public agencies know how to deal with bureaucracies—including the formidable ones that concern themselves with health issues—and may suggest avenues you can follow and agencies or individuals you can check out.

Sticking with Your Asthma Care Plan

To deal with your asthma effectively you need to have a care plan tailored to your needs and to stay with it. In practice most asthmatics do not stay with their care program faithfully, either because of the nature of the

---

Medical Resources Available to Uninsured, Low-Income Asthmatics

Although the information given below is correct as of the time of publication, change happens. Use the telephone or log onto the Web for up-to-date information.

Uninsured adults with no or very limited incomes can qualify for medical benefits that include treatment for asthma. Eligibility requirements vary from state to state. Check with your nearest state department of health and welfare office to see if you might be eligible for such aid and learn how to go about applying for it. You'll find the H&W offices listed in the phone book's local government pages.

Uninsured adults who are disabled can qualify for Supplemental Security Income (SSI) that carries Medicaid and other benefits. Medicaid helps pay doctor and hospital bills (call 1-800-722-1213 for information about SSI).

Uninsured children have a variety of resources available depending on age, level of need, and place or residence. *The Special Supplemental Food Program for Women, Infants, and Children* (WIC) provides food, nutrition, and access to health services to low-income, pregnant, and postpartum women and their children up to age five. WIC will be listed under Health Agencies in the government pages of your phone book. *The Federal Insure Kids Now* program offers free or low-cost health insurance for children. Eligibility requirements vary from state to state. Call 1-877-Kids Now (1-877-543-7609) for information or log onto http://www.insurekidsnow.gov for information on state programs and features.

In addition, some American Lung Association chapters can direct you to local physicians or clinics that offer services to asthmatics who are otherwise unable to afford and are ineligible for publicly supported treatment programs. The ALA will be listed in the business section of the phone book. Also, the American Academy of Allergy, Asthma, and Immunology maintains a list of major pharmaceutical manufacturers that offer free medications to those in financial need. Your physician can initiate the process of securing free medication. A list of participating companies appears at http://www.aaaai.org/professional/physicianreference/drugassistance.stm.

---

treatment the care program spells out or because of the characteristics of the disease.

Depending on the persistence and severity of your symptoms, your care plan may have you monitoring, medicating, and managing your condition several times daily. This routine can grow old in a hurry with the result that you abandon it simply because you get bored with it. Understandable? Yes. Smart? No.

Then, quite often medications don't do the job. Numerous studies have shown that a good half of the time metered dose inhalers are used incorrectly and, consequently, have little or no effect. Many asthma medications trigger distressing side effects, they have a bad taste, or taking them interferes with other activities. Add to these qualities the fact that taking medications may set you apart, make you conspicuous, possibly an object of pity or ridicule, and you have a bagful of excuses for not taking your medication. On top of everything else some of the activities, the PEF monitoring for instance, have no direct effect, no visible impact on your symptoms. Without this reinforcement, maintaining an habitual care routine comes hard.

To make the elements of your care program habitual (they will vary according to the severity and stubbornness of your symptoms):

- Associate airway status monitoring (PEF or FEV measurements) with other routine and ingrained health maintenance activities. For example, take readings morning and evening after brushing your teeth; keep your Asthma Diary on a clipboard with attached pencil at a conspicuous place in the bathroom.
- Get and follow instructions from doctor or nurse in the proper and effective use of medications, especially inhalers. Know when, how much, and under what conditions to take medications by mouth— with food, on an empty stomach, when symptoms reach a stated level of severity, and so forth.
- Stay with your medications if they are a regular part of your care plan. Asthma drugs can cost serious money. This cost may tempt you to play games with your medication, cutting back when your symptoms ease, upping the dosage heavily when symptoms intensify. Both of these reactions can put you at serious risk. Follow directions for use of medications strictly.
- Know the side effects that medications carry, be alert to the possibility they will turn up in your case, and report them to your doctor or nurse when they occur. If you react badly to a given medication, take heart from the fact that an acceptable substitute for it exists.

Thus, both the treatment and the disease can discourage adherence to the self-care plan.

Asthma, sly, comes and goes, waxes and wanes, even vanishes. Seemingly. If you have mild intermittent or mild persistent asthma, you will have days, lots of days, when you will go symptom-free. This intermittency and reversibility adds up to trouble for self-care programs. As symptoms fade or disappear entirely, so does the incentive to monitor or medicate them. This reversibility encourages asthmatics to believe that monitoring or medication had little or nothing to do with the easing of symptoms or, even worse, that you've been cured. This wish-fulfilling fantasy illustrates the psychological mechanism of denial at work. In fact, asthma usually carries a life sentence. Given the appropriate conditions, an asthmatic's airways stand poised to go into spasm.

Dr. Sarah, an anthropologist, received a grant to do field research in East Africa. She had had mild, intermittent asthma as a child but her last episode had happened nearly 30 years before she left to begin work on her project. Once in Africa, she settled in and got down to business. She also started to experience classic hay fever symptoms that, over a period of weeks, intensified and eventually turned into a moderate, persistent asthma with all of the usual symptoms. She sought treatment at a government hospital; the doctor prescribed use of a metered dose inhaler and it helped to keep the symptoms under control. Dr. Sarah did notice that when she left her base for brief periods of time her symptoms left her. She mentioned this to the doctor, who queried her about her living arrangements, diet, and her activities generally. Dr. Sarah had rented a house located right in the middle of a grove of cashew trees and it eventually turned out that pollen from the cashew trees had triggered her symptoms.

Under certain conditions, largely ones associated with physical maturation and enlargement of the airways, asthma's symptoms can remit and seem to vanish. However, the susceptibility does remain and the wrong set of circumstances can bring the symptoms back. Nobody wants to have asthma; nobody wants to depend on medication, so even people with severe persistent asthma succumb to the illusion of a cure, deny that they have the disease, stop monitoring, stop medicating, and live to regret their actions.

Current guidelines for the treatment of asthma recommend that you establish control of your symptoms by establishing and maintaining the lowest effective level of medication. For Dr. Sarah this simply means avoiding exposure to cashew pollen, no problem in northern California where she ordinarily works. For other asthmatics the management tactics will differ. The point here is this: With a care plan tailored to your symptoms—and followed—you can manage your symptoms handily but your susceptibility remains and slighting or ignoring the preventive measures will put you at risk.

While many, perhaps most, asthmatics do not follow care plans faithfully, adolescents and young adults are the ones most likely not to adhere. People who judge or assess their symptoms inaccurately (even when helped by spirometry), and people beset with persistent emotional reactions like anger, depression, and learned helplessness also neglect their self-management regimens.

Staying with an asthma care management program demands accurate knowledge about one's knowledge of symptoms and triggers, unflagging attention and effort, and some inconvenience and discomfort. The decision chart presented as Figure 12.3 will help you to anticipate and suggest responses to the decisions and choices you will need to make in putting together and living with your plan and the underlying symptoms.

The Outer Limits of Asthma Self-Care

Over the centuries asthma, ubiquitous, epidemic, and readily recognized, has attracted an army of remedies and "cures," many of them still around. Long on promises, sometimes gentler on the pocketbook, the shortlist has included surgery, psychoanalytic therapy, vocal gymnastics, herbal cigarettes, chiropracty, hypnosis, acupuncture, special diets, various forms of massage, meditative exercises, sweat baths, salves, nostrums, poultices, and travel and relocation, Even now, pharmacies vend over-the-counter self-care kits to control allergies. Some of the drugs in these kits, because of their sedative effects, pose a distinct threat to asthmatics. As for the other remedies cited, at least most of them will not "exasperate" the symptoms

FIGURE 12.3   Staying with Your Asthma Self-Care Program

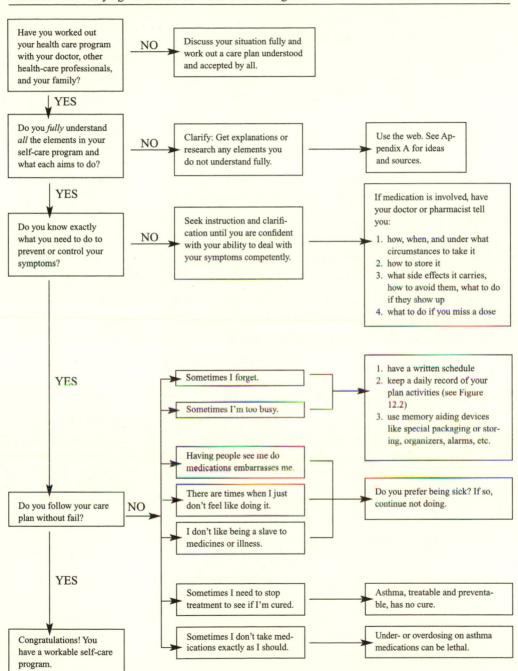

as one asthma "expert" recently remarked to Klingelhofer. We do have a sound and a constantly growing body of knowledge about the causes of asthma, its underlying physiology, and the treatment of its symptoms. With help you can adapt and use that information to construct your own asthma care plan. We beg you to do that—and then to stick to that plan come hell or high water.

Summary

This chapter deals with the self-care program you must have and follow to live comfortably and fully despite your asthma.

In it, we

- Present the elements of a self-care plan
- Stress that effective management of symptoms calls for a team approach and sketch the roles of family and friends, health care professionals, and fellow asthmatics who make up that team
- Offer suggestions on how to craft a comprehensive self-care plan with special attention paid to the difficulties faced by uninsured and/or low-income asthmatics and the strategies and resources that will enable them to overcome those roadblocks
- Discuss the widespread and nagging problem of nonadherence to the asthma care plan, nonadherence that can and often does trace to the elements in the plan itself, the medications and their side effects, and the reversibility and intermittency of the disease itself
- Emphasize that although asthma's symptoms may remit for an extended period of time, the individual's susceptibility to the disease persists for life
- State our firm belief that a carefully developed and closely followed asthma management program will enable the asthmatic to lead an active and full life

13

Medical Care

We live in an evolving health care environment. In our not-all-that-distant past, medical care—for those who could afford it—amounted to a simple fee-for-service arrangement. You had a regular family doctor who treated you when you took sick and charged you for the visit. If the family doctor couldn't handle your complaint, he or she referred you to a specialist who also charged you. If you needed medication, the physician wrote a prescription that you took to a drugstore, where the pharmacist filled it and you paid the charge. A simple system for ordinary complaints. Simple but clumsy.

An alphabet soup of plans has replaced this simple system. Now we have either indemnity or managed care plans—and managed care plans break down into preferred physician organizations, (PPOs), health maintenance organizations (HMOs), or point of service plans (POSs).

These various plans have you (or your employer) paying what amounts to an insurer who either

- Reimburses the physician and pharmacist you choose for services rendered (after you pay a deductible)—the *indemnity plan,* or
- Provides some sort of managed care arrangement wherein the strictness of management by the insurer varies with the amount of freedom you, the insured person, have to choose your primary care provider, pharmacist, or to consult a specialist varying considerably. HMOs tend to be the strictest, with PPOs and POSs allowing some-

what more discretion in choice of personal care providers and specialists. The variability in quality, flexibility, and responsiveness of the services offered vary enormously, however. Most providers have been evaluated and your employer or the provider should have such evaluations and make them available to you. Any of these plans may require deductibles or copayments for services rendered.

Government-supported plans add to the mix and make the choice of a provider even more complicated. Medicare A and B, Supplemental Security Income (SSI), Social Security, and a thicket of federal and state-supported plans designed to bring medical services to low-income families, children, and pregnant women, and programs targeting specific diseases add to the difficulty.

The health plan open to you will depend on your age, financial and employment status, health history, even your place of residence. Given the complexity of the health care world, we cannot presume to advise you on a choice. We do encourage you to find out how the various options open to you work, to select the one that fits your needs most closely, and, within whatever limitations apply, gives you the most flexibility and freedom in the choice of a care provider. In this search, as an asthmatic or the parent of an asthmatic child, you will find that Appendix A, page 245, offers helpful suggestions about using the Web. Log on to www.healthfinder.gov and search for *managed care* for information. Once you have settled on a plan, you will want to choose your doctor—the primary physician for you and your family.

Choosing a Physician

There are a number of things to look for in a physician and they apply regardless of the source of your medical care—independent, private physicians, or a large health maintenance organization. Most important, you should feel comfortable with your physician and have solid reason to believe that he or she is well trained and competent. When you call for your first appointment, inquire where the doctor received his or her training. You may find the following guidelines useful:

1. *Is the doctor a graduate of an American medical school?*

   Levels of training and standards of performance demanded in medical education vary greatly around the world. U.S. schools impose fairly uniform standards, and their graduates do perform better on medical qualifying examinations.

2. *What is the doctor's specialty, and does he or she have board certification in it?*

   Upon graduating from medical school, the doctor who has merely completed his medical school courses is awarded a license to practice "medicine and surgery." This occurs before completing any intensive clinical experience (internship) or specialized training (residency) and does not really signify that the license holder is competent to practice. Having an M.D. degree alone does not qualify its holder to go out and practice allergy or any other specialty.

   There are a number of medical groups whose members have acquired special training and background that qualify them to treat asthma—pediatricians, internists, chest or pulmonary physicians—and allergists. Depending on your age, your first asthma visit should probably be to a pediatrician (for infants and children) or an internist (for adolescents and older). Most asthmatics are adequately treated by pediatricians and internists. Make sure, however, that your prospective physician has board certification in pediatrics or internal medicine. If the receptionist or office nurse does not know about certification status, the doctor is probably not certified. Get a definite yes or no answer to the question of board certification before going in.

   You can also start with a practitioner who has had special training in family medicine. Family practitioners can manage most routine medical problems efficiently and competently, but should refer people with serious asthmatic symptoms to an internist, a pediatrician, or either a chest physician or an allergist for consultation.

3. *Choose a doctor when you are healthy.*

   Too often, people moving to a new town put off finding someone to take care of them. Then, when they get sick, they no longer have the freedom or time to choose carefully. For them it's the emergency room and potluck. It is also hard on a new doctor to examine you during a crisis, having to make decisions without knowing you, your history, or your physical exam results.

If you are new in town and have no idea where to go, call the county medical society or the nearest medical school. Ask which internists or family practitioners are located near your work or home. Then check on board certification and training, as mentioned earlier. Shop around. Ask the receptionist for names of neighbors who are patients of that doctor and solicit their opinions about the quality and cost of the care they receive. Visit the doctor's office and, when you are satisfied, arrange to have your medical records transferred.

4. *Have a family practitioner, an internist, or a pediatrician in addition to any specialists you require.*

Just because you have asthma does not mean that you should only see an allergist or a chest physician. Have someone available who cares about your whole body, someone you can consult about your headache or your infected toe, someone who can judge how good a job your allergist may be doing.

5. *Choose a doctor who asks about the "healthy things" you are doing, who cares about prevention, not just doctoring you when you are sick.*

A healthy lifestyle rests on prevention. Your doctor should want to see you periodically, even if only once every year or two, for a physical examination. Select someone who inquires about your diet and your use of vitamins, who checks your weight, asks about your smoking and drinking habits. The doctor who asks these kinds of questions cares about maintaining your good health, not just treating your disease.

6. *Do you feel comfortable with your doctor?*

This is by far the most important element in choosing a physician. Doctors are people too. They get sick and have to see doctors themselves. They can be hurried, harried, and sometimes unsure of themselves. A good bedside manner in the old days was largely a matter of knowing you as a person. It meant having a caregiver willing to stop, listen, and respond honestly and fully to your questions. Such openness should exist between you and your physician. When it is absent, you should work to establish it. Physicians who do not question or probe—who treat you brusquely and devote little time to the human side of illness, the confusion, the fear, the misunderstanding, the pain that accompanies illness and especially asthma—are not providing the best possible medical care.

What to Expect at the Doctor's Office

Once you have found the right doctor, a complete medical history and an adequate physical examination are vital to the diagnosis and effective management of your or your child's asthma. To get a proper basis for treatment—and possibly to find out what is causing your asthma—your doctor should do three main things: take a careful history, conduct a thorough physical examination, and order some laboratory tests, possibly including an X ray.

> Frances, 67, suddenly develops a persistent cough, pains in the right side of her chest, and a wheeze. Because of the wheezing she is convinced she has asthma. She goes to the drugstore and buys Primatene Mist. After using it for 10 days with no success she decides to see her doctor. By that time Frances is very short of breath. Her doctor listens to her chest and, because he does not hear air movement, orders an X ray. The X ray shows a collapse of part of her right lung. A bronchoscopy is done. During the procedure the doctor extricates a cherry pit that was apparently taken into the lung some time before. Frances does not recollect the event. "I hardly ever eat cherries," she says. "I don't even *like* them."

The Medical History

The medical history is the most important element in the process of finding out whether or not you have asthma and, if you do, what causes it. A good, thorough, well-taken history can and often does establish the validity of the diagnosis of asthma and its causes. You should be prepared to answer the doctor's questions accurately, fully, and honestly. You can anticipate what most of the questions will be by studying the Asthma Finder (Figure 5.1) in Chapter 5. (This is also a good way to get an idea about how thorough and careful the doctor is in trying to help you. If your family background goes unchecked, for instance, or if you are not asked about changes in your environment that occurred about the time of your first attack—you should take note.) The doctor will want to learn about the nature of the onset of your asthma. Was it sudden and unexpected or slow, gradual, and progressive? Was it associated with a fever or infection? Did it show up when you moved or changed your environment at work, home, or school? Do you have any pets? Any new pets? Does your asthma get worse at particular times of the year? Do you smoke? Do some foods seem to trigger your asthma or make it worse? What are they?

The Physical Examination

Your physician should give you a *complete* physical examination. You can get some idea of the caliber of your doctor by taking note of how careful and thorough the physical is. A good doctor (or staff) will carry out the routine data collecting steps, like measuring weight, height, pulse, and blood pressure. If you are over forty the doctor should do a rectal examination; women should have their breasts examined. Then should come the steps that tie in more closely to asthma, beginning with a careful listen to your chest with a stethoscope. (Many physicians believe that, for asthmatics, the stethoscope—and what lies between its earpieces—represents the most powerful diagnostic tool!) If the doctor doesn't listen to your lungs at all or does so in a perfunctory way, you've been shortchanged. The lungs are vital to maintaining all systems in your body, and asthma starves the lungs by cutting off the air flow. Thus, asthma can affect the heart, the kidneys, and the skin. Your physician, by combining the chest examination with inspection and laboratory testing of these organs and sites, can determine if they have been affected, particularly by chronic lack of oxygen.

An X ray may follow to show what your lungs look like and reveal any damage or the presence of other conditions—emphysema, for example—that may be mistaken for asthma. Unfortunately, many people balk at the idea of having a chest X ray, fearing the possibility of cancer. Although exposure to a radioactive source can be dangerous and harmful, the amount of exposure associated with today's highly sensitive and efficient devices is minimal. The small risk that radiation carries has to be weighed against the real dangers that respiratory problems carry. Tragic errors have occurred because of refusals to undergo a needed X ray.

Anthony had had asthma all his life and was used to wheezing, which he controlled adequately by taking over-the-counter medications. His doctor frequently advised him that there were much better drugs available, but Anthony paid no attention. He did not like the thought of taking prescription drugs, believing that the over-the-counter remedies were less harmful to him—a suprisingly common error. Even so, at age 40 he was able to live fairly comfortably with his complaint. Then, one afternoon at work, he began to experience aches and chills. He went home, thinking he had the flu. His wife took his temperature, which registered 101.5 degrees. He also noticed that his wheezing was getting worse. That didn't surprise him because it almost always got worse when he had a virus. Next morning his temperature was 102 degrees.

Anthony went to his doctor, who listened to his chest and concluded that Anthony might have pneumonia. He told Anthony he ought to have an X ray and be placed on antibiotics. Anthony refused. The doctor tried to insist and became angry when Anthony refused to comply. Anthony, too, lost his temper and stormed out. That night his fever suddenly shot up to 104 degrees and he became confused and disoriented. His wife called an ambulance and Anthony was taken to the emergency room where an X ray was finally taken. The picture showed severe diffuse bacterial pneumonia. Anthony was admitted to the hospital and started on antibiotics, but not soon enough. He died two days later.

The doctor, by losing his temper and not insisting more forcefully, was just as foolish as Anthony was in his stubborn refusal. A calm and reasoned approach calls on you to weigh the consequences of both actions—whether the risk of an X ray outweighs that of not knowing of the presence of an undiagnosed and possibly treatable disease. Doctors now are much better informed and prudent about ordering X rays than they were twenty years ago. If you're nervous about the X ray, speak up and listen carefully to your doctor's reply. If you're pregnant, or think you might be, tell the doctor *and* the X-ray technician. They will shield your pelvis during the process.

Laboratory Tests

Depending on your situation, the doctor may order some laboratory work. In addition to a urinalysis, which can point to any one of a large number of conditions, you may have blood samples drawn. Many individuals find this experience upsetting and painful, but it is useful in detecting anemia or infections. It can also establish the presence of allergen-specific immunoglobulin E (IgE), a strong indicator that your asthma has an allergic base. A tuberculin skin test, to determine if you have been exposed to tuberculosis, may be administered; this disease, once a rarity, is making a determined comeback. Finally, the doctor will consider and discuss with you the possibility and advisability of having allergy skin tests. Skin tests and other tests for allergies—and their place in diagnosing asthma—are discussed in detail in Chapter 5.

When to Consult a Chest Physician or Allergist

Both chest physicians and allergists are thoroughly trained and experienced in the care of patients with asthma. Most chest physicians believe that asthma is best managed by medications and that allergy shots have little or no role in treatment. Allergists, on the other hand, think that skin tests and allergy shots may be extremely important and helpful in caring for asthma.

If you have extrinsic asthma (see Chapter 1), you should certainly consult an allergist at some point in your care. On the other hand, if your asthma is intrinsic, with no seasonal aggravation and no obvious pollen or environmental triggering factors, a workup by an allergist is unnecessary.

Good allergists recognize this and—following history, physical exam, and perhaps skin tests—will return nonextrinsic asthmatics to the care of their original internist or pediatrician or perhaps refer them directly to a chest physician.

The matter of referral brings up another important point. Choose a physician who will not hesitate to seek a second opinion and will work to obtain special consultative help for you. It is your life and your health. If your physician has the kind of ego that makes it hard for him or her to seek help and guidance from other physicians, find somebody else.

On this consultative note, we should also add a few words about ENT (ear, nose, and throat) specialists. ENT specialists deal with diseases of the nose, ears, and sinuses. Allergists consult frequently with them in the management of patients with chronic sinusitis. However, ENT specialists have very little training in allergy and although many such practitioners will routinely administer skin tests and give allergy shots, we do not recommend this practice because ENT specialists do not have the training and expertise in treating asthma and allergies that an allergist has.

Other Factors to Consider in Choosing a Physician

Coverage.   People get sick twenty-four hours a day. When you check out a physician, find out if round-the-clock coverage is provided. If your doctor relies on the emergency room, then find someone else. Good physicians offer twenty-four-hour-per-day coverage for their patients. Although physicians cannot be on call all day every day for all of their patients, they can work out sharing arrangements with similar groups of specialty physicians. Thus, a group of internists may share "on call" with one another; so may a group of allergists. This assures that their patients will be adequately covered in an emergency. It also means that the physician on call has access to your medical records and knows where to reach your physician, should that be necessary.

Fees and Hours.   A physician needs to earn a living like any other individual, but money should not be his or her sole reason for treating you. We are weary and a bit distrustful of physicians who require cash payments up front before treatment. Money is important to patients too, and you should not be afraid to ask the doctor about the fee schedule and what mode of billing and payment applies. If the doctor gets touchy about money and treats you like a second-class citizen because you are concerned about money, then you are seeing the wrong person. If the doctor refuses to accept you as a patient because your resources are inadequate or your insurance coverage is unacceptable, ask to be recommended to someone else. Good physicians accept responsibility for finding alternative care for people they are themselves unwilling to treat—especially when the reasons are purely economic ones.

Don't opt for a doctor with ten patients in the office, each with a one o'clock appointment. Such a practitioner will probably be too harried, rushing from one patient to another, to give you the time and personal attention you need and deserve.

What About a Second Opinion?   Second opinions are a way of life in medicine. If you want a second opinion, ask your doctor to recommend someone. Sometimes you may be referred to an associate in the same office; often you may be sent to a medical school or a large clinic. However, do it openly and seek your doctor's cooperation. Don't go around "doctor shopping" looking for good news. It helps the second doctor if you bring all your records—after all, you paid for them—and you can legitimately insist they be provided. Without them, it's like starting to run the race all over again from the beginning—a waste of time and money.

Dr. Francis has been Pam's physician for more than 20 years. In fact, he delivered her. Pam has been seeing him for asthma for nearly 10 years. She is concerned that the treatment he recommends for her asthma may not be the most current or the best. Generally, she feels well, but on occasion she has bouts of wheezing which are not as readily controlled as she would like. She wants to ask Dr. Francis to recommend someone for a second opinion but is afraid of offending him. Instead, she goes across town and sees a specialist, Dr. Gray. She does not plan to give the specialist Dr. Francis's name, but somehow it slips into the conversation. The specialist reviews the medication she is on and makes some minor changes and suggestions. About six weeks later Pam sees Dr. Francis for her regular checkup. She is surprised when he says he is glad that she saw Dr. Gray. He explains that the specialist had been courteous enough to give him a phone call and had sent a letter describing what his results and recommendations were.

Dr. Oliver is an outstanding chest physician, one with enough board certificates and diplomas to fill an entire wall. He also has an ego to match. At a medical conference, a colleague, Dr. Madison, told Dr. Oliver that he had seen Lou R., one of his patients. In fact, Lou had called and made an appointment without a referral. Lou also requested that Dr. Madison not inform Dr. Oliver. Dr. Madison thought Lou was being too concerned about Dr. Oliver's feelings and said that he would mention it the next time they happened to meet. Dr. Oliver's reaction to the disclosure astounded Dr. Madison. Dr. Oliver went into a rage. He said that he did not want his patient seen by other doctors unless he approved it. Then, to make matters worse, he was extremely rude to Lou on his next visit. Unfortunately, Lou, like many others, considers doctors to be above reproach and continues to see him.

Being a Good Patient

In this book we emphasize how you must take charge of your asthma and be ultimately responsible for yourself and your disease. To do this you obviously need information, understanding, and the willingness to look, listen, and make decisions, some of them risky. An important part of being able to take charge of your asthma is being a responsible patient. Be prepared to describe everything to your doctor as carefully and in as much detail as you possibly can. When you consult your doctor, write down what bothers you before you get there. Be specific. Often the doctor may start out the conversation by asking you how everyone is at home and how you are enjoying the weather. The doctor is doing this to relax you, not to invite you to chat. This may divert attention from your problem and get in the way of talking about what troubles you, the reason for your visit.

There are a number of specific questions that you should prepare to ask, and to note the answers. For asthmatics, they include:

1. What are the types of drugs being prescribed?
2. Do the drugs have harmful side effects or carry risks? What are they?
3. How soon should the drugs work?
4. How long should I stay on the drugs?
5. Should I call the doctor if the treatment does not help? How soon?
6. When should I see the doctor again?
7. Is a second opinion appropriate in my case? Will the doctor recommend someone?

Establishing an honest, open relationship with your (or your child's) doctor makes coping with the illness considerably easier. It will help you both to weather crises and enjoy periods of remission.

Summary

Choosing a physician—especially a physician who will help you to care for your asthma—takes care and work. This chapter devotes itself to that aspect of the management and care of the disease.

The changes in the manner of delivery of health care over the last quarter century have profoundly altered the nature of the relationship between those giving and those receiving medical attention. Carefully consider the health delivery options available to you at the outset and then mount your search for a physician who you feel comfortable with, who stresses preventive strategies, who was graduated from an American medical school, and who has board certification in the specialty practiced.

The act of choosing a physician should help to define the course and nature the relationship ought to take—thorough, deliberate, caring, and open on the doctor's part, honest, straightforward, cooperative, and inquiring on your side. The degree of openness and receptivity of both parties to inquiry, to recognition of the need for specialized or second opinions, and the readiness to adapt to changing and difficult circumstances determine the extent to which the collaboration of patient and physician will succeed.

14

The Use of Drugs to Prevent or Relieve Asthma Symptoms

Overview of Medications Used to Treat Asthma

Twenty years ago treating asthma came as easy as "A, B, C." Physicians would start therapy by prescribing drugs that began with an "A" (like aminophylline); if the symptoms persisted or worsened, they would move on to "B" (like Beta$_2$ agonists), and, if needed, "C" (cromolyn or corticosteroids). These prescription drugs had results that resembled those brought about by weaker formulations sold over the counter, but for significant relief of symptoms, prescription drugs were the ticket.

The "ABC" days are gone. Physicians and asthma sufferers now rely much more heavily on medications that prevent symptoms, rather than treating them after they appear. Today's major classes of prescription drugs are Beta$_2$ agonists (or B), corticosteroids (or C), and leukotriene inhibitors (L). Aminophylline-type drugs are rarely prescribed and cromolyn, or drugs like cromolyn, are ordered only for children or those unable to take inhaled corticosteroids.

Your physician may prescribe any one or all of these three classes of drugs. Each has a special and enormously helpful place in preventing and treating asthma. In addition to discussing the uses, advantages, and drawbacks of these newer medications, in this chapter we provide information on the few over-the-counter nonprescription asthma drugs.

We also cover the ways in which people take asthma drugs—by mouth (orally), by inhalation using a handheld device called a metered dose inhaler, or by inhalation via a nebulization machine, a spinhaler, or rotahaler. Throughout the chapter we stress the points that medications work when the ones appropriate to your condition are prescribed, used faithfully, and taken properly (see Table 14.1).

Steps in Asthma Treatment

The first step for a physician in the treatment of asthma is to determine its degree of severity. As we noted in Chapter 1, an asthmatic will fall into one of four diagnostic categories according to the severity and persistence of his or her symptoms. The categories are severe persistent, moderate persistent, mild persistent, and mild intermittent. The degree of severity of the asthma determines treatment strategies; according to the National Institute of Health, that degree derives from the symptoms displayed over the last six months. People with normal lung function who experience wheezing attacks two or fewer times per week have mild intermittent asthma; they may occasionally wake up at night and have to use an inhaler, but do so fewer than two times per month and their ordinary activities go uninterrupted. Those with mild persistent asthma show daytime and nighttime symptoms more frequently, with regular activities sometimes affected. Moderate persistent symptoms have the sufferer showing symptoms and using an inhaler daily with nighttime symptoms showing more than once per week, and people with the severe persistent variety have symptoms continually with frequent worsening at nighttime and limitations on activity. Also, those with severe persistent asthma will often have repeated emergency room visits, hospitalizations in the past twelve months, and may experience a life-threatening episode.

With mild intermittent asthma, primary treatment will likely involve use of a metered dose inhaler containing short-acting Beta$_2$ agonists to control your problems as they appear. You probably would get along comfortably without additional drugs. People with all varieties of persistent

TABLE 14.1   Advantages and Disadvantages of Prescription Asthma Medications

Brand Name	*Advantages*	*Disadvantages*
Metered Hand-Held Aerosols		
Metaproterenol (Alupent, Metaprel)	Rapid onset of action	Short duration of action, 2–4 hours
Albuterol (Proventil, Ventolin)	Rapid onset of action	Duration of action, 3–5 hours
Terbutaline (Brethaire)	Rapid onset of action	Duration of action, 4–6 hours; "tolerance" to drug or decreased effectiveness after prolonged use has been reported
Bitolterol Myesylate (Tornalate)	Long duration of action	Takes up to 30 minutes to work
Salmeterol (Serevent)	Very long duration of action	Not used for treatment; only for prevention
Pirbuterol Acetate (MaxAire)	Slightly longer action; comes with its own built-in spacing device	Duration of action, 5–6 hours
Rotahalers		
Ventolin	Rapid onset of action	Effective for young children and those who cannot use metered-dose inhalers
Oral Preparations (short-acting)		All oral preparations are less effective than proper use of metered aerosol preparation of the same drug
Terbutaline (Brethine, Bricayl), 2–5, 5 mg, 1 mg/ml liquid		
Albuterol (Proventil, Ventolin), 2, 4 mg tabs, 2 mg/5 ml liquid		
Oral Preparation (extended release)		
Proventil repetabs, 4 mg		Less effective than metered aerosol
Solutions for Nebulization		
Alupent	Rapid onset of action	Tremors, rapid heartbeat
Ventolin (Proventil)	Rapid onset of action	Tremors, rapid heartbeat

asthma (mild, moderate, or severe) require controller medications, such as inhaled corticosteroids. Long-acting Beta$_2$ agonists can also be added for moderate and severe persistent asthma. Newer drugs like leukotriene inhibitors have been approved for mild persistent asthma. Medications such as short-acting Beta$_2$ agonists can be used for quick relief of asthma symptoms or before exercise to prevent exercise-induced asthma.

Regardless of the level of severity of your symptoms, effective care depends on keeping track of your medications and monitoring your peak flow activity faithfully.

This division into mild, moderate, and severe has major therapeutic importance. People with mild persistent, moderate persistent, or severe symptoms who do not receive anti-inflammatory therapy run the risk of sustaining irreversible lung damage. In the past, physicians believed that asthma was a reversible disease and that once treatment had been given, lung damage would not occur. We no longer believe this; people who have improperly or inadequately treated asthma do develop structural abnormalities of their lungs, a development called lung remodeling. Indeed, with poor treatment (or a poor response to treatment) over a long period of time, the lungs of asthma sufferers begin to resemble those of people who have emphysema caused by smoking.

An asthma treatment program should:

1. Establish that you really have asthma
2. Define the level of severity of your asthma
3. Have you using a peak flow meter, morning and evening, without fail, and then

Prescribe a medication program such that if your asthma is:

1. Mild intermittent—treat with a low-dose inhaled corticosteroid daily to control the onset of symptoms. A short-acting Beta$_2$ agonist can be used for quick relief of asthma symptoms
2. Moderate persistent or poorly controlled mild persistent asthma—take medium-dose inhaled corticosteroids supplemented by long-acting Beta$_2$ agonists when prevention or control of nighttime asthma symptoms is required.
3. Severe persistent—treat with a long-acting Beta$_2$ agonist, high-dose inhaled corticosteroid, and leukotriene inhibitors, as appropriate, to control the onset of symptoms.

Short-acting Beta$_2$ agonists are the ideal agents for quick relief of asthma symptoms in all categories of asthma severity.

If the preceding steps fail and your asthma remains out of control, then ask for a second opinion or query your physician about the possibility that you might have another disease (see Chapter 1, pages 22–25, for more about asthma imposters).

The regular use of a peak flow meter helps you keep track of your day-to-day symptoms and gives an idea of their severity. We discuss the use of a peak flow meter in detail in Chapter 5.

Beta Agonists in the Treatment of Asthma

The first treatment steps aim to relieve the wheezing or the spasm of airways with short-acting Beta$_2$ agonists delivered by using metered dose inhalers (see Table 14.2 for commonly used inhaler devices). For many people who have only mild intermittent symptoms, carrying a short-acting beta agonist canister and using it as needed is all that is necessary. The major beta agonists are Alupent®, Albuterol®, or Max-Aire®. All are excellent drugs and they do not differ in any significant clinical way, although most people seem to prefer Albuterol. When the symptoms are moderate persistent or severe, then a longer-acting Beta$_2$ agonist, salmaterol (Serevent®), can be added to other controller drugs such as inhaled corticosteroids. Serevent® will persist in your airways for up to eight to twelve hours and therefore can be used as seldom as twice a day. Serevent's downside is that it may need twenty minutes to take effect. Accordingly, a sudden attack would call for treatment with a short-acting beta agonist like Albuterol®. The use of the long-acting beta agonist works especially well for people with nighttime asthma, and can often be a real boon for those who wheeze with exercise, provided they take it in advance of expected need. We cannot emphasize too strongly that salmaterol must *never* be used in emergency or rescue situations.

How to Take and Use Beta$_2$ Agonists

Beta agonists, the mainstay of treatment for asthmatics, are most commonly and effectively administered by means of a metered, handheld aerosol canister. Activating the canister releases a measured puff of drug-saturated aerosol that is carried directly to the airways and acts to ease or relax the muscle spasm. This direct action of muscle relaxation quells the

TABLE 14.2   Features of Commonly Used Inhaler Devices

	Metered Dose Inhalers (MDI)	Dry Powder Inhalers (DPI)	Spacers	Nebulizers
Availability	Widespread	Increasing	Common	Widespread
Portability	Easy	Easy	Some are cumbersome	Difficult
Ease of use	Can be technically difficult	Need for adequate breath actuation	Improves effectiveness of MDI	No coordination necessary
Age range of use	Five years and older	Five years and older	Four years and older with spacer only, two years and older with mask	Any age
Available for	Long-acting Beta$_2$ agonists Corticosteroids Cromolyn Nedocromil Ipratropium bromide	Salmeterol Short acting Beta$_2$ agonists Corticosteroids: budesonide, fluticasone	Using an MDI	Cromolyn Nedocromil Ipratropium bromide
Comments	80% of dose deposited in oropharynx	Dose lost if child exhales through device	Expensive	Expensive

symptoms; beta agonists bring about this relaxation more rapidly than any other class of drugs. A canister fits comfortably in a pocket or purse.

Aerosols for the treatment of asthma have been on the market for more than three decades. The effectiveness of aerosols rests on using them properly. Here are some guidelines for the use of metered dose inhalers.

1. *Do not overuse beta agonists.* Take one or two inhalations every four hours, and no more than twelve puffs a day, unless your doctor has given you specific instructions to the contrary.
2. Be alert for side effects, including irregular or rapid heartbeat, nervousness, muscle tremors, nausea, vomiting, dizziness, weakness, sweating, or chest pain. If any of these symptoms appear, discontinue use of the medications and monitor the symptoms carefully. If they persist or worsen, proceed immediately to the emergency room.
3. Do not use beta agonists unless you have specifically discussed them with your physician. If you have high blood pressure, hyperthyroidism, or cardiac disease, these drugs may not be right for you.

How to Use a Metered Aerosol

1. Shake canister.
2. Begin inhalation and at the same time place the aerosol canister just in front of your mouth and release a properly aimed puff of aerosol. (Aerosol should go straight to the large airways; it should not hit the back of the throat or the tongue.)
3. Inhale at a moderate rate with open mouth.
4. Hold breath for five seconds.
5. Exhale.
6. Repeat steps 2–5, one time only, if necessary.
7. If you still have problems using metered dose inhalers, consult your doctor, who may prescribe use of a spacing device such as Inspir-Ease.

Even children as young as four can be taught to use metered aerosols. Parents can help by working the canister valve as the child inhales. In both adults and children, however, an incorrectly aimed canister will have the medicine land uselessly on the roof of the mouth or the tongue and fail to reach the lungs. Studies in children using inhalers (and in seniors as well) have revealed that as many as one-third of them do not use the device properly and thus lose most of its benefits. To overcome these deficiencies, two other delivery systems have been developed.

The first and older remedy for this deficiency introduces a "spacer" into the process. A spacer is simply a device that makes it easier to deliver the drug to your lungs by coordinating timing, aiming, and breathing. The cardboard cylinder found within a roll of toilet paper or a disposable paper cup with its base removed make cheap, effective spacers. The user activates the inhaler to release the drug into the spacing device, then slowly inhales its contents. Most of the time this works quite well. However, we recommend that you use a commercial spacer. There are many of these available and we suggest that you ask your pharmacist for advice; there is virtually no difference between brands other than in cost. They usually cost approximately $15 and consist of a mouthpiece followed by a long hollow tube into which you insert your metered dose inhaler. The pharmacist will show you how to use it.

Another short metered dose inhaler that delivers a drug called Max-Aire® comes with its own built-in spacing device, a larger mouthpiece that allows for more effective delivery. Although it frees users of the need to buy or create their own spacer, Max-Aire® also has an autoinhaler version that activates delivery of the spray when you inhale. It sounds like a good idea but many people do not like it and we do not recommend it.

The Rotahaler represents another useful effort to improve the drug delivery system. It consists of a three-inch plastic cylinder housing a little pin and propeller. The beta agonist drug for use here comes as a powder encased in a capsule. When inserted into the cylinder, the capsule is punctured by the pin. When you inhale, you set the propeller in motion and its spinning disperses the powder into the airways. An extremely effective and simple system for very young children to master, the Rotahaler delivers drugs as efficiently as a metered-dose inhaler; studies of children have shown it to be particularly useful. Often young children will preload their Rotahaler, put it on their night table, and take and use it during the night if they wake up wheezing. The Rotahaler does not offer major advantages over metered dose inhalers for most people, but it is a particularly useful alternative for children or for other people who have difficulty coordinating inspiration (breathing in) with closely timed hand movement. We like it.

You need to take care when using metered dose inhalers. Nasty accidents happen. All the metered dose inhalers (except MaxAire) have caps. Sometimes users forget to remove the cap, and when they press on the canister, the cap gets propelled into the mouth—and even, on occasion, into the airways. The MaxAire's hinged cap, which folds up and becomes part of the mouthpiece, avoids this problem but with all inhalers—including MaxAire—foreign objects such as coins, dirt, and other small objects may lodge in the mouthpiece and be blown into the airway.

Almost all of these aerosol beta agonists have liquid or pill take-by-mouth versions but these forms carry worse side effects—rapid heart rate, tremors, and muscle shaking. We prefer the metered dose aerosols or the Rotahaler because of their rapid action, effectiveness, and immediate availability. And, note that dry powder inhalation (DPI) devices, late additions to the list of medication delivery systems, are especially effective and easy to use. The long-acting Beta$_2$ agonist, salmeterol, available as Serevent Diskus®, can be had in DPI form. This version carries an especially useful feature, an indicator that tells users the number of doses remaining. Another and even newer dry powder inhalant is Advair™ Diskus® that delivers both salmeterol xinafoate and fluticasone propionate. A potent anti-inflammatory, it provides greater improvement of pulmonary function and control of asthma symptoms than do either of its two main components. We have had a great patient response from Advair™ Diskus®.

Finally, you should know that Alupent and Albuterol are both available in a solution that can be delivered by nebulization in a home air compressor. This is by far the most effective way of delivering beta agonists. For people with moderate to severe asthma or for very young children, the use of home air compressors is strongly recommended. We discuss the features and use of nebulizers a bit further on in this chapter.

Treating Persistent Asthma

Asthma sufferers who have persistent symptoms—or those for whom the beta agonists do not work—need therapy that will control the inflammation of their airways. Corticosteroids, leukotriene inhibitors, or under certain conditions, cromolyn sodium or nedocromil sodium, can achieve this control. These drugs act as preventatives and anti-inflammatories but do not treat acute symptoms.

In asthmatics with acute or severe exacerbations, it is important that the doses of the preventive drugs be optimized so as to cut down on the number of episodes; measuring and keeping track of peak expiratory flow is critical to this goal. It is important to tailor treatments to the individual and to base them on his or her detailed history, physical findings, and peak flow meter readings.

Corticosteroids in the Treatment of Asthma

One of the most important advances in the treatment of asthma came with the discovery of steroids in the 1950s. Use of these drugs, potent agents that inhibit inflammation of the airways, has greatly helped many asthma sufferers. Unfortunately, in this oral form, they carry major side effects including weight gain, development of a moonlike face, thinning of the bones, eye cataracts, and even dissolving of the joints. Even today asthmatics with severe or acute flare-ups of their asthma may need to take oral bursts of corticosteroids for periods of up to one or two weeks to get their symptoms under control. About twenty-four years ago, however, it was found that steroids introduced in an inhaled spray, much like beta agonists, could prevent the onset of asthma's symptoms and largely avoid the nasty side effects of the oral medication; there are now many such preventive inhalers on the market. These agents include, among others, Azmacort, Flovent, Beclovent, Vanceril, and Pulmicort. Flovent has a major advantage because it can be prescribed in a range of dosages suitable for use with children and adults with severe persistent symptoms. Pulmicort can now be had as a nebulized solution for use with the very young. The daily and chronic use of these agents may be the best way to prevent the onset of asthma symptoms.

If used for long periods or if your doctor prescribes a high dose, you should have your eyes tested regularly for glaucoma. In children, they may inhibit growth slightly but only if used regularly for most of a child's life.

Leukotriene Inhibitors in the Treatment of Asthma

The use of leukotriene inhibitors has been one of the more exciting recent advances in the prevention of asthma. Over the past ten to fifteen years, it became clear that asthma is an inflammatory disease and if one wishes to control the symptoms of asthma, then it is absolutely essential that the inflammation be inhibited. Many clinical studies showed that the severity of asthma varied directly with the amount of leukotrienes that patients were producing and that were found in their lung fluid. Hence, much research went to finding ways to inhibit production of these enzymes. Three such enzyme-controlling drugs have now been approved. They are Accolate, Singulaire, and Zileutin. They work equally well but they differ in cost and in their side effects. For most people, the drugs are tolerated uneventfully but Zileutin can affect your liver and its use requires periodic testing of your liver function.

Leukotriene inhibitors come into use when persistent symptoms do not respond to beta agonists or inhaled steroids. Many asthma patients whose symptoms do not yield to beta agonists resist taking inhaled steroids, and leukotriene inhibitors work well with them as well as with people that are sensitive to aspirin, have exercise-induced asthma, or have problems with compliance with inhalers either because they don't like to use them or because they can't work them properly.

Leukotriene inhibitors must never be used in the treatment of acute asthma (because of their slowness in taking effect) and they do carry one rare side effect we should mention. A small number of people on leukotriene inhibitors have developed an intractable form of asthma called eosinophilic vasculitis, or the Churg-Strauss syndrome. Those most likely to develop this disease from these drugs had been on high-dose oral corticosteroid therapy before the leukotriene inhibitors were added. Symptoms of Churg-Strauss syndrome include pneumonialike lesions that show in a chest X ray, a skin rash, and sometimes, cardiac problems. Should any of these signs appear, abandon the use of leukotriene inhibitors. To decide about using leukotriene inhibitors, consider the following guides:

- Do *not* use for mild intermittent asthma alone.
- Do *not* use as the sole treatment for acute severe asthma.
- Do use for moderate persistent asthma and severe asthma.
- Do use for aspirin-sensitive asthma.
- Do use for exercise-induced asthma.
- Do use to reduce the dose of corticosteroids.
- Do use it for those who either fail at or adhere poorly to taking inhaled corticosteroids.

Other Drugs in the Treatment of Asthma

Atrovent.   Atrovent belongs to a class of drugs that inhibit what are called "cholinergic receptors." These receptors appear to be very important in patients with chronic lung disease, accompanied by a cough. Atrovent (or Ipratropium) inhibits these cholinergic receptors and offers significant relief to individuals who have chronic obstructive pulmonary disease that results from either emphysema or bronchitis. It works to dilate the airways by inhibiting the vagus nerve and it acts swiftly. In asthmatics, taken in tandem with a beta agonist, the combined dosage greatly enhances the response to therapy. You can be prescribed two separate inhalers, one holding Atrovent and the other a Beta₂ agonist, or else a combination canister drug called Combivent®, which carries both drugs in the same inhaler. The use of Combivent® is not as common as using a beta agonist alone, but for some patients who have mild intermittent asthma that occasionally exacerbates and who do not want to take inhaled steroids, sometimes using the Combivent® can be a real help.

Theophylline.   At one time, theophylline was the drug of first choice in treating asthma. Its chemical structure resembles the caffeine in coffee.

Medications incorporating theophylline can help asthma by relieving airway bronchospasm. They also possess the virtue of having been used and studied for many decades, so we know a lot about them. Theophylline, if used incorrectly or if it interacts with other drugs, may trigger significant side effects, including nausea, vomiting, skipped heart rates, seizures, and even death. For these reasons, theophylline is rarely prescribed nowadays. Some asthmatics do respond so well to theophylline that they and their doctor insist on using it. In such instances, the correct dose needs careful calculation, with the drug prescribed in either one- or two-dose-a-day forms, and the level of theophylline in the blood measured regularly. Intravenously administered, aminophylline, once routinely used in the emergency room for the treatment of asthma, no longer gets general use but still fits the needs of an occasional person in an asthma crisis. Actually, recent evidence suggests that aminophylline in an emergency might be more effective than we once believed.

Cromolyn and Nedocromil. Inhaled cromolyn used to be the choice of medication for children and adults who had moderate persistent asthma, but it has given way to the more effective inhaled corticosteroids. (Outside the United States, cromolyn finds more use because the strength of the dose is much higher; Intal-Forte, a high potency cromolyn, enjoys popularity elsewhere.) Cromolyn works by inhibiting inflammation by blocking the release of histamine and other vasoactive amines from your mast cells. It also seems to stabilize your airways. Only Cromolyn's lack of strength has cut its popularity but it still finds use in children, in people who do not want to or cannot use inhaled steroids, and particularly in infants and pregnant women. A second-generation cromolyn sodium is nedocromil. This drug is only slightly more effective than cromolyn sodium and is also not widely used because neither of these agents are as good as inhaled steroids.

A Special Word on Cough Medicines. Coughing acts as both a symptom and a cause of asthma. A cough, especially a nighttime cough, may be the only sign that your asthma is active. Unhappily, coughing also makes your airways tighter and your asthma worse. Because of this, many people, including many doctors, recommend the use of cough suppressants. Mild, over-the-counter cough suppressants generally won't work but they won't hurt you; prescription cough suppressants (including those containing codeine) pose a real danger for asthmatics. They may make you sleepy and reduce your breathing effort; they may dry out your lung secretions as well, making mucus harder to raise. We advise asthmatics to avoid taking cough medications containing codeine. We advocate going after the cause of the cough, not the cough itself. Stomach acid reflux or gastroesophogeal reflux (GER) can also cause nighttime cough and aggravate your asthma. If you have chronic heartburn tell your doctor and get treated for it. Azmacort, the topical steroid mentioned above, is especially helpful in relieving nighttime asthmatic coughs.

Home Air Compressors.   For severe persistent symptoms, a home air compressor represents a good way to administer both beta agonists and cromolyn. Much more effective than metered handheld canisters, the home compressor works particularly well for small children, the severely ill, or the elderly.

To use these durable and dependable devices, a solution of the medication is placed in a small cup attached to a face mask or mouthpiece. When the machine is turned on, the solution is *nebulized*—made into a fine, easily-inhaled mist.

Where drugs need to be administered daily to small children or to severe asthmatics, these air compressors are strongly recommended. The cost, about $200–$400, may seem like a drawback, but avoiding one emergency room visit will pay back the investment. Most health plans—even government-subsidized insurance for the needy—will pay for a compressor if your doctor takes the time and trouble to prescribe it and defends his decision. Many chapters of the American Lung Association recycle donated nebulizers and distribute them to people in need.

Compressors come in several forms and are made by several manufacturers, including models that work on a battery pack or plug into the wall or a car's cigarette lighter. Most units are about the size of a shoe box or smaller.

Over-the-Counter Asthma Medications.   At one time the woods were full of over-the-counter asthma medications. Most of them served up doses of Epinephrine or theophylline in varying strengths but they fell out of favor with the discovery and widespread use of the newer beta agonists or metered dose corticosteroids. Table 14.3 names and describes the surviving members of this vanishing tribe. Primatene Mist is the most heavily advertised and widely used of these medications, but it and other such drugs declare that a medical diagnosis of asthma should precede their use and they all warn of the distressing side effects we have named in Table 14.3. We do not recommend use of any of these medications. In other countries, the much-to-be-preferred Alupent is available over the counter but there is little reason to believe that it will be released for OTC use in the United States any time soon.

Although OTC medications have made life more bearable for many asthmatics, they have had other, less agreeable consequences. The dramatic results they produce have encouraged people to become overreliant on them and to ignore the other aspects of an effective, comprehensive program of asthma self-management—exercise, breathing improvement, careful avoidance of allergens, scrupulous monitoring of respiratory states, and so on. As noted, these medications, especially if overused, can and do carry dangerous—perilous—side effects and render chronic asthmatics a disservice by encouraging them not to seek out the best prescription, the one right medicine for their asthma (see Table 14.3).

Summary

Over the past quarter century the discovery of a stunning variety of drugs has revolutionized asthma treatment. The severity and stubbornness of your symptoms will determine which of these asthma medications you will use. You will most likely relieve mild and intermittent symptoms through use of a prescription short-acting $Beta_2$ agonist delivered by means of a metered dose inhaler. For more persistent or severe symptoms, you will aim to control their onset or severity with longer-acting $Beta_2$ agonists, inhaled corticosteroids, leukotriene inhibitors, or, if circumstances warrant their use, oral steroids.

TABLE 14.3   Names of and Agents Found in Common Over-the-Counter Asthma Medications

Drug Name and Form	Active Ingredients	Dose	Side Effects
Primatene Mist Nebulizer	Epinephrine 5.5mg/ml	.22mg Epinephrine per puff 2 puffs per use each 4 hours	Nervousness, rapid heart rate
Bronkaid Mist* Nebulizer	Epinephrine 5.5mg/ml	.22mg Epinephrine per puff 2 puffs per use each 4 hours	Nervousness, rapid heart rate
Primatene Tablets (Oral)	Ephedrine HCI USP 12.5 mg in each tablet	2 tablets taken 2 to 4 hours apart; no more than 12 tablets over 24 hours	Nervousness, rapid heart rate
Bronkaid Caplets* (Oral)	Ephedrine sulfate 25mg/tablet	1 caplet every 4 hours	Nervousness, rapid heart rate

* Bronkaid nebulizers and caplets are generally marketed under the name of the distributor.

NOTE: All these medications carry the warning that a doctor's diagnosis of asthma should precede their use and that their use by individuals with certain conditions or their overuse may carry dangerous side effects. Their use in lieu of prescription drugs is not recommended. Note, too, that the FDA is expected to authorize the sale of Zyrtec Claritin and Allegra over-the-counter in the near future.

We describe and assess the various types of medications fully, explain how they address asthma's symptoms, tell about using them, describe and appraise the various ways used to deliver them, and spell out side reactions associated with them. The Asthma Care Plan presented in Chapter 12, pages 158–161, will guide you in the when, why, what, and how of medication usage.

We do mention other medications occasionally used in the treatment of asthma, name the risks run by asthmatics who employ certain kinds of remedies to treat their coughs, and offer a brief analysis of over-the-counter asthma medications, including a tabled list of the active ingredients found in these drugs whose only advantage is their availability.

15

Allergy Shots and Asthma Treatment

How Do Allergy Shots Work?

Allergy shots aim to make you less sensitive to the substance that triggers your symptoms. Thus, desensitization, the reduction in your allergic state, can be brought about by administering a series of increasingly more potent shots of the allergen that causes your discomfort. An accepted and commonplace method of treating certain allergies, this desensitization process has an uneven record of success for asthma. For hay fever sufferers with positively identified causes whose symptoms are not easily controlled by other means, desensitization usually works. The procedure formerly represented a real blessing, but these days the drugs used to treat hay fever are so effective that allergy shots don't get the use they once did. When it comes to asthma, allergy shots rarely pan out.

Desensitization rests on a homeopathic principle whose roots go back to the very beginnings of medicine. It relies on the discovery that the body can tolerate minute amounts of substances that in larger quantities cause severe reactions. These miniscule doses can systemically be made more potent by small degrees so that, after a period of time, the individual can tolerate quantities of the substance that would earlier have caused serious or even fatal illness. For allergy sufferers, this gradual process of desensitization elevates the threshold of reaction to the point where the concentration of allergen occurring naturally in the environment no longer produces allergic symptoms.

The Role of Allergy Shots in Asthma Treatment

A series of allergy shots may be useful if you and your doctor know for sure that your asthma represents a reaction to a specific allergen. Take allergy shots for asthma *only* if strict and careful avoidance strategies have not worked and if medications have proven ineffective after extensive tryout. Allergy shots or immunotherapy should rarely (if at all) serve as the *sole* treatment for asthma.

Allergy shots have been used for years in attempts to reduce allergic reactions. The basic method of making allergenic extracts has improved very little during the last fifty years, although the means to standardize and control manufacturing, testing, and storage do exist. The standard practice has been to soak an allergen such as grass pollen in a solution containing saline (salt) or some other buffered solution to leach out the allergen. Then the allergen is sterilized by filtration. Obviously, there are several conditions one hopes (but cannot be sure) are being met. The material being injected should be free of extraneous material; it should be potent, stable, and efficacious.

Unfortunately, in only a handful of instances are there standard potencies for allergy shots, and almost never is the final product tested to determine its exact strength or even its composition. Recently there have been major efforts to standardize the potency of allergenic extracts by expressing it in protein nitrogen units (PNU), which describe the concentration of allergen in a given preparation. This has worked well with such allergens as insect venoms in which the compound responsible for the allergic response has been isolated. However, in the case of molds this level of standardization has not been achieved. At present, allergy is the only field of medicine to employ injectable substances that are not required to have guaranteed potency or authoritative dosage recommendations based on intensive studies or evidence-based medicine.

Some extracts are prepared crudely, while others are carefully made under acceptably controlled conditions. At one extreme there is house dust. A large number of people with allergy and asthma are allergic to house dust, and it is found everywhere. However, it is very difficult to determine what house dust contains because it holds all sorts of particulate matter as well as dust mites and the remains of other insects. Its basic biochemical composition varies enormously from house to house. There is persuasive evidence that the triggering agent in house dust may be the feces of the house dust mite.

In past years, some allergen manufacturers harvested the house dust they used in preparing their extracts from vacuum cleaner bags. Other suppliers used the dust found on mattress covers. It comes as no surprise that house dust allergen potency and efficacy varies tremendously from batch to batch and company to company.

At the other extreme end of the quality continuum is the extract prepared to treat allergy to bee stings. Allergy to honeybees and other stinging insects like wasps, hornets, yellow jackets, and fire ants shows up in individuals who reside in the country, in beekeepers, and in people who work outdoors. For many years individuals allergic to bee stings were treated (desensitized) by receiving injections of extracts made from the ground-up bodies of honey bees. This was considered a highly effective procedure until about twenty years ago when some imaginative studies demonstrated that these whole-body extracts of bees did not work. The experiments proved that the allergen from a bee sting is the venom itself. They went on to demonstrate that injecting the venom into susceptible individuals produced a blocking antibody. Consequently, bee venom shots ultimately eliminate allergic reactions to bee stings in most people. As a result of this discovery, rigorous procedures have been developed for producing venom extracts of known and controlled potency.

The Food and Drug Administration has addressed these critical issues. The next decade should see major new pioneering efforts to develop bioengineered allergens that meet approved criteria. Our ability to clone biological molecules will play a significant role in preparing allergenic extracts that are pure and have accurate concentrations.

Who Should Receive Allergy Shots?

You should receive allergy shots for asthma only if you have extrinsic or IgE-mediated (atopic) disease as revealed by skin tests, a clear unequivocal history, or both. Nonatopic (intrinsic) asthmatics do not need and would not find help by having allergy shots. Young children who have asthma brought on by virus infections should not receive allergy shots, nor should individuals with negative allergy skin tests. Generally, children under four should not even have skin tests. In most cases a physician can tell by your history whether you might benefit from allergy shots. But turning up with positive skin tests does not necessarily mean that you would benefit from shots.

Evan has had eczema, hay fever, and asthma all of his life. His eczema, a year-round problem, gets worse in hot weather. Usually mild to moderate, applying cortisone creams and avoiding caustic agents keep it under control. Evan's hay fever is generally similar to his asthma in that both sets of symptoms worsen in the spring and the fall when things pollinate. He also reacts to dust throughout the year. Evan's allergist suspected that Evan would be allergic to most pollens as well as to house dust, but she wanted to confirm her hunch. She did the skin tests; those for pollens and dusts turned out positive. Evan, elated, thought that, because he had a positive skin test, his allergies and especially his asthma might be relieved with allergy shots. The allergist told him that she didn't want to give him allergy shots because of his eczema. "They could make your eczema worse," she said. "I'd prefer to up the medication in the spring and fall when the hay fever and asthma are worse." Evan decided to see another allergist. He sought out a physician who advertised that he treated allergies by nutritional and "preventive medicine" means and advocated the use of a whole variety of "ecological" procedures, including something known as cytotoxic testing. Cytotoxic testing should be history but there are still those out there using it. This new physician said that Evan should receive allergy shots and Evan, abrim with hope, readily agreed. He began a program of twice-a-week injections. After about three months his hay fever and his asthma showed no improvement while his eczema became much more severe and stubborn. The ointments didn't help and the itching intensified. Evan acknowledged that the first allergist had it right. He stopped the shots and went back to the first allergist.

Although some allergists will occasionally use shots to treat people who have hay fever, asthma, and eczema, we believe that unless there is some overriding reason—failure to respond to other drugs or treatments—people with eczema should not have allergy shots.

Nevertheless, the exception proves the rule—some asthma patients with positive skin tests do respond well to desensitization.

Allen first developed asthma at age 12. His wheezing, made worse by smoke, polluted air, and exercise, persisted 12 months a year. His asthma was particularly bad during the spring and for a short period during the fall. Thus, although he had asthma year-round, it worsened according to the season. He was referred to an allergist who did a panel of skin tests that turned out positive for trees, grasses, weeds, and dust. The allergist began a program of weekly hyposensitization shots for Allen. After a period of about six months Allen saw that his asthma remained pretty much the same, but during spring and fall the rise or the exacerbation that he normally experienced fell off and his asthma was considerably easier to manage.

How Are Allergy Shots Done?

The first step in preparing an immunization—vaccination—schedule for your allergy shots, is to find out what you are allergic to by having you undergo skin or RAST tests. Then, with the tests completed and the offender pinned down, the doctor prepares a dilute mixture of your antigens. The first injection will be a very weak solution—possibly one part vaccine to one million parts saline solution. Thereafter, once or twice a week you will receive an injection of allergen in your arm. Following each injection you will stay in the doctor's office for thirty minutes in case you show a systemic reaction. Before you leave your doctor will also inspect your arm to see whether or not you have had a local reaction to the shot. If you develop any discomfort at all following the shots, a physician will check you out immediately.

Assuming that you show no local or systemic reactions, the strength of the dose of allergen will increase with successive visits. If things go well, a dose strength of 1 part allergen to 100 parts of the carrier solution will eventually be reached and maintained.

Some physicians make a cocktail of all the allergens that trouble you; others prefer to administer separate shots for each offender. Thus, you may have one or a number of separate shots for trees, grass, house dust, and so on, depending on your allergist's preferences and your own degree of sensitivity.

We do not endorse testing or immunizing asthmatics to control their food allergies. Skin testing for asthma resulting from food allergies rarely helps and may even provoke life-threatening reactions (see Chapter 5).

How Long Should Allergy Shots Be Continued?

Allergy shots usually go on for a period of approximately one year. If, after that time, your allergies do not seem to be under better control (fewer and/or less severe episodes), discontinue the shots. On the other hand, if your symptoms get better, continue the shots for up to five years. At that point, depending on your response and the nature of your allergies, the frequency should decrease so that instead of having a shot once a week, you may eventually require a shot every other week or even once a month. This individual decision rests with you and your doctor.

The Dangers of Allergy Shots

Allergy shots are potent extracts of the material that you are allergic to. Injected directly into your body, they have the potential to induce an acute anaphylactic reaction, a form of shock that may result in death. In fact, the leading cause of anaphylaxis is injection of allergy extracts. Anaphylaxis turning up when you are getting an allergy shot is the most scary thing the doctor—or you—may ever encounter and you certainly do not want to be the cause of his of her panic. And you can do without the symptoms too. For this reason, allergy shots should always be administered under a doctor's (not nurse's) supervision with emergency equipment to treat anaphylaxis on the site and *immediately* available. People having allergy shots should let their doctors know of any local reactions and any systemic complaints that may develop. Systemic complaints may include wheezing, shortness of breath, swelling of the face or throat, and hives; cardiac complaints or even severe abdominal pain can also turn up. If any of these problems occur, the doctor will probably either stop the shots forever or else severely reduce the strength of the allergy shot. If a dose at 1:1000 dilution causes large local reactions, you should have your dose cut back to a dilution of perhaps 1:10,000 and maintained at that level for a while. Later, by the time the dose is increased, you should have developed some immunity to prevent these reactions. Yet many highly sensitive people cannot tolerate large doses of allergy extracts, and others are so sensitive to specific agents that they must omit them from their treatment vial or else have them administered singly in extremely dilute solution.

Allergy Shots to Counteract Sensitivity to Pets

One of the more melancholy chores of an allergist entails advising an asthmatic's family to remove the family dog or cat. All too often the family rejects this advice entirely or falsely claims that the pet stays outdoors. Allergies to animals can provoke serious symptoms on their own or the pets may not trigger obvious symptoms, but will have enough impact to push you over the edge into a full-blown episode when you begin wheezing from other causes. Often people found to be allergic to their pets want to have shots that will desensitize them to the animals. Although available, we discourage people from undergoing these vaccines. The small amount of evidence available suggests that such shots often fail to work and the extracts prepared from skin cells from animals may contain viruses that can trigger infections or diseases.

Only individuals necessarily exposed to animals should undergo allergy shots for animal dander. Veterinarians allergic to pets make up the bulk of individuals who get this treatment. Families who insist on allergy injections rather than giving up their pets sometimes find help but should know going in that the procedure is risky, expensive, prolonged, and frequently ineffectual.

Bacterial Vaccines

For a number of years some practitioners treated recurrent infections and asthma and sinusitis by administering bacterial or autologous vaccines. In this process, the doctor cultivates a culture containing bacteria from the individual's throat or sinus. The bacteria are then heat killed and vaccines are prepared. Alternatively, commercially prepared vaccines containing extracts of the common bacteria that infect people were available. Despite the theoretical possibility that this procedure ought to work, it never panned out and, in some cases, toxic responses followed administration of bacterial vaccines. Use of bacterial vaccines to counteract asthma was never recommended, and we strongly discourage their clinical use.

Gamma Globulin

Gamma globulin contributes to the working of our immune systems. People with impaired immune systems—those whose bodies cannot produce it themselves—sometimes receive injections of gamma globulin. Some researchers, in the hope of relieving asthma symptoms, have injected asthmatics with gamma globulin, but to little effect. We believe that gamma globulin should be given only to the few asthmatics who have severe symptoms that do not respond to conventional drugs. Besides being very expensive, gamma globulin carries the risk of provoking serious allergic reactions.

Summary

Allergy shots work by gradually and over a period of time desensitizing individuals to substances that provoke allergic symptoms. Once routinely used to control allergic rhinitis (hay fever), the procedure has seen less use recently with the development of medications that perform more effectively, conveniently, and economically than the vaccines do.

In rare instances allergy shots may be prescribed for asthma sufferers, but only as a tactic of last resort. The danger of serious complications or side effects heavily outweighs the limited prospect of favorable results of shots when used to manage or limit asthma's symptoms. Such vaccinations when used to counter food allergies or allergic reactions to pets—regardless of the form the allergic reaction takes, asthmatic or other—are inherently risky. Simple avoidance of the triggers, in those cases, represents a better, more effective control tactic.

Bacterial vaccines developed to counter infection-triggered asthma and sinusitis have, despite their hypothetical promise, failed to produce favorable results, and sometimes deliver toxic side effects. Gamma globulin injections used as a means of boosting asthmatics' immune systems have also yielded disappointing results and can also provoke severe allergic side reactions. Neither of these tactics live up to the promise held out for them; indeed, asthmatics need to know what desensitization amounts to so that they can avoid it in all but the most extreme of cases.

16

The Treatment of Acute Asthma

In a severe asthma attack your or your child's chest gets tight, so tight that it almost feels as if it had an iron band around it. Breathing becomes rapid, shallow, and difficult, and even the slightest exertion—a spell of coughing, for example—will leave you or the child spent and panting. Wheezing will be loud enough to be heard halfway across a fairly large room, and there will be an overabundance of thick, clinging, yellow-tinged mucus, which will be extremely difficult to raise. If these conditions develop, do the following:

1. Try and determine what, if anything, triggered the reaction; did an infection, exposure to an allergen, a recent period of exercise, or something you cannot single out cause it?

2. Make sure you are taking the recommended doses of medication. If you know that you must increase your medication during a bout of asthma, do so at once.

3. Boost your fluid intake. Rapid, shallow breathing causes a drastic loss of body fluid, which must be replaced. You need an adequate supply of liquid to keep mucus thin.

4. Try to raise your mucus to prevent clogging of your airways. The presence of mucus is a serious sign; have your physician evaluate it or else go to the emergency room.

5. Avoid any other medication that may make your asthma worse. In particular, *do not take aspirin or any sedatives*.
6. Take your temperature; watch out for fever.
7. Monitor the respiration rate. Adults usually take in sixteen to twenty breaths per minute; children breathe at a rate of twenty to twenty-five breaths per minute, and infants take between thirty and forty breaths per minute. If you or your child's respiratory rate becomes consistently elevated, take note and alert your physician.

When to Call a Doctor

If any of the following conditions turn up during the course of an asthma attack, consult your doctor as soon as possible.

- Fever
- Vomiting and abdominal pain
- Persistent rapid respiratory rate that does not return to normal
- Wheezing and shortness of breath that does not respond to medications

Fever may indicate the presence of infection and other conditions that can drastically complicate ordinary asthmatic episodes. Mucus sometimes ends up being swallowed into the stomach, causing vomiting, particularly in children. Some of the medications used to treat asthma can lead to gastric irritation and vomiting, and the chronic cough and the air hunger that asthmatics have may cause stomach bloating, which can also lead to abdominal pain and vomiting.

Vomiting represents a very serious complication for asthmatics because it causes you to lose body fluids and become dehydrated. Dehydration in turn makes mucus thicker and reduces air flow. Also, vomiting prevents you from keeping your medication down. If this occurs, see your physician immediately! Likewise, if your respiratory rate remains persistently above normal or if usually effective medications do not relieve wheezing or shortness of breath, call your doctor.

A Special Warning About Sedatives

People die from asthma. One of the most common things found about people who do die from it is the fact that they had taken sedative agents or tranquilizers. If you have an acute asthma attack, you must keep your respiratory drive as strong as possible while maintaining all of your mental function. If you take a sedative, you become sleepy and your respiratory muscles get sluggish. As a result, you may drift off; this can lead to a further decline in respiratory function, unconsciousness, and death from lack of oxygen. *Under no circumstance should anybody with asthma ever take a sedative.*

Jill is eight years of age and has had asthma for the past four years. She becomes terribly anxious whenever she begins to wheeze. Her mother has often felt that her anxiety and the fact that Jill is often hyperactive anyway caused the asthma in the first place. She consulted her pediatrician, who told her that he did not want to give Jill any tranquilizers for asthma. He explained that they can make asthma worse. However, Jill's mother decided she would give her some of her own tranquilizers. She gave Jill 2 mg of Valium about three times a day. Jill's hyperactivity actually seemed to get better for a few days. However, Jill was sleepy much of the time.

About two weeks later Jill developed a cold; it began to settle in her chest and made her wheezing worse. Jill's mother doubled the dose of Valium. Although Jill had been wheezing for the past four years, she had never required hospitalization. However, during this episode, Jill just couldn't seem to get enough air; she got sleepy and her respiration became shallow. Her mother panicked and rushed her to the emergency room. Jill was examined and found to be in *status asthmaticus* (the most dangerous form of asthma), with severe obstruction. The doctor determined that Jill's respiratory reserve was insufficient; he hospitalized her and performed an intubation to put her on a respirator. Jill's pediatrician could not understand what precipitated this severe episode until Jill's mother, under severe questioning, finally admitted she had been giving her daughter tranquilizers.

Nighttime Asthma

For many asthmatics the nighttime period is the worst—we don't know why. At bedtime they feel well, take their medicine, and go to sleep. Then in the dark hours of the early morning they wake up wheezing. Explanations advanced to account for this include: nighttime accumulation of mucus in the lungs; the body's different rhythms in the daytime versus the nighttime; dust being released through the air vents during the night; other allergens present in the room, such as dust mites in the bed or bedding. Take your pick.

If you have nighttime asthma and wake up with it more than twice per month, your asthma is not under effective control. You should mention it to your doctor, who may adjust your medication, possibly starting you on an anti-inflammatory drug like an inhaled steroid or a leukotriene inhibitor. We also suspect that your peak flow meter reading at bedtime would not be in the green zone. If your child is affected and begins coughing or wheezing in the middle of the night, you may have to wake him or her up and administer an inhaler (beta agonists). This beats having the child continue to sleep fitfully and restlessly, only to awaken the next morning with tight, constricted, mucus-jammed airways. Note that the beta agonist represents a quick fix with the symptoms calling for anti-inflammatory therapy.

Hospitalization for an Asthmatic Emergency

Admission for acute severe asthma ranks among the most frequent causes of hospitalization in any community. There is nothing more dramatic and frightening than the acute shortness of breath seen in a wheezing individual. The inability to get enough air arouses tremendous feelings of fear in observers and victims, even though it usually looks worse than it actually is.

When you or your child is being evaluated in the ER for acute asthma, the doctors or attendants will do a number of things. First, they will assess the severity of the symptoms so that they may provide the kind of acute care needed. Acute care may entail administering oxygen, fluids, and medications. In making the fast decision about what must be done, emergency room personnel may appear brusque, impersonal, and dispassionate. This does not mean they are uncaring. On the other hand, if the staff has you fill out insurance forms or supply information while you or your youngster can't breathe, complain. If you sense that a doctor is urgently needed, *demand one!* An asthmatic episode serious enough to have you at the emergency room requires special, prompt attention.

In transporting someone to the hospital, move swiftly but without endangering yourself and others. Don't risk an automobile accident. Keep cool and calm. If you don't have transportation or symptoms are very severe, dial 911. The fire department and rescue squad carry oxygen and will bring the victim directly to the closest available hospital.

Emergency Room Procedures

Entering the emergency room in the throes of a severe asthmatic reaction sets off a series of events. First, you or your child will be taken to a station and seated. If necessary, oxygen will be administered. Then someone will record vital signs—heart rate, blood pressure, respiratory rate, and, sometimes, temperature. Next, a physician or nurse practitioner will probably listen to the lungs. At this stage the first direct countermeasures will be taken.

A child having a severe asthmatic attack once received an injection of Adrenalin (epinephrine). Nowadays they receive an aerosol treatment. Most physicians now prefer to administer aerosolized bronchodilators such as albuterol because of their relative safety and limited side effects.

Adrenalin, or epinephrine, can make the heart race alarmingly and produce feelings of nausea. Some individuals develop pounding headaches or even a migraine after receiving Adrenalin.

Albuterol is administered as a fine mist using a nebulizer. The mist is inhaled and, like Adrenalin shots, the nebulized drug works within minutes, producing a dramatic remission of symptoms.

If the inhalation therapy does not produce improvement, other steps will be initiated. At this point the child or adult is usually admitted to the hospital and intravenous drugs and fluids started. The purpose of the intravenous tube is to supply fluids to fight off the dehydration that comes with rapid, shallow breathing.

The intravenous line may also be used to carry other asthma-fighting drugs. Usually the drug administered at this point (assuming a clear diagnosis of asthma) will be corticosteroids.

Once the acute attack is controlled or stabilized, additional tests may follow. These can include a chest X ray as well as a test to determine the amount of oxygen in the blood. The chest X ray shows whether there are any abnormalities within the lung, other than the effects of asthma itself, leading to the impairment of breathing. Here the physician will look for underlying pneumonia, a collapsed airway, or some defect in air movement through the lung that has permitted air to leak out into the chest wall or into the lung cavity itself. This last, a pneumothorax, along with the other conditions, requires special immediate treatment.

The test for the amount of oxygen in the blood, the arterial blood gas test, capitalizes on the knowledge that the arteries carry oxygen directly from the lungs. By taking blood from an artery, the laboratory can tell the physician how much oxygen is dissolved in the blood. This gives a precise indication of the severity of the asthma and also offers an excellent way to monitor the effectiveness of the therapy being given. In most cases the arterial puncture, or "stick," needs doing only once. The improvement that occurs with ER treatment is usually so dramatic that further arterial punctures are not necessary. In the few instances where repeated sticks are necessary, there will be some local discomfort, but the test is only a bit more painful than any other routine blood test. The major complication of the arterial stick is excessive bleeding. Your doctor should hold pressure over the stick site for several minutes following the test before applying a pressure bandage. (As with any blood test, if the person doing it is having trouble finding the artery, ask for an "expert" to help. You or your child are probably miserable enough without having a novice practice on you. Asking for an anesthesiologist to help with arterial sticks is sometimes a good idea. These specialists have the most experience in drawing blood.)

A new way to measure oxygen content in the blood, pulse oximetry, does not require a needle stick. It does not provide as much useful data as the arterial blood gas test, but it is less painful and is often chosen for that reason.

In the hospital it may also be necessary to get help from an inhalation therapist. These specialists will administer beta agonists—like the albuterol given as a handheld, metered aerosol. The inhalation therapist will deliver the medication through the special ventilating equipment used in the emergency room. These machines provide good aerosolized medication.

In addition, patients admitted to the hospital almost always receive high doses of intravenous steroids or cortisone. This is probably the single best drug available to break off an acute attack but it requires several hours to take effect and then must be continued for several days before the attack is considered completely gone. Even then, there may be some residual wheezing, and certainly, if pulmonary function testing is done, some abnormalities may persist. Probably the biggest mistake in the treatment of severe asthma is the failure to give enough steroids or to stop them too soon. Although prolonged use of steroids can carry serious side effects, you should take them as long as your doctor prescribes them. If you stop too early, the acute asthma may rebound, often worse than the initial episode. When this happens, another hospital trip and replay of the pain, discomfort, and anguish of the first visit happens. Generally, hospitalization for acute asthma should last no longer than three or four days.

The Use of a Respirator or Ventilator

Asthmatics rarely need to be put on a respirator, but one may be pressed into use when a person becomes exhausted and unable to breathe independently. It may also be ordered when the results of the physical exam, the pulmonary function tests, and the blood gas analysis are so ominous that the physician fears a sudden respiratory or even heart collapse. In that case, the doctor may elect to put you on a ventilator before the crisis happens, rather than have to try an emergency intubation during a cardiac or respiratory arrest. Realistically, only your physician will know what signs to look for and only he or she can decide on this drastic step. Cyanosis, a dark blue or purplish coloration of the skin owing to lack of oxygen, is one of the signs physicians encounter that concern them mightily. A *late* sign, cyanosis, denotes a severe lack of oxygen and truly signifies an emergency.

If your physician elects to intubate you, he or she usually calls in an anesthesiologist and places you in intensive care. At that time you will receive some medication to make you sleepy and thus less likely to experience the trauma of having a tracheostomy or air tube inserted and being hooked up to a machine. Although most people absolutely dread the thought of having a tube down their throat, virtually all admit afterward that it was not nearly as bad as they feared.

Roger has been on a camping trip in the Sierra Nevada for the past week. Although he has had asthma for many years, he finds that it no longer troubles him and he lives a full, active, and vigorous life. Unfortunately, he was not used to climbing, and although his body was in good shape for ordinary athletic activities he found that climbing, with its reduced level of oxygen and the extreme exertion, was too much for him. At about 9,500 feet he collapsed. He developed an acute shortness of breath and turned blue. His companion had no means to summon help; he had to leave Roger on the mountainside and descend to the base camp for assistance. It took a relief team several hours to get to Roger. By that time he was unconscious and unarousable. He was airlifted to a local hospital where treatment of his acute asthma, as well as the acute pulmonary edema that he developed from climbing, was begun. The physicians wanted permission from Roger to intubate him. By this time Roger was conscious but not especially coherent. He balked, but his terrible shortness of breath and desperate struggle to breathe finally led him to give grudging permission. Although the process was uncomfortable for Roger, he found, within a few hours, that he tolerated it quite well. Moreover, it relaxed him and relieved him of the need to breathe as hard and as deep as he could because the machine did most of the work. Roger left the hospital after four days, pretty much restored to normal.

Whatever else may be said about hospitalization, it provides an excellent opportunity, after the acute problem is resolved, to find out why it happened. This is also the time to review your management and prevention tactics. Did it grow out of a poorly controlled asthma that could have been managed more competently? What lessons does it hold? Critically review your own care procedures. Review the services and care provided by your physician. Was your medication and treatment schedule optimal? Why did it fail? Did you know as much as you should have when you entered the hospital? Were you inadvertently exposed to an allergen that precipitated your attack? Upon discharge, go over the medicines you carry with you to make sure that you understand the instructions, dosages, and treatment schedules.

Can Asthma Kill?

Although most patients with asthma, particularly adults, never require hospital admission for this disease, deaths do result from asthma. In fact, in spite of our increased knowledge about asthma, the mortality rate for asthma has increased sharply over the past fifteen years. People die from asthma because:

1. *They are given sedatives.*

   The panic that occurs from shortness of breath agitates asthmatics severely. Accordingly, some may take or be given tranquilizing agents that have been either prescribed for other family members or sometimes incorrectly prescribed for themselves. Sedatives or tranquilizers (Librium, Valium) should *never* be used by asthmatics.

2. *They overmedicate, especially with beta agonists.*

   Often asthmatics in the throes of an attack think that increasing the dose of the medicine will control their symptoms. To some extent this is true, but only within limits; continuing to increase medication when the increase does not relieve the symptoms is foolhardy. Some of this toxicity may affect the heart and produce heart irregularities. Instead of significantly increasing your dose, go to the emergency room or see your doctor immediately.

3. *They undermedicate, which can lead to a sudden, severe episode or even a lethal attack.*

   Know and be sure of the correct doses of your medication and take them faithfully. Do not decide you can undertreat yourself and try to get away with taking the least amount of drug possible.

4. *They recklessly expose themselves to allergens because they can control their symptoms with medications.*

    Medicines that relieve aggravating symptoms don't remove the allergy itself. Increased exposure to substances that incite asthma can lead to more attacks of greater severity.

Summary

The symptoms of asthma are much easier to prevent than they are to treat. Taking medication on a regular basis and using a peak flow meter are essential for taking charge of your asthma. Make sure you are taking the recommended doses of medication, boost your fluid intake, and try to raise your mucus to prevent clogging of airways. If you develop fever, vomiting and abdominal pain, a rapid respiratory rate and wheezing/shortness of breath that does not respond to medication, then you should see your doctor as soon as possible. People with asthma should not take sedative agents.

    Hospitals and emergency rooms follow standard operating plans (SOP) for dealing with acute asthma. The whole experience is frightening, but the procedure's goal is to elevate the amount of oxygen in your blood and reduce the inflammation in your lungs. The use of steroids is essential.

    Although uncommon, people with asthma sometimes need to be put on a respirator. This is usually done by an anesthesiologist in an intensive care unit. Most people dread the thought of having a tube down their throat, but virtually everyone admits afterward that it was not as bad as they had feared.

    Asthma, sadly, still kills. Most deaths follow the use of sedative agents, overmedication, especially with beta agonists, undermedication with corticosteroids, or reckless exposure to allergens.

17

Summer Camps and Care Programs for Asthmatics

Programs designed to provide comprehensive and aggressive treatment of asthma have appeared in the past few years. They feature broadly based education about the disease and training in its self-management. Primarily aimed at providing help to children with moderate to severe or intractable asthma, these programs vary greatly in focus, duration, and intensity of therapeutic intervention. They include:

1. Summer camps
2. Community-based programs for training or outpatient treatment

Summer Camps

Summer camps for asthmatic children began in the late 1950s when a group of young physicians rejected the then prevailing notion of what constituted appropriate treatment for asthmatic children. These rebels contended (correctly) that asthmatics did not need to lead an isolated, sedentary existence and that with proper care, training, and supervision they could participate in and enjoy many activities previously denied them. This led to the establishment of summer camps especially designed for moderately to severely asthmatic children. These camps offered ongoing medical supervision and a program of activities aimed at accomplishing two goals. First, they tried to provide experiences, enjoyable for their own sake, that these children had been denied in the past. Second, they wanted to help the campers (and, in some instances, their parents) develop a knowledge of and control over all aspects of the disease and its treatment—to have the children attain the ability to manage and control their symptoms more effectively. These educational programs vary widely from camp to camp, from the basic transmission of information to a tightly organized self-management training program that may even consider the psychosocial issues that so often complicate the disease.

This once daring and hotly debated move has proved to be extremely successful. Summer asthma camps with names like Camp Superkids, Camp Wheeze, and Camp Huff'n Puff have sprung up throughout the country. These are generally sponsored and financially supported by local lung associations or chapters of the Asthma and Allergy Foundation of America, but they have attracted a wide range of other backers: thoracic, pediatric, and allergic societies; religious groups; Children's Aid; medical societies; and private organizations all fund and staff these camps.

To locate the nearest asthma camp, call the American Lung Association for information and referrals. Their phone number appears in your local white pages. Appendix A tells you how to pull up a nationwide list of camps from the web. Unfortunately, not all localities offer this valuable resource for children. The number of applicants to any camp may exceed the spaces available, so preference is usually given to children with moderate to severe symptoms who have had no prior camping experience. A doctor's statement is invariably required, and the application asks for a complete history of the child's episodes and an enumeration of causes and special dietary, medication, and other needs.

The camps are often staffed by former campers, themselves asthmatics, who understand—and respond sensitively to—the needs, problems, and anxieties of the children, some of whom are away from home for the first time and understandably frightened at the prospect. Medical needs, including adherence to medication schedules and management of any medical emergencies, are attended to by a resident medical staff (doctors and nurses), often volunteers from local pediatric or allergy societies. Dietary restrictions are noted and provided for, and the possibility of individuals violating their food restrictions is kept to a minimum.

In the last few years there have been two interesting developments. One of them is the establishment of camps where all sorts of infirmities are welcomed and managed together. In these camps it is not uncommon to have children who suffer from any one of a score or more of disabling conditions—asthma, cystic fibrosis, sickle cell anemia, muscular dystrophy, spinal cord injuries, diabetes, cerebral palsy—to be in camp at the same time. A second development is "mainstreaming" asthmatics, that is, having them attend camp with "regular" children. Whereas the asthmatic camper still has his or her special needs looked after, and some program elements continue to be directed specifically at managing the disease, the aim here is to have asthmatic and well children encounter and learn from one another. The anecdotal reports indicate that this sort of experience is especially valuable for asthmatic and nonasthmatic children alike. (See also Chapter 18 for considerations when attending regular summer camp for children with mild or seasonal asthma.)

Although the curriculum varies from one camp to another, most camps offer a course of instruction in the disease, provide skill training in use of medications, use an ingenious collection of breathing exercises (for example, "Puff Hockey," where teams arranged on sides of a Ping-Pong table try to blow a Ping-Pong ball into a goal), and run according to a settled routine that carries over to the home situation. In some instances parents are encouraged to participate as well. Follow-up indicates that much of the information is retained for a significant period after camp and that campers show a drop in number of ill days, days absent from school, and emergency room visits in the year following camp.

Added to these benefits for the children is one for the parents. It is a period, however short, during which they are spared the ever-present burden of caring for their asthmatic child. To have the load lifted, even for a brief time, and placed on competent, knowledgeable shoulders is a rare gift.

Your decision whether to send your asthmatic child to a special camp should be based on your knowledge of your child's condition, your physician's recommendation, and a consideration of the facilities offered by the camp. The camp staff have or have seen problems similar to your child's, and know how to manage them. If they cannot handle your child's problem they will be the first to let you know. (In most instances, a medical panel evaluates each application and decides whether the camp facilities are sufficient for any special problems that your child may present.) Camp is an exceedingly worthwhile experience for most moderate to severe asthmatic children, and we strongly recommend that you seriously consider having your child participate. The potential benefits to you and the youngster far outweigh the risks.

Community-Based Programs for Training or Outpatient Treatments

It is fair to say that most asthmatic symptoms, with appropriate treatment, can be either prevented or quickly controlled. That this ideal often does not occur in practice has more to do with breakdowns in communication between physician, parent, and asthmatic than deficiencies in available medical measures. Misunderstanding, failure to comprehend or adhere to procedures, inappropriate or unnecessarily heroic measures in response to crisis, and ineffectual, panic-fueled reactions growing out of feelings of helplessness all conspire to make asthma more of a problem than it needs to be. Recognition of this side of the asthma problem has led to the establishment of a number of different kinds of community-based programs aimed at helping asthmatics and their parents know more about asthma and develop skill in the management of its symptoms. These self-management programs are offered by hospitals, schools, and community groups.

Hospitals

There are a few hospital-based allergy centers in the country. Your health provider should know of them. In addition to providing up-to-the-minute treatment and care, these institutions offer outpatient programs designed to educate asthmatics in the effective management of asthmatic symptoms. The programs vary from place to place. Most of them have the participants come together once weekly for an hour or two over a brief period. The programs ordinarily include educational sessions that entail distribution and study of written materials, family and peer group support sessions, and behavior training exercises. They may also provide recreation, a telephone hot line during (and after) the course of instruction, and long-term follow-up. Parents are expected to accompany their children; sessions may be either separate or joint, depending on the program.

These programs aim to increase understanding, to teach self-management skills and techniques, to cut down frequency and severity of attacks (including reducing the frequency of emergency room visits), and to reduce school absenteeism. Evaluations of the programs indicate that most of the objectives are achieved with some degree of success.

Although hospital-based programs are not widespread, they offer a valuable adjunct to routine medical care for those with severe, persistent, and hard-to-control symptoms.

Schools

The school is an obvious place to offer primary educational programs aimed at asthmatic children. Considering the number of schoolchildren with asthma—estimates have run as high as 10 percent—and the roughly 50 percent higher days absent from school rate for asthmatic (as compared with nonasthmatic) children, an aggressive educational program to systematically bring together these youngsters would benefit not only the children but the school as well. Such a program, using American Lung Association (ALA) materials, could be run by the school nurse, through the counseling office, or even by qualified volunteer personnel in the community. Additional self-management training materials are available through a variety of sources. The National Asthma Education and Prevention Program provides a resource book titled *Asthma and Physical Activity in the School,* which spells out a model plan for serving students with asthma. Asthmatic children should be able to participate in all school activities.

The ALA has developed a variety of programs designed to help students breathe easier and to inform teachers about asthma and alert them to symptoms. Schools can secure these materials from their local Lung and Heart Associations and to incorporate them in the school's general health education program. The ALA's *Open Airway* Program is intended for use in schools.

Community-Based Groups

Community-based educational or support programs have been attempted in a number of places, primarily under the auspices of local chapters of the American Lung Association. One serious drawback to the effective use of these programs is the tendency of asthmatics or caregivers to participate only in time of crisis—when the stress generated by the disease becomes acute. Without a crisis brewing there is unfortunately little incentive and consequently little obvious reason to give up time, energy, and comfort to attend these sessions. Obviously, the crisis-generated approach fails to capitalize on some of the real advantages that a rational program of prevention and preparedness provides. We heartily encourage you to search for such a program, to enroll in it *in advance of need,* and to stay with it faithfully once enrolled. You will find the benefits worth the effort.

In addition to local programs, three national asthma training programs for children have been developed. *Open Airways at School,* a school-based program, aims to give elementary school children more self-confidence, self-control, and know-how in dealing with their asthma. ALA has developed and sponsors this program as well as *A Is for Asthma,* designed for use with preschoolers.

ACT (Asthma Care Training) *for Kids* is supported by the Asthma and Allergy Foundation of America (AAFA). Your local allergy society will know the location of the program, which consists of five one-hour sessions aimed at asthmatic children ages six to twelve and their parents. It is usually offered to small groups and tries to develop mastery skills and provide practice in decisionmaking for the child. Parents are taught how to nurture the child and create an environment conducive to decisionmaking. AAFA also offers *You Can Control Asthma,* directed at eight- to twelve-year-olds.

There are four other formal asthma training programs for children that may be offered in your community: *Open Airways*/Respiro Abierto, *Living with Asthma, Air Power,* and *Air Wise.* Development of these programs has been supported by the National Heart, Lung, and Blood Institute (NHLBI), and may be sponsored locally by private medical practices, hospitals, clinics, American Lung Association affiliates, health maintenance organizations, and schools. The target groups, teaching techniques, curricula, and objectives sought vary from one program to another. Your local ALA branch will know of and be able to direct you to any of these programs that are being offered. NHLBI has also developed *Breathe Easier*, a program for adults.

In some communities local support groups have been formed. These groups hold regular meetings, discussions, and (sometimes) maintain a telephone hot line network. These groups are effective in disseminating information and are particularly valuable in teaching parents and children how to manage the psychological complications of asthma, notably the fear and helplessness that so often accompany it.

Enrolling in community-based programs repays the effort involved in seeking them out. Get in touch with your local American Lung Association chapter. They will know of any local programs going on in your community. In addition, check with the allergy department of your hospital, or the local chapter of the Asthma and Allergy Foundation (call the local medical society to find out the one nearest you) or pediatric society for information about community training and self-management programs. Your care provider—insurer or HMO—will also know about and may even offer such programs—many do. Seek them out and take advantage of them.

Summary

Asthmatics need to and can, with help, enjoy activities most of us take for granted. Summer camps and community-based care programs have been developed to help them attain their goal of fullest possible participation.

Your community probably offers such programs. In this chapter we tell you what they consist of and how you can learn of them. Your local chapter of the American Lung Association can help you. The references cited in Appendix A also supply information about camps and community and school-based management and care opportunities.

18

Traveling with Asthma

General Precautions

Here are some general rules you can follow to travel safely and comfortably.

- As an asthmatic you should never leave home without your medications and never fail to carry enough medications to see you through your entire trip.
- Carry your medications where you can get to them *immediately* if you need them. Always stow your medications on your person or in your carry-on luggage. If perfumes set you to wheezing and you get a seatmate who reeks of musk or lavender, having your Albuterol inhaler in the suitcase buried in the baggage compartment won't help you. Nor will it help you if you are bound for Atlanta and your luggage (and the medication it holds) winds up in Denver.
- Some recent evidence reveals that airline companies have systematically cut back on the supply of conditioned air to reduce their fuel costs. Take note of this possibility, and if poor air quality sets you to wheezing, complain and ask for full operation of the air conditioning equipment. (This degradation of air quality often happens when the plane waits on the runway or at the gate.)
- If you know that you could need emergency treatment for your asthma, be sure that you wear a Medic-Alert bracelet and carry a statement spelling out what could cause a severe reaction in you

and how it ought to be handled. (Your physician can provide you with a letter carrying this information. Keep it in your billfold, not in your passport. We have had reports of people being denied entrance to foreign countries after immigration officials read such instructions.)

The surest way to prevent asthmatic episodes is to know and avoid whatever it is that provokes them. This is tricky enough ordinarily, but it can represent even more of a problem for the traveling asthmatic. You can circumvent it, though, by carefully relating the *cause* of your asthma to the *when, where,* and *how* of your trip. Although we cannot anticipate every situation every asthmatic might run into, an example or two will help you to develop your own plan for steering around possible travel troubles.

Robert has severe asthmatic reactions to pollens, especially ragweed (cause). He wants to fly (how) to his sister Margaret's wedding, which is to be held in Iowa City (where) on August 20 (when). He wants to decide if he should attend or not.

For the asthmatic traveler susceptible to pollens, first find out is what the pollen situation will be like at the destination or destinations. For travel in the United States or Canada you can determine in advance the likely conditions for any destination at any time of the year. Your allergist, hospital, or medical school libraries would have the most easily accessible source, *The Manual of Allergy and Immunology,* edited by Drs. Glenn Lawlor and Thomas Fischer and published by Little, Brown and Company. This book tells what pollens turn up where and when. www.carti.com gives daily air quality forecasts and pollen counts for fifty cities and www.about.com lists pollen allergy seasons by region as does www.claritin.com. Drug companies like Hollister-Stier or Center Laboratories offer extremely useful pollen guides that are available on request. All of these references agree that ragweed pollen production peaks in Iowa during August and September. By seeking out these references and knowing what to expect, Robert can decide about attending the wedding and work out the precautions he ought to take in the form of preventive medication, housing, and so on. In Robert's case, flying is probably the best way to go because travel by automobile through ragweed country at the height of the pollen season would undoubtedly cause him considerable distress—even with the windows up and the air conditioning going full blast.

Statistics about airborne allergens other than pollens that trigger asthmatic attacks have not been compiled, although you can find today's air quality forecast listed in any major U.S. city by going to www.weather.com and clicking on the name of the place you intend to visit. If smog triggers an asthmatic reaction for you and you have to make a trip to Denver in June, your local weather service or local library can pull up air quality readings for June a year ago. When the data arrive, use your knowledge or your reaction to polluted air to decide about the wisdom of a trip to the Mile High City at that time. If you cannot put off the trip and June is bad for smog in Denver, carry appropriate medication and observe the other precautions we spell out in Chapter 6. Also bear in mind that air pollution readings—"low," "moderate," and so on—relate to ordinary, nonasthmatic people. A low reading may affect a person with asthma more drastically than moderate pollution affects someone without asthma.

> Celeste is excited about her safari of the East African game parks. She will fly (how) to Nairobi, Kenya (where), in July (when). She expects to have a marvelous time, but she is a little worried about accidentally consuming sulfites, a preservative (cause), which always trigger a serious asthmatic reaction in her.

Celeste will have to watch her step all along the way. She is likely to run into sulfites in the airline salad dressing and in other processed foods she will be exposed to in Africa and any other continents en route. Worse, the requirements about package labeling of contents are not as stiff in many other countries as those in the United States, and the contents, if named at all, will be listed in the language of the country. Celeste should try to stay away from preserved or processed foods entirely when she is out of the country. She should also let the tour director know of her problem in advance so that he or she can help Celeste find safe things to eat and is aware of the possibility of a severe reaction in the event of a slip-up. Tours usually provide some variety in food choices, so Celeste should be quite safe as long as she keeps alert and takes no chances.

If you are going to a part of the world where the food differs radically from what you usually eat and you react asthmatically to some foods, identify everything you are about to consume. Check it against a food family chart (see Chapter 7, page 111). If what you are about to eat belongs to the same family of foods that cause you to wheeze, put it aside no matter how appetizing it looks.

For the other major causes of asthma—vigorous exercise, exposure to extreme cold, and upper respiratory infections—following the same precautions you do at home and faithfully keeping up with exercises and medication should see you through. If you do react severely to extreme cold or low humidity, you should consider choosing a travel or vacation site that is compatible with your condition. Swimming in Barbados would be considerably less troublesome than trekking in the Himalayas.

Sleeping in New or Different Quarters

If you have intrinsic asthma, new environments and strange rooms will make little or no difference in your breathing or respiratory problems. On the other hand, if you have extrinsic asthma due to mold, animal dander, or dust, new rooms and new beds pose special problems.

Susan is extremely sensitive to house dust and animal dander. While on a trip she checked into a motel. The motel and the room looked clean enough, but Susan began to wheeze severely almost as soon as she entered the room. It did not take her long to figure out that some previous occupants had brought their cat into the room with them. Susan had already paid the night's fee but was smart enough to realize she was in trouble. She packed her bags and went to a motel that did not allow pets. By explaining the problem she even got her original room fee refunded.

Other problems with hotels, inns, and motels include the fact that years of use, abuse, and careless cleaning have left dust, mold, dusty drapes, and worn carpets that hoard dander and dust. Before you consider bedding down for the night, don't pay until you've inspected the room carefully and asked yourself:

- Does the room smell moldy or musty?
- Is there dust on the surfaces? In the corners? Under the furniture?
- Have animals been in the room?
- Does the room smell of cigarette or other tobacco smoke?

If you answer yes to any of these questions, and if the condition brings on your asthma, move on.

Travel and Medication

Traveling with medication generally poses no problems. The pills or capsules and the metered aerosols take little space and can be carried in your purse or hand luggage where they are immediately available in case of need. They can be taken easily and inconspicuously. However, if you use a DeVilbiss Pulmo-Aide or other similar air compressor delivery system, you may run into difficulties. This device, as we indicated in Chapter 14, is simply a compact air compressor that nebulizes and efficiently delivers beta agonists like albuterol. These machines have to be plugged into an electric outlet to work, and this can pose a problem on long automobile trips. It is inconvenient to have to stop the car and go into a rest room at a gas station or a fast-food place to plug in the Pulmo-Aide and service station and fast food rest rooms can harbor mold and dirt so that the compressor merely sends dirty air into your or your child's lungs. DeVilbiss, as well as other companies, makes a device with an adapter that plugs into and works off of the car's cigarette lighter. One model, the Travelmate, has a battery pack and can also operate off of a wall socket or a car cigarette lighter. It costs approximately $400; the other, less adaptable models cost between $250 to $300. Minaturized models are also available; one that we like is called the Dura-Neb 3000. Airports and large bus stations generally have first-aid rooms with provisions to plug in such machines. The machines are small enough to be carried easily and will fit under your airplane seat.

Foreign travel may pose a problem to the person who relies on an air compressor. Electrical outlets and current abroad differ from those in the United States. If you plan on traveling abroad, take a supply of socket adapters and a small transformer that will convert the local current to 120 volts. These converters are available in several forms from large department stores, luggage stores, or retailers who specialize in travel gear. Or choose a unit that comes with an adapable transformer of its own.

Summer Camps

Most summer camps that have been in business for a number of years will have had experience in dealing with asthmatic children. If your child has mild or seasonal asthma and wants to go to camp, you should send along medicine and discuss its use and your child's complaint beforehand with the camp physician. However, children with mild asthma may experience some new and different problems when they first attend camp.

- Going to camp means meeting new people. New people mean new sources of infection. Infections, especially respiratory infections, can make asthma worse.
- Camp housing, often in older, poorly ventilated, dusty, mold-ridden buildings, can house plenty of allergens.
- Exercise, a major feature of summer camp, can make asthma worse because it is more strenuous or different from what your child usually does.
- Children, embarrassed at having others see them take their medication, skip medicating and have their symptoms appear or intensify as a result.

By anticipating these problems and taking appropriate action, camp can be a happy experience for your child. In choosing a summer camp for an asthmatic child, make sure the camp has immediate access to medical personnel; has previous experience dealing with children with asthma; has clean housing arrangements, free of obvious asthma-exacerbating factors like dust, mold, and so forth; and has a counselor sensitive and concerned enough to look out for your child knowledgeably and discreetly.

Children whose asthma is so severe and chronic as to make summer camp impossible for them should consider attending special camps for children with respiratory or other severe problems. The features and advantages of these special camps for moderate to severe asthmatic children are sketched in Chapter 17, which also tells how to locate the ones in your area.

Summary

This chapter sketches how asthmatics, with care and planning, can travel comfortably and safely. The keys to asthma care in general—and certainly to traveling with the disease—are:

- Knowing and avoiding the disease's causes
- Using medications appropriately

Planning entails:

- Taking account of the causes of the symptoms and developing tactics beforehand to avoid them on the road and at the destination
- Assuring an adequate and readily accessible supply of medications for the entire trip
- Being alert to and prepared to deal with the possibility of radically changed environmental conditions
- Assuring that means exist to satisfy any special treatment requirements—having strategies for emergencies in place, knowing that needed equipment like compressors can be operated competently

These principles apply across the board, whether the trip has you venturing to Baffin Bay or your asthmatic child going off to summer camp.

19

Home Remedies and Alternative Strategies in the Treatment of Asthma

Asthma's stubbornness and its capacity to disable its victims repeatedly for varying periods of time understandably makes those victims prime candidates for experimentation with various treatments. The chronic asthmatic wants nothing so much as to be free of symptoms and will try anything to achieve that freedom. This yearning makes the treatment of asthma attractive to unscrupulous operators who promote a variety of abstruse schemes and devices. In seeking help, beware of what is being offered and who offers it.

The approach to care that we have followed in this book is essentially a traditional medical one, although we strongly emphasize the importance and benefits of an informed and aggressive program of self-care. To be effective, such a program depends on the determination and the ability to act intelligently and knowledgeably in finding appropriate and congenial help. In earlier chapters we presented procedures to follow in finding the best resources for treatment and control of asthma. See also Appendix A for the names and addresses of national organizations and associations that will help you in your search for medical, educational, and self-care resources.

Alternative Nonmedical Treatment Options

If you or your child have moderate to severe persistent asthma, any or all of a raft of alternative nonmedical treatment options may attract you. These alternatives are likely to be mentioned or discussed in a number of places such as the classified advertisements in "alternative" publications, uncritical or undocumented accounts of "cures" appearing in the popular media; reports by family, friends, or neighbors who have heard of the treatment, who know somebody who benefited from it, or who themselves attest to its efficacy in their own case; or, most recently, radio and TV programs that feature lay health commentators who are eager to report a "medical breakthrough" no matter how fragmentary or tentative the evidence behind it may be. Anyone who has had to endure the pain, the discomfort, and the feeling of helplessness brought on by persistent asthma is likely to be intrigued by—and tempted to try—any remedy that seems to offer quick, complete relief. We believe, however, that these alternative strategies for the treatment of asthma are not as effective or time-efficient as conventional medical treatment. But we (and we hope your own personal physician) respect your right to choose and would view sympathetically your search for alternative therapies. We would also hope that your doctor would remain informed of what you are doing and would provide medical advice and treatment when appropriate or requested. Although any of these treatments may bring some relief of symptoms, such remedies most often do not provide genuine, sustained relief. In some cases they actually make matters worse by diverting individuals away from appropriate treatment measures.

The major alternative approaches to treatment of asthma are:

- Acupuncture
- Herbalism
- Homeopathy
- Naturopathy
- Chiropractic

Alternative treatments differ from conventional forms of medical treatment in two important ways. First, alternative approaches assume that what is wrong with the individual can be traced to something systemically wrong with the body. Their practitioners are more apt to consider disease entities as the result of a breakdown of bodily defenses; conventional medical thought, on the other hand, is inclined to regard bodily breakdown as effect rather than cause. The nontraditional view is not completely at odds with current medical thought and practice but mainly represents a difference in emphasis.

Second, alternative approaches derive from a different set of assumptions about the nature and workings of the body. Conventional medical thought grows out of the Western scientific view, which is inclined to emphasize precise diagnosis and equally narrow treatment efforts.

> Ed hardly recognized Maurice, who had wasted away, gone completely gray, lost most of his hair, and was obviously under chemical treatment for cancer. They had lunch together. Maurice indicated that he had just come from his biweekly treatment at the acupuncturist's. "Is it helping?" Ed asked. "I believe in it, so it helps," Maurice replied. He died two months later.

Maurice's case illustrates an important point about traditional medical and alternative therapies. The acupuncture did not cure him, but conventional chemical treatment had not been effective either. The alternative therapy did provide reassurance, relief of pain, and a source of support that proved comforting.

Acupuncture

Acupuncture (which has many variations) proceeds from the premise that disease is the result of an imbalance in the "energies" that course or flow throughout the body. This imbalance, for example, is said to permit bacteria to proliferate. By inserting long, slender needles (or by administering minute electrical charges or medication through needles; or by using acupressure, which does not require needles at all) at various points along the energy paths ("meridians"), the practitioner is able to normalize or stabilize the energy flow, and health is restored.

Acupuncture has enjoyed something of a vogue in the United States in the past twenty years. It has had considerable acceptance by physicians who use it to treat migraine, psoriasis, osteoarthritis, and joint pain, among other complaints, and for treatment of pain generally. It apparently relieves the pain associated with a number of chronic conditions.

Some acupuncturists recommend specific procedures for the treatment of asthma. However, there is *no* scientific evidence to indicate that, even when administered properly, acupuncture brings about even modest improvement in respiratory flow, decreased need for medication, or a decline in subjective reports of symptoms. Save your money.

Herbalism

Herbalism is certainly a companion to, and has been an important element in, medicine for thousands of years. It is still followed by those who believe in the efficacy and the essential conservatism of the method. Indeed, many medications still in favor and use grow out of the herbal tradition, and there is a recent, renewed interest in discovering the ability of herbs to affect body processes. For example, cromolyn was originally found in a weed.

Herbalists are likely to take an exquisitely detailed history. They then usually outline a program of diet, exercise, and herbal treatment aimed to improve the general health status. Underlying the treatment is a whole-body approach, based on the view that the body is an aggregation of systems, some of which (according to the symptoms) may need toning or cleansing if health is to be restored. Thus, in addition to herbal remedies, dietary and stress-reducing measures might be recommended.

Coupled with the more general systemic treatments, there are a large number of herbs (herbs are defined as plants used as medicines) that are said to relieve asthmatic symptoms. Teas made of mullein, elecampane, ephedra, eucalyptus, horehound, lungwort, and pleurisy root are recommended to ease asthmatic coughing and to raise mucus; so is an infusion of garlic, ground ivy, blackthorn, and blue vervain; yerba santa mixed with cayenne, gum plant, vervain, and blackthorn and simmered in water is said to relieve bronchospasms.

These herbs are listed in standard medical references as treatments for asthma; the fact that they are not relied on to any great extent nowadays is because they are nowhere near as swift and powerful in their effect as the medications that have come to supplant them. Herbalists acknowledge this readily and contend that although herbal procedures take time, they are more effective in the long run in that they may strengthen the body's natural tendency to seek health.

Serious herbalistic treatment with adequate follow-through might be expected to result in some reduction in the frequency and severity of asthmatic symptoms, but neither it nor conventional medicine is capable of overcoming the underlying genetic and physiological disposition to the disease. But there are no standards for herb preparation in the United States and it is a consumer-beware market. At this junction we do not recommend herbs for your asthma. We also worry that taking herbs may interact with your conventional medications, rendering them either less effective or more toxic. At the least, if you use herbals, make sure your doctor knows about it.

Occasionally we are asked about the use of marijuana for asthma. There is no evidence that it is of any value; moreover, marijuana is extremely irritating to the airways and the lungs. We strongly advise everyone (and especially asthmatics) to avoid it!

Homeopathy

Homeopathy is a "natural" system of healing or therapeutic method. It is based on the premise that a remedy can cure a disease only if it is capable of triggering symptoms similar to that of the disease in a well individual. Established by Samual Hahnemann, a German physician, in the early part of the nineteenth century, it advances a law and set of postulates that provide a guide to treatment. While the system and the arguments for it are much too elaborate to be repeated here, the essential philosophy can be summarized as follows:

- Any pharmacologically active substance can cause symptoms to appear in a healthy individual, and these symptoms are characteristic of that substance.
- Anyone suffering from any disease shows a set of symptoms that are characteristic of the disease.

- A cure (the disappearance of symptoms) may be obtained by administering the substance whose symptoms *exactly* match those presented by the disease.

This is analogous to what happens in the process of desensitization through the administration of allergy shots. The ill person takes extremely dilute solutions of the substance, which produces the symptoms that match those produced by the disease. The result is immunity and loss of symptoms. If the symptoms do not vanish, try again until you find the one substance that perfectly matches the symptoms.

Certainly, some elements of homeopathic thought do appear in traditional medical practice, and, as we have noted, immunization and desensitization rest on what Hahnemann advanced as homeopathic principles. To a limited extent it is useful as a concept, but in practice the method is so highly individualized, arcane, and slow that it is of little or no value in the treatment of anything but the mildest type of asthma symptoms. Apart from that, we have already indicated that desensitization, insofar as asthma is concerned, is rarely appropriate and carries with it substantial risks. Finally, homeopathy seems to assume that all diseases are unitary and that any "interconnectedness" (of allergic complaints, for example, where symptoms may be extremely diffuse and in conflict with one another when it comes to treatment) would pose a difficult therapeutic decision.

Naturopathy

Naturopathy is a very old belief system whose keystone is the mechanism of homeostasis—the tendency of the body to seek and maintain a state of equilibrium, or balance.

Naturopaths (who are not recognized as medical specialists in the United States) are apt to refer to themselves as holistic healers whose efforts are directed at people rather than at ailments. In practice they regard each person as unique, having a constellation of capabilities, characteristics, and needs different from those displayed by any other person.

The naturopath tries, through history and observation in a variety of modes and levels, to discover this whole, unique individual and to establish the underlying causes of illness.

Once established, treatment is directed at eradicating causes rather than attacking symptoms; treatment itself may use some combination of herbalism, homeopathy, massage, psychological counseling, acupuncture, biofeedback, or any of a variety of other approaches.

We believe that, although naturopathy is based on some fundamentally sound principles, such discovery and treatment of the unique, many-faceted individual represents a task beyond the present capability of any specialty or specialist.

Chiropractic

Chiropracty (and osteopathy) share belief in some tenets basic to pursuit of those professions. However, they differ greatly in the amount of training required for certification. In all states osteopaths are accepted as coequal with physicians and practice on an equal footing with them.

Chiropractors must have a state-issued license, but their training period is considerably shorter and narrower than that for osteopaths or physicians. Physicians generally dismiss the assumption that certain kinds of mechanical adjustments to the body (especially of subluxations or misalignments of vertebrae in the spinal column) can bring about improvement in asthma; osteopaths and chiropractors hold the assumption in varying degrees.

Not all chiropractors will try to treat asthma. Many are now likely to be interested in the dietary and other habits of their patients and to recommend a broadly based holistic treatment regimen.

Nevertheless, most physicians contend that strict chiropractic or osteopathic treatment of asthma is futile. Certainly there is no persuasive scientific evidence indicating that chiropractic treatment of asthmatics has led to the easing or remission of their symptoms, and there is no obvious reason to believe that the manipulations and adjustments that are an integral part of this sort of therapy would have any effect either on the agents that cause asthmatic reactions or on the bronchospasms that are the result of the asthmatic's hypersensitive airways. Despite this, many clinical reports of chiropractic success with asthma do exist. These may have occurred possibly because of the relief of underlying psychological stress or tension that aggravated the bronchospasms and the resulting symptoms.

Nontraditional Methods of Testing and Treatment

The history of medicine is filled with examples of treatments that enjoyed great popularity for a time until they were found to be ineffectual or even made symptoms worse. Asthma has had its share of dubious treatments over the years, and there are three treatment strategies currently in vogue that proceed from the contention that nutritional status underlies asthma's symptoms. These strategies are hair analysis, cytotoxic testing, and Candida testing. A fourth general approach to asthma treatment is clinical ecology.

Hair Analysis

Hair analysis may be recommended to measure your nutritional status. Hair analysis is a very precise, accurate procedure when done *correctly*. A properly conducted hair analysis would first have you wash your hair completely and not put any hair preparations on it until the test is complete. Next, an area on your scalp would be shaved and new hair allowed to grow for the next few weeks. It is this new, never-been-washed hair that is analyzed. Otherwise, all you are analyzing is the chemical composition of your shampoo or hair spray.

Nutritional deficiency has not been established as a cause of asthma. However, many people do have legitimate problems with nutrition. They may suffer from diabetes, intestinal disorders, or may even have a rare genetic disease that prevents normal metabolism. If those individuals also have allergies—including asthma—they should consult their physician and, if necessary, refer themselves to somebody skilled in clinical nutrition. Be sure that the nutritionist has had formal training in a nutrition department in a university medical school. Unhappily, there is no board certification in nutrition, so anybody can hang up a shingle as a clinical nutritionist. It is up to you to check their credentials. The best place to start your search for a qualified nutritionist is at a local university or your county medical society. Unfortunately, people who advocate hair analysis are likely to have vested financial interests in the laboratories that do hair analyses and therefore have something to gain from ordering them.

Cytotoxic Testing

Cytotoxic testing is likely to be done by a physician who is interested in or claims to practice something called "ecological" or "orthomolecular" medicine. This practitioner believes that your asthma symptoms are most likely linked to your reactions to different foods or chemicals and will have you undergo a series of tests to identify what it is that is causing your asthma. In this form of testing, the white cells are removed from a sample of your blood. Then the cells are mixed with extracts of foods or chemicals believed to be responsible for your symptoms, and the mixture is studied under a microscope. If the white cells seem to be dead, you are said to be allergic to whatever has been mixed with the cells.

This is an attractive and superficially plausible procedure, but it has one basic shortcoming: *it does not work*. Laboratory studies have compared individuals known to be free of allergies with people with known allergies. Cytotoxic testing did not differentiate between the two groups and failed to identify the specific allergens reliably.

Cytotoxic testing has been judged to be useless by the Food and Drug Administration and by the American Academy of Allergy and Immunology. California physicians using cytotoxic testing have been sued by the California Board of Medical Quality Assurance for, among other things, fraudulent advertising, unfair business practices, and conspiracy to violate the state's business and professions code. If a physician or other health practitioner recommends that you undergo cytotoxic testing, seek other help.

Candida

There have been a number of reports circulated of people suffering from weakness, tension fatigue, and even occasionally mild to moderate asthma who are said to have Candida or Monilia (yeast) infections throughout their body. The reports contend that these infections are occult, not revealed by conventional methods of detection. Nonetheless, it is believed that a yeast infection is present in the body and releases certain products, including alcohol, which bring about personality change and produce a wide variety of symptoms, including allergic ones. The reports go on to claim that when these people are treated with antifungal antibiotics, they often get better.

The Candida connection to asthma is even more flimsy than some of the alternative therapies we have already discussed. If you did have Monilia or Candida in your body, you would almost certainly be gravely ill. Your body simply cannot tolerate fungal infections beneath the skin. Although you may get yeast infections in your intestinal tract, mouth, or vagina, these areas are all considered to be external. To suggest that Candida infections inside the body are producing these infections is absurd; to treat it with broad-spectrum antibiotics is not only pointless but may cause unnecessary and potentially harmful side effects.

Clinical Ecology

Clinical ecology is not an established medical specialty like orthopedics or dermatology. It is simply an outlook or an approach to the practice of medicine, particularly the treatment of individuals who are troubled by generalized stress-fatigue symptoms or allergic-like reactions, including asthma.

The assumption behind clinical ecology is that these reactions and fatigue-stress symptoms are the result of subtle and insidious effects of any of a multiplicity of possible causal factors. To these practitioners much of what ails people—from itchiness to madness to obesity—is traceable to allergic or hypersensitive reactions to something in the environment. Foods are saddled with much of the blame, but synthetics, chemicals, plastics, and emissions come in for their share of criticism.

To the clinical ecologist there is no such thing as intrinsic asthma—everything is extrinsic; that is, everything has a cause somewhere in the environment that can be located if one looks hard and long enough. This is an attractive notion, but the search for the ecological villain may be long, expensive, and, in the end, futile. Sometimes the therapeutic strategy will be the preparation of an ecologically "pure" environment, which can use up a good deal of your cash and achieve no more than much simpler avoidance tactics supplemented by an appropriate and judicious course of medication that anticipates and controls your asthma symptoms.

A second problem with clinical ecology is that, whereas its practitioners are messianic in their zeal, and there are many individuals around who attest fervently to what, in retrospect, seem to be their near-miraculous cures, there is no persuasive evidence to bear out the contention that many of the vague, annoying, debilitating symptoms are the result of allergies or hypersensitivity to anything. We have no quarrel with advice to eat sensibly and to live in an environment that is as free of contamination as it is possible to make it. When carried to extremes, however—and this often seems to be the case with clinical ecology—it is an overwhelming and ultimately limiting outlook.

A Note About Vitamins

There are some people who claim that asthmatics have some genetic or familial abnormality in body metabolism that leads to vitamin or mineral deficiencies or abnormalities in sugar metabolism. The evidence for this abnormality is very weak, although there is no doubt at all that adequate nutrition is vital for good health. However, this does not mean that suboptimal nutrition will result in asthma or allergies.

We discussed earlier in this book the necessity for a good, sound diet, one likely to give your body the nutrients and minerals it needs. We believe that the recommended daily allowances for many vitamins and minerals may not always be sufficient for asthmatics. These recommended daily allowances are based on limited observations and often do not take into account the additional stresses and needs brought on by chronic illness, by interactions of diet with medications you are using, and by possible changes in requirements as you get older. For this reason we unhesitatingly recommend the use of a good multivitamin preparation, should you have any doubts at all about the adequacy of your diet. It does not have to

TABLE 19.1   Essentials of a Good Multivitamin

Vitamin A 5000 IU (20% as Beta Carotene)	Magnesium 100 mg
Vitamin C 60 mg	Zinc 15 mg
Vitamin D 400 IU	Selenium 20 mcg
Vitamin E 45 IU	Copper 2 mg
Vitamin K 10 mcg	Manganese 2 mg
Riboflavin 1.7 mcg	chromium 150 mcg
Niacin 20 mcg	Molybdenum 75 mcg
Vitamin B_6 3 mg	Chloride 72 mg
Folic Acid 400 mg	Potassium 80 mg
Vitamin B_{12} 25 mcg	Boron 150 mcg
Biotin 30 mcg	Nickel 5 mcg
Pantothenic Acid 10 mg	Silicon 2 mg
Calcium 200 mg	Vanadium 10 mcg
Phosphorus 48 mg	Lutein 250 mcg
Iodine 150 mcg	

*These amounts are equivalent to what is found in Centrum™
Silver and are meant to be a guide only.

be expensive. It should contain all of the B vitamins and vitamin C as well as minerals including zinc. Table 19.1 lists what we think should be in your multivitamin or family vitamin. These vitamins, incidentally, are generic and can be bought over the counter. They are identical to and much less expensive than heavily advertised, brand-name vitamins.

Summary

Asthma, like any other chronic disease, has its fair share of treatments that fall outside the boundaries of conventional medical practice. Some alternative strategies for the treatment of asthma do have tenuous links to contemporary medical thought; others originate in unsupported ideologies about the nature of disease and the work of the body.

Although the major alternative approaches to the treatment of asthma—acupuncture, herbalism, homeopathy, naturopathy, and chiropractic—may do little or no harm, on balance they do little or no good when it comes to preventing or controlling asthmatic symptoms.

Other treatment modes that claim a medico-scientific basis cleave to the view that nutritional deficiencies or environmental toxins spawn asthma. When put to empirical test these views, too, have proved without value in the treatment of asthma. Yet the great majority of people with persistent asthma will try alternative treatments or home remedies at some point in their efforts to cope with their symptoms. These trials, unhappily, will not succeed.

Appendix A: Keeping Current with Asthma Care

How to Find Up-to-Date Information on Asthma and Its Treatment

Any book about health care starts going out of date the same day it gets published. Although most of the contents of *Asthma: Stop Suffering, Start Living* have a usefully long shelf life, new discoveries and new treatments will certainly appear. You can keep up on these new developments by consulting the resources we've listed below.

The fastest, easiest way to stay current with asthma treatment resources is to connect to the World Wide Web. If you already have a computer and can log on to the Internet at home, splendid! But, even if you don't have such easy access, you do have options:

- Your local public library, more than likely, can connect you to the Web and help you to find what you need to know.
- Many colleges (and community colleges) allow nonstudents to use their Internet resources during low-use hours. These facilities are usually housed in the library.
- You probably have friends or relatives with computers and access to the Web. Get them to help you with your medical sleuthing.
- Various kinds of private enterprises—cybercafés, office supply, and copy chains—offer Web access for a fee.

Here are a few of the literally hundreds of sites that carry information and suggestions about asthma and its care and treatment. (These addresses are provided as a service to our readers and do not imply endorsement or support of any programs or organizations.)

http://www.healthfinder.gov. This valuable site, compiled by the U.S. Department of Health and Human Services, describes itself as a free gateway to reliable consumer health information. Bring up the site, type "asthma" in the Search for: bar, click Go, and you will be rewarded with an extensive list of Web topics and organizations that you can pull up directly. They include:

- Asthma Information Home Page (general information provided by the American Lung Association)
- Asthma Camp Directory (a state-by-state list of summer camps for asthmatics)
- For Kids and Teens: Asthma and Allergy Web sites of interest
- Living with Asthma: Special Concerns for Older Adults
- Allergy, Asthma and Immunology Online (takes the user to the medical library and easy access to a large collection of publications from various sources graded for their relevance and degree of complexity)

The healthfinder site also lists organizations concerned with various aspects of asthma treatment and care. They include:

American Academy of Asthma, Allergy, and Immunology
　　611 East Well Street
　　Milwaukee, WI 53202
　　1-800-822-2762 http://www.aaai.org/

American College of Allergy, Asthma and Immunology
　　85 West Algonquin Road, Suite 550
　　Arlington Heights, IL 60005
　　1-800-842-7777 http://acaai.org/

*American Lung Association
　　http://www.lungusaorg/index.html

---

*Identifies user-friendly organizations, ones that within certain limits respond to questions put to them on the Web or by telephone.

See the White Pages of the telephone directory for phone number and address of your local Lung Association. (Your ALA is an especially valuable source of information about self-management programs and summer camps for asthmatic children.)

Asthma and Allergy Foundation of America
    National Headquarters
    1233 20th St. NW, Suite 402
    Washington, DC 20036
    1-800-727-8462 http://www.aafa.org/

*The Allergy and Asthma Network/Mothers of Asthmatics Inc.
    2751 Prosperity Avenue, Suite 150
    Fairfax, VA 22031
    1-800-878-4403 http://www.aanma.org/

National Asthma Education and Prevention Program
National Heart, Lung and Blood Institute Information Center
    P.O. Box 30105
    Bethesda, MD 20524-0105
    1-301-251-1222 http://www.nhlbi.nih.gov/nhlbi/htm

*National Jewish Medical and Research Center
    1400 Jackson Street
    Denver, CO 80206
    1-800-222-LUNG http://www.nationaljewish.org/

The organizations listed above provide considerable information about asthma's causes, symptoms, treatments, self-care and management strategies, and resources. Much of what they have to offer is freely available and can be downloaded from the web. Particularly useful are lists of providers of products and devices and responses to FAQs—frequently asked questions.

Also useful for its links to other sites and the easy access it provides to organizations and topics that concern asthmatics is the ERP Asthma Site. Your web search engine (we like google) can bring up this resource when you type its name in the entry bar and hit go.

Getting to Know More About Your Medications

New asthma medications keep turning up; we've covered the current ones in Chapter 14. When prescribing or dispensing any drug, the physician and the pharmacist ought to tell you about it and the medication itself should come with a sheet that describes it, tells how, when and when not to use it, gives dosages, and enumerates possible adverse reactions. Where this information is not supplied, look for it in Chapter 14; then, where necessary, go on to the *Physician's Desk Reference* (PDR). Your doctor will have a current copy of this huge volume (which is updated annually); so will your community public or college library and your HMO. It will list your medication, display a photo of it, give its chemical makeup, tell you how it works, give dosages, warn you of possible side effects, and instruct you what to do in the event of adverse reactions.

The PDR represents your best informational source about medications, but the web can also tell you about drugs. Simply type the name of the medication in your search engine's entry bar and hit go. The big problem here is that you'll probably wind up with a mountain of results and will have to spend serious time separating the clinically and therapeutically useful material from advertising claims, testimonials, and highly specialized technical reports.

Most asthma sufferers will try complementary (alternative) treatments at some point. Keep your physician informed about your excursion into self-treatment; all physicians know about this tendency, can live with it, and can keep you from harm if you try something that proves to be hazardous. The Center for Complementary and Alternative Medicine Research in Asthma (http://camra. ucdavis.edu) at the University of California at Davis is busy identifying, supporting research into, and communicating information about these products and procedures.

Knowing What to Do in an Asthmatic Emergency

We cover the steps you need to take in the event of an acute asthmatic attack—see Chapter 16, pages 208–217—but with the incidence and severity of acute episodes on the rise, repeating what we say there won't hurt. Tightness in your neck muscles, lips or fingertips going gray or blue, or skin around your ribs being sucked in signal a severe attack of asthma. When one hits, take your asthma medication, get emergency help right away, and go to your doctor's office or the emergency room immediately.

Appendix B: Sources of Products for People with Asthma

On balance, you will be better served if you secure asthma care products—air purifiers, cleaning devices, hypoallergenic products of all descriptions—from local suppliers. Buying locally permits you to assess quality prior to purchase, sometimes allows use for a trial period, and makes seeking recourse easier if anything goes amiss. With allergies and asthma so commonplace, even smaller cities support businesses that specialize in or at least stock goods and devices needed by asthmatics. To find these suppliers:

- Use the phone book's Yellow Pages. Here are a few telephone directory classified listings that you may find helpful in your search for products for asthmatics:

> Air Cleaning and Purifying Equipment/Services
> Air Conditioning Equipment and Systems/Rooms
> Allergy Treatments and Products
> Dust Control Materials
> Health and Diet Food Products—Retail
> Health Plans
> Medical Equipment and Supplies
> Safety Equipment

In addition, the Yellow Pages will list distributors of name items—vacuum cleaners, air conditioners, and so on.

- Consult With Your Physician, HMO, Insurer, or Hospital. All of these care providers ought to be able to suggest local sources of supply for materials or devices and may provide insurance coverage for acquisition of some of them—peak flow meters, nebulizers, and other pieces of medical equipment essential to the monitoring or management of your symptoms.

- Ask Your Local Branch of the American Lung Association for help in locating local suppliers of equipment and (in some local chapters) loan of used and reconditioned therapeutic devices.
- Tap into the World Wide Web. Refer to Appendix A for tactics to follow in taking advantage of the resources of the World Wide Web. Log on and then ask your search engine to name suppliers of asthma care products. This will yield an astonishing number of resources and checking through them will give you a very good idea of the availability and costs of supplies or devices. Narrowing the search by naming specific products—peak expiratory flow meters, for instance—will also yield a large number of sources. In addition the Allergy and Asthma Network/Mothers of Asthmatics (http://www.aanma.org/) vends a variety of asthma-related products.

Most large mercantile chains like Sears, J. C. Penney, and so forth, carry some of the products that people affected by asthma may require.

Index